a friend
like
henry

NUALA GARDNER

a friend like henry

HODDER &
STOUGHTON

Copyright © 2007 by Nuala Gardner

First published in Great Britain in 2007 by Hodder & Stoughton
A division of Hodder Headline

Some names and identities have been changed

The right of Nuala Gardner to be identified as the Author of the Work has been
asserted by her in accordance with the Copyright, Designs and Patents Act 1988.

A Hodder & Stoughton Book

3

A CIP catalogue record for this title is available from the British Library

ISBN 978 0 340 95274 0

Writing by Lindsey Hill

Typeset in Sabon by Hewer Text UK Ltd, Edinburgh
Printed and bound by Mackays of Chatham Ltd, Chatham, Kent

Hodder Headline's policy is to use papers that are natural, renewable
and recyclable products and made from wood grown in sustainable
forests. The logging and manufacturing processes are expected to
conform to the environmental regulations of the country of origin.

Hodder & Stoughton Ltd
A division of Hodder Headline
338 Euston Road
London NW1 3BH

This book is dedicated with love and admiration to my amazing son Dale, for allowing me to tell his story. Without his support and participation, this book would not have been possible.

Contents

Prologue

My husband, Jamie, and I didn't want a dog. That's not to say we didn't like them – I had had one myself as a child, and although Jamie wasn't used to dogs, he had nothing against them. No, we just didn't want one at the time, because we had enough responsibilities. Our young son, Dale, was locked deep inside his autistic world, terrified by every little thing, yet totally unable to communicate his fears or understand our reassurances. Every waking minute with him was a maelstrom of conflict as we plunged from one violent tantrum to the next. He didn't even know who we were, and our efforts to interact with him were deeply frustrating, completely draining and ultimately, it seemed, quite futile.

Then a chance encounter with Jamie's cousin's dogs gave us a glimmer of hope . . . and so began the road to finding our puppy. Even at six weeks old, Henry stood out from the rest of the litter; but we didn't choose him, he chose Dale. Whether or not he was at that tender age able to sense our wee boy's troubles and feel he could be of assistance, I don't know. All I can say is that his beautiful, stoical, saintly nature was the key to unlocking a personality we never knew our son had. What happened was beyond our wildest imaginings – nothing could have prepared us for the impact on all our lives of finding a friend like Henry.

I
The Words

I wept with joy as the midwife placed my first-born child into my arms: a tiny, neat baby boy, weighing 5 pounds 13 ounces. In only two short years, I had extricated myself from a bad relationship, met the man of my dreams and become a mum.

'It doesn't get much better than this,' I thought, as I wiped away my tears and gazed down at my new son.

And then my stomach heaved with fear when I saw his head.

A midwife myself, at St Luke's Maternity Hospital, I had only once before seen a baby admitted to the neonatal unit for excessive moulding of the head. I now vividly remembered my shock at that sight and was haunted by the words of my colleague at the time: 'It'll be a miracle if this baby gets away unscathed.' I never did learn what became of that child, but all I knew now was that the shape of my new baby's head was terrifyingly worse than anything I had previously witnessed.

His head was quite flat at the back, severely elongated and virtually touched the tops of his shoulders. It was also bruised all over, even on his face. I knew immediately that he would be admitted to the special care unit to undergo tests, but I glossed over this with my partner, Jamie: 'It's because he's premature,' I reassured him.

We had chosen our baby's name months in advance, when we were excitedly anticipating the big event: Dale for a boy, Amy for a girl. But for all the simplicity of his name, Dale's entry into this world had not been without drama. On Saturday, 11 June 1988, at only thirty-five weeks pregnant, I had started to have contractions while putting the finishing touches to the newly renovated bathroom of the flat where Jamie and I lived. As it was too early for me to be in labour, I concluded I must have a bladder infection. Because of my medical training, I wasn't particularly worried, but Jamie drove me to the hospital just in case. I was admitted and was somewhat surprised when the contractions continued in earnest. They were regular and strong, but no real progress was made until five o'clock the following morning, when my waters broke. I now knew for sure that my baby would be delivered at some point within the next twenty-four hours because the risk of infection had superseded those of a premature birth.

I laboured and laboured, getting precisely nowhere. Then, at about 7 a.m., the night sister examined me and announced her suspicions that the baby was in a breech presentation, despite all previous assessments having in-dicated to the contrary. Some thirty-six hours after my admission, in agony and exhausted, I was X-rayed and the sister's suspicions were confirmed. Jamie was hauled out of his office, in the middle of eating his bacon roll, and he joined me in surgery for the inevitable Caesarean section. Eventually, at 11.04 a.m. on 13 June, Dale entered the world, screaming enthusiastically.

The moulding to Dale's head was caused by the fact that he was an undiagnosed breech and his head had become caught in my ribcage, which was why the labour hadn't progressed naturally. Only time would tell whether any lasting damage had been done as a result of this trauma.

Despite my misgivings, I tried to keep things in perspective. Becoming a mum was a blissful continuation of the wonderful journey that had begun with meeting Jamie. Having ended my previous relationship, I had moved into St Luke's nurses' home with just a suitcase and bitter memories. Although I was only forty miles from my home town of Greenock, it felt at times as though I was in another country and I missed my friends and family dreadfully. Fortunately, in spite of the exhaustion induced by the rigours of my working life, my close friend Lorraine would from time to time ignore my protestations and demand my return to the Greenock social scene. I had known Lorraine since the summer of 1978, when our paths had coincided at Ravenscraig Psychiatric Hospital in Greenock. As part of our nursing training, we were there to gain some practical experience of psychiatry. I think it's fair to say we gained rather more practical experience of boozy nights out, and in the process bonded like sisters.

One Friday evening in 1986, my presence was required by Lorraine in the popular Greenock music bar Tokyo Joe's. As the night wore on, and the drinking and dancing intensified, I became aware of a tall, dark-haired man propped up at the bar, watching me. He was alone, but seemed totally at one with himself. When he opened his mouth to mumble a hello, vodka fumes assailed my nostrils.

'You're a fine-looking woman,' he slurred pleasantly.

Despite his condition, I think my reply was along the

lines that he wasn't so bad himself. There was a pause as he wondered whether he was capable of pursuing the discussion. Then he shook his head, wryly declaring, 'Time to send myself home.' In spite of his inebriated state, he came across as a polite, very funny character. He said that he hoped to see me again sometime, when he'd got his 'sensible head' on.

I'm not sure whether he found me irresistible or simply forgot that he'd said goodbye, but before he left he came back over and invited me to a party at a mate's flat the following night. For some reason, I was sufficiently intrigued by this man to want to know more.

The next evening, I found him at the party, still nursing the effects of the previous night's binge and determined to take things easy.

'Remember me?' I introduced myself. 'You really suit your sensible head.' Suspecting amnesia would have set in straight after he'd left Tokyo Joe's, I hoped this would be enough to remind him of our encounter. There was a moment of slightly startled blankness, but then recognition flooded across his face – and no doubt relief across mine.

Jamie and I totally clicked. We spent the evening together, talking and laughing, before deciding to abandon the party early and retreat to his flat, which was round the corner. It was on the top floor of a ninety-year-old red-sandstone tenement in Roxburgh Street and Jamie had just moved in – his first bachelor pad.

Despite being in our late twenties, we were like a pair of young teenagers, playing music and talking late into the night, before finally falling asleep in each other's arms on the sofa until morning. Phone numbers were exchanged, and, after a caring goodbye kiss, I returned to the confines of the nurses' home at St Luke's and Jamie to National Semiconductor, where he worked as a physical design engineer, designing microchips.

Within only a few months I found myself strangely secure and happy with Jamie. We became inseparable, yearning to be with each other when work divided us. It was perhaps inevitable, therefore, that at one of our Saturday night post-pub parties, 'the words' were said. Still drenched by the torrential rain that had fallen as we left the pub, and both pleasantly pickled in alcohol, we were lost in each other and oblivious to the party. As I laughed at yet another dry one-liner, Jamie suddenly grabbed me and said 'the words'. For a confirmed bachelor, this was something of a giant leap, but I seized the moment and told him I loved him too.

That Christmas, I was the first girlfriend ever to dine with the Gardner family and our future together was cemented. I moved into Jamie's flat in June 1987, eight months after meeting him.

The flat desperately screamed for a woman's touch and we set about renovation work. This was no easy task, given that everything we threw out or brought into the property had to be transported up or down a total of sixty-five big, cold, concrete steps, the first fifteen of which were in the form of a spiral staircase. This climb to the flat would become like the north face of the Eiger in later years.

Despite the physical challenge, we had great fun with the renovations, not least because we were aided and abetted by 'the team', a group of Jamie's crazy friends, who would think nothing of turning up somewhat the worse for wear at one o'clock in the morning. Their demands for coffee, meals and more drinks were always met – in return for slightly more sober assistance later with the work on the flat. So, after many months of sweat and hard graft, combined with the electrical and joinery skills of Jamie's dad, Jimmy, an unprepossessing, poorly modernised flat was restored to its former Victorian glory. More importantly, it was home, and even the painful dent in our bank balance could not dampen our delight.

After a Christmas-party outing, the revelling continued at our place and we spontaneously celebrated our new abode with 'the team' and their partners. Big George decreed the dump had become 'a palace', while Big Kenny and John Turner did their best to break in the new lounge carpet by encouraging all present to dance on it into the wee small hours.

Jamie and I were besotted with each other and gradually developed a series of 'rules' to anchor our relationship. It would be based on mutual trust and respect and we would at all costs avoid one of my pet hates: clichés. I saw no value in a compulsory bunch of flowers on Valentine's Day or by way of apology and so Jamie promised that on at least one random day a year he would bring me flowers. Since then, he has never disappointed or failed to surprise me, one year waiting until the stroke of midnight at Hogmanay to present me with a stunning bouquet of roses.

Our trust extended to such things as opening each other's mail and throwing in our assets together. I sold my two-year-old Ford Fiesta to use the money to furnish the flat, and Jamie returned the gesture big time by legally placing the ownership of his flat in our joint names.

The only domestic irritation came as no real surprise, being itself something of a cliché about the nature of men. Jamie seemed to think that part of the package of setting up home together was that he had acquired a live-in maid. One day, I found a solution in the form of an item I had spotted while browsing through a magazine and duly placed an order. While waiting for my purchase to arrive, I laid the groundwork by threatening Jamie that I would have to get in hired help because of my hefty work schedule. He didn't seem to believe this would really happen. Then, a few days later, when he arrived home, I met him in the hall.

'I've found a lady we can hire,' I announced. 'She's waiting to see us in the lounge.'

Jamie was suitably embarrassed that I had had to go to these extremes and promised he would be more considerate in future. Perhaps rather cruelly, I insisted that he himself should explain to Myrna, the maid, why her services were no longer required. He was all for legging it to the pub, but I dragged him inside. There, 'Myrna' was waiting . . . in the form of a vacuum-cleaner cover designed to look like a Victorian domestic worker. Jamie took one look at the cute, doll-like face and introduced himself forcefully as her new master. We laughed, but secretly I think he felt he had finally met his match in me.

While our relationship was all I could have wanted, the daily stress of travelling from Greenock to work at St Luke's was beginning to take its toll. My shift pattern and tiredness meant that Jamie and I hardly saw each other. I was also staring my thirties straight in the face and becoming increasingly aware of my biological clock ticking. This was compounded by the fact that I was constantly handing over new babies to couples, while at the same time yearning for one of my own.

One night, as Jamie and I polished off a bottle of wine together, he suddenly declared, 'Hopefully, that'll be your last.'

'I may like a drink,' I protested, 'but I'm no alcoholic.'

His meaning became clear when he ceremoniously flushed my contraceptive pills down the loo. Within a year I was delighted and excited to be pregnant.

Being a dutiful midwife, I was careful to obey all the usual prenatal and pregnancy rules to ensure the development of a healthy baby. I also reduced my workload down to two night shifts a week, and the hospital were happy to let me stay at the nurses' home for my nights on. I missed Jamie, but it was safer this way, rather than travelling back and forth, pregnant and exhausted.

I quickly became huge and, to give Jamie a laugh, would break into a mock tap dance whenever and wherever the mood took me . . . like in the aisle of a supermarket. He would fondly call me 'Tubs', much to the consternation of one fellow shopper, who seemed disgusted a man would refer to his partner in this way – until I turned round to reveal my mammoth bump.

Tap-dancing aside, perhaps, I did everything I could for the health of my growing baby. And yet here I was now, cradling my newborn son in my arms, unable to shake off a feeling of deep unease. My friends Barbara and Eleanor, also midwives, tried all they could to reassure me with regard to Dale's head, and it was a great relief when the hospital tests he subsequently underwent revealed no abnormalities. I was pleased, too, to be able to get Dale breastfeeding really well, as I wanted him to have all the benefits this would bring.

A steady stream of friends and family visited over the following days, so happy for us and bearing gifts and cards galore. Jamie's old teddy bear, which I had washed and re-stuffed in readiness, sat with great pride in Dale's cot, as if watching over him. We christened the toy Teddy Gardner.

Finally, ten days after the birth, we made our way back to our lovely refurbished home. Jamie took a week off work and we just enjoyed being a family, little knowing of the harrowing journey that lay ahead.

2
A Different Child

In terms of Dale's early behaviour, it seemed we had the perfect baby. In many ways, he appeared unique. He was passive, placid and exceptionally easy to care for. He would go to anyone, not missing me in the slightest, and friends and family would often comment on how good he was. I must admit I sometimes wondered whether he was unnaturally so. It seemed strange to have to waken or lift him for breastfeeds during the day, after not feeding for as long as five hours, and he slept through the entire night without a sound. He rarely cried, though when he did it varied between a pathetic whimper and screeching howls as if he were in pain. Sometimes the only sign that indicated he was awake was that he would scratch the sides of the vinyl cover of the pram with his tiny nails.

Nothing seemed to faze him. He didn't react to the sound of the telephone or noise from the TV, and I remember one day when I left Jamie in charge so I could go to the shops, I came back to the sound of rock music blaring from our flat. I found Jamie in the kitchen, casually making coffee.

'Where's Dale?' I shouted, horrified by the deafening volume.

'In the lounge. He's really into Whitesnake.'

I hurried in to rescue my son, and found him calmly

bouncing in his little baby chair, quite oblivious to the racket. Only when I turned down the music and lifted him up did he cry, apparently distressed at being disturbed. Jamie thought it was good that Dale didn't mind the music, but the experience left me chilled.

On the second routine visit from the health visitor, I expressed my feelings of doubt about Dale's welfare. She thought it unusual to hear a mother complaining that her baby was 'too good' and was reassuring, although she did dismiss me with the words 'Just enjoy that you have such a happy and contented baby.' In a way, I felt she was right, but on some deeper level my niggling sense of unease persisted. Nonetheless, I continued to love and appreciate Dale for the wonderful little baby that he was.

My son remained totally undemanding, seemingly at one with everyone and everything around him. He would smile at random, and I found that actually to prompt a smile I had to go over the top, bouncing him up and down and making silly noises. Even then, the resulting smile didn't quite seem natural; it was more as though he was smiling to himself. I remember one time when Jamie had Dale on his knee and was talking to him about taking us all on a weekend break to St Andrews. Every time Jamie said 'St Andrews', Dale would give a big, beaming smile. We loved seeing him smile at our request and so thereafter continued to use those magic words to get our reward.

As with his smile, Dale's eye contact seemed a little 'out of sync' somehow – again, just not quite natural. Despite this, I was reassured when he made burbling baby noises or laughed heartily at something, even though we couldn't work out what he had found so funny.

I did all the usual things to stimulate a new baby and ensure Dale was as happy and thriving as any other child. There were rattles and toys attached to his cot, such as Dozy Daisy, who squeaked when she was pulled, and a musical sheep mobile that played 'Baa, Baa, Black Sheep', which I sang along to many a time, particularly while Dale fed. Teddy Gardner still kept watch, along with a new little bear whom we had christened Happy Ted. The cot bumper and duvet had a train scene, along with a matching sheep from the mobile. I had no idea then how significant trains were to become in the future, or how special this particular duvet would be.

My mum and dad, Dale's Granny Madge and Granda George, regularly came round to help out and babysit so that Jamie and I could go out for a meal or see a film. Madge relished this time with Dale, singing to him and stimulating him with games for the entire evening. He loved the songs she made up and she found he particularly liked the same lines hummed over and over again, never tiring of them. Despite his placidity, we soon found Dale wouldn't sleep in his bed, only in his pram, and then only as long as it was moving. He seemed addicted to the motion. Mum could also easily get him to settle into a deep sleep for the night by holding him upright, his cheek next to hers, and swaying him to and fro as she sang. She could even achieve this after he'd been screaming at full fury when all my efforts had failed. Her patience and love for my child knew no bounds.

During the day, I would take Dale in his bouncy chair from room to room as I did the housework, talking to him all the while to try and gain his attention in any way.

Sometimes he would play casually with the big, colourful wooden beads on his chair; at other times he would just sit, seemingly content to gaze into oblivion. To try to stimulate him further, I changed the beads for a 'gym' with Disney characters dangling from it, but his play remained unchanged. He seemed to have only a fleeting interest, generally hitting the toys by accident with his arms or legs, rather than getting stuck in as I had seen other babies do.

Around this time, I was pleased to discover that two local health visitors had taken the initiative to start a breastfeeding support group, where mothers could get together and exchange ideas and experiences. I embraced this opportunity to meet other parents and felt it would be excellent for Dale's development to socialise with other babies. All was well to begin with, and the other mums appreciated having someone there with knowledge of midwifery. It was also good for me to see how the other babies were developing and note, for example, that in sitting up at six months, Dale was holding his own with them. I had no idea how all this was shortly to change.

Now that Dale had reached six months, I felt it was a good time to get back to work, but at this point only wanted a part-time post. This I found at Inverkip House, a local home for elderly people who needed nursing care. My ultimate goal was to pursue a career in health visiting, but I felt the job at Inverkip would at least get me working again until something more suitable came up. Happily, all of Dale's grandparents shared in looking after Dale so that I could work my three shifts a week and they continued to find him easy to care for. He was perfectly happy with the same few familiar toys, particularly a red rubber car, and would contentedly 'mouth' them most of the time. Sometimes, like at Jamie's mum's, he would prefer to play with pots and pans, which would amuse him for an unnaturally long time. Granny Dorothy would sit him on his play mat with wooden spoons and pots containing lots of clothes pegs, and he would simply transfer all the pegs from one pot to another and back again, seemingly happy to repeat this process endlessly. When I think back, he showed no symbolic or imaginative play – another child might have stirred the pegs in the pot or played appropriately with a toy, rather than just mouthing it.

Although Dale would occupy himself contentedly in this manner, I was concerned that he didn't seem to be aware of anyone else's presence. To attract his attention, we would have to shout, clap our hands or simply pick him up, which would often prompt loud wails and tears, as if he resented the intrusion; and while he would sit contentedly on my or anyone else's lap, he seemed to regard this as just a seat, rejecting all attempts to interact with him. Also, I noticed that, unlike other babies, he would not lift his arms to be picked up and nor did he point at any item of interest. When he started to crawl, at eleven months, I remember him only ever crawling away from us, despite our efforts to engage and play with him.

I had to learn to rotate Dale's toys, otherwise one item would be mouthed to death, which seemed such a futile form of play. Once he had laboriously exhausted a toy's use, I would put it away for a rest and introduce a new one for him at his cognitive level. It would then become difficult to move him on to something else, but we learned to divert him by playing boisterously with him, especially tickling, which he would want to go on for hours.

Tickling sessions aside, our son didn't seem to have the slightest interest in us or anyone else. Nor did he respond to our enthusiastic efforts to produce his first word. Our exaggerated facial expressions were entirely lost on him, and he seemed to have no comprehension of even the simplest language. Try as we did for that crucial 'Ma-ma' or 'Da-da', it never came.

Instead, we tried to get him to understand the two most basic and useful words in the English language: 'yes' and 'no'. After a great deal of effort on our part, Dale finally learned to love the concept of the word 'yes', as it brought all good things his way. 'No', however, was a different story: whatever we tried, he simply refused to register or respond to a word that was going to prevent him doing or getting what he wanted. It's as if he liked the tone of the word 'yes' but hated the tone of 'no'.

I had to go into town to meet a friend one day with Dale still clutching the shiny saucepan from which he had refused to be parted, despite countless 'no's from me. In time, when out in public, I would learn to get used to the strange looks and negative reactions prompted by Dale's bizarre behaviour.

Inevitably, I continued to have real doubts about my son's progress, or lack of it, and voiced these concerns to the health visitor during his many check-ups. As he was so young, however, it was simply a case of wait and see.

Dale developed a fascination for water and loved visits to the local swimming pool, where he would turn into a prune before we could get him out, despite being oblivious to everything that was going on around him. Another favourite was bath time. Around the time of his first birthday, I decided I wanted to try to get him off his dummy as I didn't want it to obstruct any potential for him to talk. I wasn't sure how to go about this, as I knew if I simply removed it, he'd be desperately upset. One night, however, while I was drying him after his bath, Dale solved the problem for me by throwing the dummy down the toilet. I let him see it flush away, using the words 'all gone', which he was used to hearing when we finished feeding the birds at the local pond. For some reason, Dale found this highly amusing and laughed heartily, as indeed did I, such was my delight at sharing an enjoyable moment with my son. Although later there were times when he demanded, in his own screaming way, a replacement, I never gave in.

From that moment, it became vital to lock the toilet seat as anything that could go down the pan did. Because of his lack of response, the only toy we used at bath time was Diver Dan, a wee man in a swimming costume who would dive off a springboard into the bathwater. Sadly, one night, before I could lock the toilet seat, Diver Dan went the same way as the dummy, with Dale chortling gleefully as his toy whooshed down the U-bend like a flume. After that, whenever Jamie and I were at the Battery Park on the beach, throwing stones into the water to keep Dale amused, one or other of us would periodically issue a reminder to 'keep a lookout for Dan'.

When Dale was fourteen months old, we headed north to Auldearn for a week's holiday. The quiet, family-run hotel we stayed in was where Dale chose to take his first steps. On our first night, he was crawling and trying to get up, so we encouraged this enthusiastically, taking turns to help him. The next night, after our meal, we were debating going for a walk to explore the village when Dale seemed to answer the dilemma for us. He simply stood up and walked the two metres from Jamie at the bar to me in my seat at the dinner table. During the rest of that week, he literally found his feet. There was no in-between stage; Dale was on a roll.

As his walking progressed, I noticed that Dale was developing a strange gait, and mentioned this to the health visitor. She was unconcerned, but as time went by, it became more obvious that my son was 'tiptoe walking', a trait that would take him some fifteen years to overcome. Despite many years of our efforts to help him, it would take a friend of ours, who understood Dale's problems, to get through to him.

Now that Dale was mobile, our difficulties were compounded. One day at the breastfeeding group, a new mum was sitting with her baby beside her in a car seat and I watched with delight while Dale toddled over to the baby and sat next to her. He seemed intrigued as he studied her, carefully touching her tiny hands . . . and then he whacked her forcefully in the face with a toy car. The poor wee thing screamed accordingly, but thankfully it was quickly established that no real damage had been done.

The mother herself was very understanding, reassuring me that Dale was young and didn't realise what he had done. Even so, perhaps because of my knowledge of his other anomalies, I was devastated; it felt as though I had hurt the baby myself. This wasn't helped by the fact that not all of the mums were so understanding. My guilt, as well as a deep fear that I could not prevent a recurrence of this type of incident, was such that I never returned to the group.

I did not have much time to dwell on what had happened, however. Shortly after that event, Jamie and I were driving along the coastal road, Dale sitting silently in the back of the car, when Jamie said casually, 'I suppose it's time to make an honest woman of you.' There was no preamble or fanfare – just this simple statement – but it sounded like a marriage proposal to me, so I quickly said yes, adding for good measure that we might as well get the piece of paper as we'd effectively been married since the birth of our son.

We married at the Registrar's Office in Greenock on 6 April 1990, with the reception afterwards at the Tontine Hotel. As a wedding present, Jamie's friend George had offered us the use of his dark-brown 1960s Ford Zodiac, which he drove dressed up as a chauffeur. I think the car got more attention than I did. I coordinated well with it, however, adorned in my favourite colour, sky blue. Jamie's cousin Pamela had made the cake for us, tinting the icing exactly the same blue as my dress. The only confusion on the day was that when we arrived at the hotel, the head waiter was somewhat flummoxed by the lack of anyone dressed in white. He finally approached me and cautiously asked if I was the bride. 'Of course I'm the bride,' I retorted. 'I match the cake.'

A friend of mine from work arrived with Dale at about six o'clock, explaining that he had been no bother as he had happily spent most of the afternoon in the bath. All she'd had to do was top the water up every so often to keep him warm. Dale was so obsessed with water that, if allowed, he would stand at a sink at anyone's house and fill a mug with water via the trickle of a tap, using a teaspoon. If we put a stop to this, he would go ballistic, but it did allow us to visit friends in peace.

Dale clung to me like a limpet for the whole evening; Jamie and I even danced together with him between us, clutching on to the silk of my dress. He seemed to like the sensation of silk, often wandering around with my silk pyjamas or slips, and sometimes falling asleep clinging on to one of them. All things considered, however, his behaviour at the reception was fine and we and our guests enjoyed ourselves hugely.

As if the wedding wasn't enough, Jamie spoiled me further the following day. I'd heard tales of new brides being whisked off to surprise exotic honeymoon destinations, but surely no one could have predicted what my spouse had in store for me. I was instructed to dress warm . . . and taken not to the airport, but to Firhill, Glasgow, to see Jamie's team, St Johnstone, win another crucial game in their bid to clinch the football league. This outing was at least followed up with a night in a luxurious hotel and then we went home to continue our life with Dale.

Dale's strange gait did nothing to hinder his mobility. This, and his limitless supply of energy, became one of our biggest challenges. He would run constantly, both in the house and outside, but not at all like any other energetic youngster. His running was repetitive, almost ritualistic and without purpose. He would charge across the room, bounce himself off the wall to gain momentum and race back again – droning continuously, sometimes in a happy tone, sometimes anxious. This would go on for hours and he never tired. He did this so often that the plaster on the walls started to bulge and separate where he bounced off them. He had an unusual tolerance to cold or rain and would run outside in his pyjamas, soaked to the skin, given half a chance. If anyone tried to stop him, he would respond with a challenging tantrum.

When not pursuing his *Chariots of Fire* running, Dale would often perform his 'circus spinning trick'. He would spin like an ice-skater on the exact same spot for ages, always in a clockwise direction, eyes deviating to the left so much that we could barely see his pupils. He would keep this up far longer than you would expect before the apparent reward of dizziness set in. Then he would stop for a few moments, before having another go. And then another.

Dale's greatest talent, though, was for climbing. This, coupled with a complete absence of a sense of danger, made for some uncomfortable moments. We had to move the dining table away from the single-glazed window in front of which it had always stood; being on the top floor of the building, any loss of balance on Dale's part while conquering the table could have had dire consequences.

If I moved an object that had piqued Dale's interest, I had to ensure that he didn't see where I put it, as he would go to frightening lengths to retrieve it. I remember putting some scissors on the top of a high shelving unit in our lounge and when I came back into the room a couple of minutes later, Dale was clinging on to the top shelf like a mountain climber, hand stretched out for the scissors. He had established his toy rocking elephant as base camp and from there had scrambled on to the top of the TV, before ascending to the summit via the lower shelves. I also remember him climbing on to the top of the cooker, using the kitchen drawers as a ladder. Like any toddler, he had no concept of danger, but I felt that he showed the intelligence of an older child in figuring out how to use the drawers.

Mealtimes were another challenge. Dale was rarely hungry, and in order to get him to eat at all, I tried various innovations such as arranging the food in the shape of cars or Mickey Mouse, or serving it on novelty plates. Sometimes this worked, but even then more food was thrown all over the floor and Dale's clothing than was actually eaten. What's more, he was a nutritionist's nightmare, rejecting everything except sausages, chips, chicken nuggets and pizza. Jamie and I tried to follow a healthy diet ourselves, but Dale was having none of this. There wasn't an approach or piece of advice I hadn't followed to encourage him to eat, but none worked. If I introduced so much as a single pea or slice of carrot, he would protest by vomiting at will. More worryingly, he would sometimes choose to regurgitate food simply if things were not going his way.

I also tried to get Dale to use cutlery like other toddlers, but even his plastic Mickey Mouse knife and fork would get stuck into my face or eyes rather than his food. My son preferred to eat with his hands and that was that.

Drinking was slightly more straightforward. Fortunately for his teeth, he wasn't keen on sugary drinks, preferring just water or milk. He would take as much as a pint of water in one go, which would sustain him until a similar urgent thirst kicked in. A small breakthrough came one day when Granny Madge persuaded him that he liked milky tea

– again, no sugar – and to this day, some sixteen years later, he has never refused the offer of a cuppa.

By the time he was about two, I felt that, now he was a little older, Dale should be around other children. Despite the daily grind of living with him and trying to get through to him, I hoped that being around other children might help him to learn. But I couldn't shake off the sense that my son was like a slowly ticking bomb. Deep inside me was a feeling that something about him was going to explode – I just didn't know when or how.

3
'Tree'

I found the local mother and toddler group in Peat Road, about a mile away from our flat. While somewhat nervous about how Dale would react, that first morning I was relieved to see a friendly face; Anne, a nursing colleague, and her young son seemed pleased to see us, too.

I let Dale explore the toys and did my best to familiarise him with a couple of the other children. I took my eye off him for a moment to talk to Anne, and turned back just in time to see him push a little kid to the ground so he could reach a toy fire engine. Before I could get to him, he had pushed this into another child's face, just as he had all those months ago at the breastfeeding group. I spent the rest of the visit glued to his side, desperately trying to help him to engage safely and appropriately with any child who was brave enough to go near him. It was, however, impossible; if he wasn't having a screaming fit due to me constantly saying no to him, another child would be screaming because Dale had hurt them or snatched a toy from their grasp. Anne courageously tried to take over, to let me sit and have a cup of tea, but Dale threw himself on the floor in noisy protest.

Seeing my embarrassment and despair, Anne and the other mums were generous enough to attribute Dale's behaviour to the fact that it was his first day and a new environment. I was nonetheless acutely disturbed by Dale's extreme behaviour and the extraordinary level of vigilance required by me to ensure that he and the other children survived the session unscathed. This time, however, I was not going to give up as easily as I had with the breastfeeding group.

On the next visit, although it was my turn to help set up the toys and drinks, Anne did this for me as I needed to stay by Dale's side at all times. For the next hour and a half, I tried valiantly to teach Dale to engage properly with the other children, but it was blatantly obvious to all concerned that my efforts were futile.

I persevered in attending the group, but became increasingly used to comments from the other mums such as 'I think you must be spoiling him', 'He doesn't seem to understand that what he's doing is wrong' or, most helpful of all, 'Why don't you smack him?' I grew adept at politely deflecting such interventions.

After the toddler group, as Dale clearly didn't want his play session to end, I would take him to the Wellpark, a large park round the corner from our flat. Granny Madge and Granda George would spend many hours here with him on the days when I was working and I quickly came to understand how exhausting they found it.

Dale's behaviour in the park mirrored that of the playgroup, with the added disadvantage of the potential to bolt across the acres of parkland at his disposal. He would not let us hold his hand and would throw himself on the ground if we tried, so Jamie and I, together with Mum and Dad, had developed the 'three-metre rule', whereby one of us was always within three metres of Dale, ready to catch him if he decided to take off. He seemed to enjoy the 'game' of an adult chasing after him, and many a passer-by had to seize and restrain him on our behalf.

Dale would want to stay in the park for hours, and the whole experience would be entirely on his terms. When I needed to leave, no amount of bribery or preparation such as saying, 'Time to go soon,' could end the visit, even in torrential rain. The only way to achieve this was simply to lift him up and go. His disapproval would be registered with a tantrum of mammoth proportions. I had to carry him while he screamed, punched, continually kicked my shins, scraped his fingernails down my face or tried to bite me to demonstrate the full force of his rage. Then, when I had finally got him to the bottom of the stairs to the flat, and by now exhausted, I had the north face of the Eiger to deal with.

The first curve of the spiral staircase was particularly tricky: with Dale fighting against me, if I didn't get it right, I would lose my balance, fall back down the stairs and Dale would tumble after. So I had to develop a technique to get the two of us to the top safely.

Wherever I went, I always carried my 'survival bag', a large shoulder holdall loaded with essentials such as nappies, a change of clothes, a favourite toy, sweet rewards and anything else that might help me get Dale through the day. To climb the stairs, I would put the bag strap over my head and shoulders, leaving both hands free, and then hoist Dale into a horizontal position, supporting his body on my waist. He was of course writhing and lashing out as I tried to do this, but I would eventually manage to pin his arms to his side, with his head facing away from me so he could not bite. Then we would start to climb, my right arm locked round him, my left free to grip firmly on to the handrail to help pull us up. Sixty-five stairs in all.

Occasionally, the combination of Dale's anger and extraordinary strength would mean that I couldn't even start the ascent. If I was lucky, one of the neighbours would come to assist, alerted by Dale's screams. It was easy if there were two adults: one would grip Dale firmly under his arms, the other by his feet, and he would then be lifted bodily up to the flat.

My parents, Madge and George, learned to employ this technique also and it was to become a familiar sight to the public in Greenock as Dale would be carried out of whichever shop or bank he was trying to wreck at the time.

Jamie, I knew, had still been clinging to the belief that Dale's behaviour was as a result of his premature birth and that things would improve in time. Somewhere deep within me, however, the feeling of doom about the future was steadily becoming stronger. I wondered if Dale had not got away with the damage suffered to his head at birth after all, or whether something equally sinister was going on, but 'what' I still didn't know. If Dale was perhaps developmentally delayed or had learning difficulties, then I knew I would do my utmost to help him catch up. I didn't have the faintest inkling of what was to come.

I hoped eventually to follow a career in health visiting and, to make such a transition possible, thought it would make sense if I left caring for the elderly and returned to the National Health Service. If I could reduce my shifts as well, I would be able to spend more time with Dale in the long run. I managed to get a perfect post to enable this, as a senior staff nurse, working two nights a week at Raven-scraig Hospital. I would be looking after patients in an assessment and rehabilitation ward, many of whom had suffered strokes and required rehabilitation to assist with their speech and comprehension. My mum and Jamie's mum, Dorothy, were immensely supportive, in that they would have Dale over to stay on the two nights that I worked and I would get a blissful six hours' sleep during the day, after finishing my shift. Given that Dale only ever slept for an hour or so at a time, uninterrupted sleep was a rarity for Jamie and me. Sometimes, too, Dale could be awake in the morning and start moving about but make no noise – we had to have a baby alarm to alert us in case he was up and about and doing something dangerous unbe-knownst to us.

While I was sleeping, Granny Madge and Granda George would take Dale to the Wellpark, armed with a picnic lunch as they knew they had no chance of getting him home to eat – they would be there for the long haul. But Dale was happy, the park having become his own version of Disney-world. He loved to climb up the twelve big steps of the enormous slides, touching each one ritualistically as he scaled them. Typically, he would barge in, pushing any other children in the queue out of the way. To him, they were just objects blocking his path. Then, as soon as he had slid down, he would hurry back round to the steps again, with no intention whatsoever of waiting his turn. It was the same at the swings: if he didn't get his way, or there was no swing free, a horrific tantrum would ensue in protest.

Dale would spend an hour or more on the equipment and then accept that it was lunchtime, though his participation in the picnic was more for the purpose of replenishing his energy supplies than any form of enjoyment. After lunch, he would race off to the big cenotaph, the park's crowning glory, where he would run around recklessly, climbing over the chains and playing peek-a-boo with Granny Madge as she gamely tried to engage with him. Sometimes passers-by would comment on how this was disrespectful to the war dead, but they didn't understand our desperate need to stimulate and encourage this wee troubled boy who was over two years old and still had not spoken a single word. For us, therefore, the park was too important a learning experience for Dale. He was in a place that he loved and it was a relatively controlled environment for us to try to teach him, so removing such a valuable resource at this difficult time in his life was not an option.

It was Granny Madge who made the breakthrough with Dale that was to give us all immeasurable hope for the future. I owe so much to my amazing mother. Very much an ordinary working-class woman from a large and poor Dublin family, she left school at thirteen and went straight into full-time employment. Because of the hardships in Ireland at that time, she moved to Blackpool, started work in hotel kitchens and progressed to waitressing. Extreme hard work was what my mum became used to, and this, together with a healthy dose of common sense, would prove invaluable when it came to interacting with Dale – though, endearingly, she was entirely unaware of her special attributes and qualities.

One day, as Granny Madge tried to get Dale to leave the Wellpark, he managed to break away from her and ran into a large tree by accident, not surprisingly hurting himself.

He was really upset, which prompted Granny Madge to pretend to hit the tree back. She stood there shaking a large branch, saying, 'Bad tree, don't hurt Dale.'

The next time they were due to leave the park, Madge anticipated the usual tantrum and grasped Dale firmly by the hand, but instead of freaking out, he dragged her over to the tree. Although he had no language, she nevertheless understood that he wanted a repeat performance of shaking the branch. She decided to humour him as it might be a means of getting him out of the park without a tantrum. My poor mum stood there shaking that branch for almost an hour before Dale was satisfied; but it did the trick and he left the park peacefully. 'Shaking the tree' became a regular part of the Wellpark experience and considerable time for it had to be built into the programme. It was, however, a great means of toning the arms for the 'shaker', so all was well.

On leaving the tree, Dale would insist on inspecting the caravan that was permanently parked on the road outside the park. This would easily take half an hour as he touched and stared at it, paying particular attention to the hubcaps and wheels. At least this was on my mum's route home, and she knew that once all of his obsessions and rituals had been dealt with, he would be happy to accompany her.

The breakthrough came when Granny Madge was dutifully shaking the tree one day, patiently saying, 'Tree, Dale, tree.' She had been doing this for the last several outings, but Dale's only response was to jump up and down in delight; he so loved watching the branch rise and fall, with the occasional leaf being detached in the process. Madge repeated, 'Tree, Dale, tree,' and on this day was utterly stunned to hear in reply a wonderful voice she had never heard before.

'Tree,' Dale shouted back with considerable enthusiasm. 'Tree!'

Through dogged persistence, my mother had got his first word – at twenty-six months of age. She answered him back with great glee, 'Yes, Dale, tree!'

That evening when Mum brought Dale home, she told me cautiously, 'I think I might have a wee surprise for you.' I watched, intrigued, as she lifted Dale up to the kitchen window and pointed. 'Look, Dale, it's a . . . ?'

After a dramatic pause, Dale's matter-of-fact response was, 'Tree.' Mine was to dissolve into tears. Then I grabbed one of his books, my heart pounding, and pointed at a picture of a sycamore. Once again he answered, 'Tree.'

I gently hugged him, tears still in my eyes. 'Good boy, Dale. Yes, it's a tree. I love hearing you say "tree". You're a good boy. Tree. Tree! It's a tree!' Still better was that Dale looked really happy because of my delight. I gave him a sweet reward, repeating, 'Good boy, it's a tree.' I wanted him to learn how much I loved hearing him speak.

I beamed at my mother, who observed in her soft Irish lilt, 'If this is what it takes, so be it. If we can get one word, we can get two.'

Dale seemed very chuffed with his new word, but the enormity of what would be involved in teaching him more soon became apparent. He had taken the meaning of the word 'tree' literally, thereafter assigning it to everything remotely similar and green, whether it were a real tree, a plant, bush, watercress or broccoli. Nonetheless, I couldn't ignore this momentous breakthrough.

I was so heartened by my mum's achievement that I decided to abandon my hopes of a career in health visiting. This would have meant working full-time, which I knew was not an option if I wanted to help my son, and so I chose to stick with my two shifts at Ravenscraig. My mum had shown that it *was* possible to get through to Dale, and even though I suspected that progress would be in millimetre steps, I wanted to spend as much time as I could with him. Because of the accidental approach with Dale's tree, I now realised that comprehension had to come before language. To achieve this, our own language would need to be reduced to very basic components, modified down to Dale's level. The event with the tree had taught me that we had been trying to teach Dale on our terms, bombarding and overloading him with 'our' language, although his own understanding was so poor. With Granny Madge being led by Dale on his terms, through the basic repetition of shaking the tree and reinforcing that this alone was a tree, she had finally found the key to reach him.

It wasn't so much a first word that my mum had prompted as a whole new approach, and I knew that our future efforts should be tailored to the same method that had finally produced that wonderful, glorious 'tree'.

4
The Explosion

Now that we had that one precious word, I wanted Dale to learn that if he made any further attempt to communicate, I would be 'switched on to receive'. It may sound a little extreme, but Jamie and I agreed that as far as possible all sensory interruptions in the house, such as TV, radio and music, would be turned off when we were with Dale. We also kept the answering machine permanently in answer mode: not even a phone call was going to interrupt any chance of communication or sharing a special moment with our son.

As soon as these distractions had gone and all focus was now on Dale, I noticed there were in fact many times when he would give me subtle 'invitations' to engage with him. These were as simple as coming into the kitchen to look at what I was doing, and then walking away, or even just a fleeting moment of eye contact with me. When I picked up on these invitations, Dale often allowed me to interact with him, and I felt that, in contrast with the time it had taken to get the word 'tree', this new approach had at least set us on the right path – albeit still travelling at a snail's pace.

As always, Granny Madge gave us her full support, with the result that Dale probably received as much as fifteen hours a day of one-to-one input, seven days a week.

It wasn't long before our efforts paid off. Mum and Dad

lived in full view of Greenock Central Railway Station and Dale used to love to look at the trains with his granny. When coming home from the park, he would drag her up to the entrance of the station and she would always apply the appropriate word, albeit a very simple one. Sure enough, the day came when she got her reward as Dale chanted back, 'Choo-choo, choo-choo.' He had doubled his vocabulary!

Dale's fascination with hubcaps reaped further benefits. I wasn't embarrassed to sit on a pavement with him as he scrutinised a hubcap of particular interest. I would give a simple running commentary, always trying to reinforce the names of things and what he was doing with them: 'This is a *wheel*. Dale is *touching* the *wheel*.' Then, as he would try to take me to inspect another car, I would hold back a little to get his attention. '*Car*, Dale. You want to see the *car*?' He would attempt to pull me towards the car and I would repeat my words, so that with each pull he learned that it was the car he wanted to see.

Eventually, the day came when he rewarded me with his third word, 'car'. I excitedly confirmed, 'Yes, Dale, car. Let's see the car,' and on seeing my delight, Dale repeated his new little word over and over. To reinforce the power of communication, I rewarded him with a new toy metal car in the same colour as the one he had pointed out to me. This and my praise he accepted with great pleasure.

Heartened though I was as Dale's collection of little cars grew, there was no denying that the occasional words he now echoed back to us were always spoken without expression or intention to communicate. Also, delighted as Dale was with his collection of cars, here again the absence of symbolic or imaginative play was all too evident: he would simply line up the cars, with not the slightest attempt to make engine noises. He would form and re-form these lines for hours on end if we allowed him to, and it was hard to envisage what possible enjoyment he was gaining from the activity. Yet he was totally locked into what he was doing. If I tried to engage in his play by attempting to lift one of the cars, a tantrum would result. If I stepped over his line of cars, fury would be unleashed. I had to sneak by when he wasn't looking.

While to us progress had still been made, no matter how painstakingly slow, others did not share our optimism. An increasing number of family and friends were now voicing concerns about Dale's unusual behaviour and lack of speech and interaction, and soon, as life became more challenging by the day, we would be forced to accept that we could no longer handle the situation on our own.

During yet another disastrous visit to the bank where I needed to pay a bill, Dale started pulling out all the promotional leaflets and throwing them around – much to the disapproval of other customers and staff. When I stopped him and tried to coax him back to the queue, he threw himself on the floor and went into a full-throttle tantrum. Queues were something he just didn't get – and of course it was impossible to explain to him that there was a reason for the fact that I was apparently standing around doing nothing and needed him to do the same.

I abandoned my quest to pay the bill and struggled outside with my writhing, bellowing toddler.

Two passing policemen stopped. 'Are you all right, love?

Do you need us to call an ambulance?' They thought he was having some sort of seizure.

'No, no, we're fine, thank you,' I stuttered, desperately trying to restrain Dale. 'This is quite normal.'

Fortunately, they weren't about to leave me there with him in that state and so we had a taxi home in the form of a police panda car. What a treat it was for me, with only my survival bag to carry, to have two strapping policemen make the Eiger climb back up to the flat, my son still in the throes of his violent tantrum.

'I could do with you full-time,' I told them, before thanking them profusely.

They were remarkably understanding, but did express their concern that Dale's behaviour was anything but normal.

'Maybe you should think about getting some help, love,' they offered as they left.

That night, we had a visit from a friend, Linda Reilly, who happened to be the assistant manager at the bank where Dale had made such a scene earlier. Coincidentally, she was learning British Sign Language at the time, as she had an interest in this area, and she cautiously ventured that Dale was displaying similar behavioural traits to those of a deaf child. She added, 'And if he's not deaf, then something else is seriously wrong.'

Jamie and I could not ignore the combined force of the comments from Linda, the policemen and friends and family. We resolved that we would request a hearing test for Dale from the GP, though we did feel a little confused by Linda's observation. Dale might ignore people's attempts to speak to him, but how did he get his few words?

More puzzling still was the fact that Dale was able to react to the whisper of a chocolate biscuit wrapper or the rustle of a crisp packet from about fifty paces. My hunch was that while something was obviously wrong, it wasn't deafness; but it felt right to seek a hearing test anyway, just to make sure.

In October 1990, at the age of two years and four months, Dale's hearing was pronounced normal, although the audiometrician commented that he seemed sensitive to certain pitches. Interestingly, at about that time, the health visitor twice commented in her notes that Dale seemed 'a very stubborn child'. While I didn't then understand the true nature of Dale's condition, I strongly felt that he wasn't stubborn, but frightened, confused and lost. It was as though he became overloaded as people bombarded him with their language, terrified him with their mere presence. This was never more apparent than the day our attendance at the Peat Road toddler group came to an abrupt end.

Even though Dale appeared to be learning nothing at the playgroup sessions and remained a danger to the other children, buoyed by his progress with speech I had persevered in attending the group. At the end of this particular session, as we were clearing away the toys, one of the other mums noticed that Dale had a tiny yellow teaspoon from the toy kitchen set clasped firmly in his hand.

'He can't keep that,' she ordered. 'It's got to be locked in the cupboard with the other toys.'

'I'd rather not take it from him just now—' I began.

'The children aren't allowed to take toys away,' she interrupted. 'You know the rules.'

'It's just a teaspoon,' I protested, and promised it would be safely returned for the next session.

She was having none of this and demanded the spoon from Dale. I pleaded to her that while of course I understood the need for the rules, removing the spoon now would cause the most horrific tantrum. My friend Anne also tried to reason with the mother, reassuring her that my word was good for the safe return of the spoon, but to no avail. It became clear that, come what may, I was going to have to take the spoon from Dale, and I knew that no amount of gentleness, explanation or bribery was going to prevent his devastated response.

Sure enough, as soon as I had forcibly prised the teaspoon from his welded grasp, he hurled himself to the floor, screaming, thrashing and banging his head as fast and hard as he could against the linoleum tiles. The noise and thuds from each impact were terrifying and I took hold of him as best I could, at least to try to stop the head-banging. Anne did her best to assist, but the only reaction from the other mother was, 'We've had enough of his behaviour – all of us. Don't ever bring him back here again.'

Anne offered me a lift home, but she was a stranger to Dale and his distress increased as she tried to help me get him into the car. We abandoned this idea and I said I'd wait for the bus. Then I realised that Dale's fury was too great even to contemplate this and both Anne and I were at a loss as to what to do. Eventually, she helped me get him to the bottom of the road, but it was clear that her presence was making Dale worse. I thanked her and said I'd sit with him a while and let him calm down. She understood and left, but not before urging me to get help. I promised I would call the health visitor as soon as I got home.

Without Anne's kindness and empathy, I don't think I would have had the mental strength to keep going – every scrap of which was now required for the journey home. I sat on the pavement for a while, my back against a wall as I tried to restrain Dale, but no matter what I did, his torment continued. In the end, I had no alternative but to carry this kicking, screaming, seemingly alien being the whole mile back to the flat, blood running down my face where he had managed to dig his nails in. I could of course have avoided this injury if only I had been able to keep Dale's nails cut short, but this, as well as cutting his hair, was nigh on impossible. The latter could only be achieved, when absolutely essential, if I wrapped Dale in a double sheet to restrain him, while my hairdresser sister Linda gave him a quick trim. I hated his hair being untidy, as it only compounded the public view of a mother who neither had control over her child nor concern as to his appearance. True to form, on this particular journey home I received several 'tut's from passers-by, along with bits and bobs of unsolicited advice such as that dispensed at the toddler group.

I finally made it to the enclosed area at the bottom of the stairs to the flat. Here at last I had some privacy, and although it was a relief to be free from the judgemental stares and comments, I could no longer keep a rein on my emotions. I sank on to the cold, dusty concrete floor and wept with despair, hot tears flowing freely as I clutched Dale to me. He was a little calmer now, but totally detached and oblivious to my distress. At least my outpouring of grief allowed me a brief physical rest before beginning the ascent to the flat.

As soon as we had made it upstairs, I put on Dale's *Disney's Sing-a-Long Songs*, which Jamie's dad, Jimmy, had bought him, and at last he began to calm down. I gave him a large drink of water, knowing his throat would be raw from screaming for what was now well over two hours. The video had been something of a discovery: he would watch it over and over again, never tiring of its jolly little tunes. Then he would be almost as amused by the constant droning sound and white-line screen that signified the end of the video. All this helped to cheer him up if he was upset, and it would have been so easy for us to 'plug him in' to the video to get a break from him; but we felt that in the long term this would be counterproductive, and it was in any event of little assistance if he was having a major tantrum. On this day, however, he was now exhausted and settled down to watch – and there was no way I was going to disapprove.

I moved through to the bedroom to steal what was meant to be a moment of peace, but again I was overwhelmed by emotion and this time I sobbed as never before. I had been holding it all in for so long, perhaps knowing on some unconscious level that if I let go, it would be impossible to stop. After a while, though, my grief was interrupted by the sound of breaking glass, accompanied by Dale's cries of joy and laughter. Smash, laugh, smash and a louder laugh. I hurried through to find him standing barefoot at a cupboard door in a sea of broken wine glasses. I froze as he lifted up the next glass. Then, before I could grab him, he noticed me and calmly started walking towards me, quite unaware of the danger, but somehow managing to avoid by millimetres the fragments of glass strewn all around him. While I felt momentary relief at this near miss, I was completely drained and exhausted by the tidal wave of emotion that had earlier engulfed me. I knew I couldn't go on like this. Taking a huge deep breath, I composed myself and at last resolved that it was time to get help.

In response to my telephone call, the health visitor carried out a home assessment on 7 December 1990, when Dale was two and a half. She offered little advice about his general behaviour, but did agree that his speech was poor and said she would make a referral for him to see a speech therapist. She also observed in her notes, of which I subsequently obtained a copy, that his concentration was poor, but that he could build a tower. She was referring to his efforts with Duplo, which was a set of large Lego-type bricks for young children. I'm not sure her brief note quite reflected his achievements: he had built something resembling the Manhattan skyline. He had covered the baseboard in a series of different-sized towers, each in a different colour and all having a definite structure and colour sequence. I was intrigued by how he was capable of creating more than the random jumble of bricks that might be produced by other children of his age. He was also able to complete jigsaw puzzles, some of which were advanced for his age, without reference to the picture on the box, but simply by studying the pieces themselves. He could even do this when looking upside down at the jigsaw. Our excitement at observing these abilities, however, was tempered by the fact that he would obsessively repeat the puzzles over and over again, rather than becoming quickly bored like most other children. I was also upset to read in the health visitor's report that the efforts I had made to try and socialise Dale at the Peat Road toddler group and his violent tantrum there – the very reason for her visit – were recorded simply with the words 'Not meeting any peer group.'

Despite our distress, Jamie and I were nonetheless immensely relieved that we were to receive professional help. We were looking forward to meeting the speech therapist and, hoping this might be the turning point we needed, took the opportunity to consider how else we might improve our lives. Dale had become a monster child, barred from playgroups; I had become totally isolated as a result, seeing only my parents or Jamie's; and it was all too clear that the north face of the Eiger was something we shouldn't have to deal with on a daily basis. Although we loved our home, we decided to put the flat on the market. Even this was not straightforward, as Dale did not take kindly to strangers in his house. Every time we had a viewing, one of us would have to take Dale out for a walk while the other showed the viewer round. It was a cold and wet December and these outings were scarcely enjoyable; added to which, they seemed to increase the frequency of Dale's tantrums.

Now desperate to get help, I phoned the speech therapy department at the health centre to chase up my appointment and was horrified to be told there was a nine-month waiting list. I pleaded with the secretary, who thankfully was sufficiently receptive to my distress to call back a few days later to offer me a cancellation. The appointment was to be in three weeks' time, after Christmas.

*   *   *

Shortly before that Christmas in 1990, when Dale was two and a half years old, he and I were invited to a children's party held by the staff at Inverkip House, where I had previously worked. I could barely get Dale through the front door; he seemed petrified of the whole affair. I lifted him up and he wrapped himself tightly round me, his head buried in my chest as he wailed and cried. I tolerated this for as long as I could, but Dale was upsetting the other children, not to mention some of the elderly residents of the home. Before I abandoned ship, Jean Bassett, the matron, tried to help me at least get Dale's present from Santa. In Dale's eyes, though, Santa was the devil incarnate and we had to beat a hasty retreat into Jean's office. She eyed me seriously for a moment, before saying kindly, 'I've seen this type of behaviour before.' My heart sank: I could tell from her expression this wasn't going to be good news.

I had previously told Jean about some of the problems I was experiencing with Dale and now that she had seen him at first hand, she told me he was very similar to children she had worked with in the past. She took a deep breath and said gravely, 'All of those children were autistic.'

Although at that time I didn't understand the implications of this, it still felt as though Jean had just told me my son had cancer. I had never even heard the word 'autistic' before, not even once during any of my nursing or midwifery training. I just knew that the very sound of it was terrifying, and that it was obviously a serious condition as no professional to date had even hinted at anything along these lines. Telling me was such a hard thing for Jean to have done, but I still felt she had done me a big favour. I needed to know, and the sooner I knew, the sooner I could really help Dale and make sense of him and his condition.

I made it my business to find out exactly what the word 'autistic' meant. I rushed to the local library, and as I started to read up on the subject, it was chilling how each and every book was all about Dale. I was stunned: even traits that I had thought were just part of his personality, like scratching the sides of the pram, which we had thought was quite sweet, regurgitating his food, spinning round and even his strange tiptoe gait, were all signs of classical autism. I felt as though the authors had used him as a test case.

A few days later, when there was nothing on autism in the library left to read, I gently spoke to Jamie about my findings. But he either couldn't or wouldn't process this news. He had somehow become convinced that our son had glue ear, a problem his mother, Dorothy, had told him about. Once diagnosed and treated, such children improve and I could readily understand why Jamie's own ears were closed to what I was saying. I tried again, telling him that although I, too, was terrified at the very thought of the condition, I couldn't ignore that the word 'autism' seemed to have been invented to describe Dale and that it made sense of his problems. Unfortunately, this was too much for Jamie to accept.

Devastated though I was, I remained determined that despite this condition, Dale was first and foremost my amazing son and I would do all in my power to help him.

Despite my sense of shock and Jamie's denial, we tried to go through the motions of Christmas. Dale had no awareness of the concept, but we nevertheless wanted to try to make it a special time and buy him a present he would appreciate. His favourite video was now *Mickey and the Giant Beanstalk* and while out shopping in Greenock, we saw a two-foot-tall Mickey Mouse doll, which talked when a string on its back was pulled. We thought this would be ideal for Dale, not just because he loved Mickey Mouse, but also because the few phrases this Mickey spoke might encourage Dale to respond. With 'Hi, I'm Mickey Mouse', we could reinforce that things and people had names. With 'I love you', Mickey might help Dale to understand affection. Every night when Dale started to burn out, Jamie and I would take turns to lie with him or rock him to sleep in our arms and tell him how much we loved him. We doubted that he understood, but wanted to let him know, anyway. Whether or not Mickey would make any difference remained to be seen.

We generally tried to keep our flat clutter-free, so as not to overload Dale. In the hope that he might get something – anything – out of the occasion, Christmas was no exception. The only signs were the tree and cards from friends and relatives. We bought a real tree and involved Dale in the process of choosing it at the garden centre, right through to decorating it; with manipulating and prompting from us, he selected train ornaments and some tinsel. We ensured that no presents were under the tree until Christmas morning, so as to reinforce that Santa had visited on Christmas Day; otherwise we felt Dale would have been confused.

Dale would never usually go to bed until he finally ran out of energy and so what we called 'bedtime battles' would start at around nine o'clock and end somewhere between eleven and midnight. Christmas Eve was no different and Dale finally fell asleep in Jamie's arms at about a quarter past eleven. I remember so well my sorrow at not being able to enjoy the simple pleasure of reading Dale a bedtime story; whenever I tried, he was not the least bit interested and the process generally made him more excitable and hyperactive.

We popped him into his bed that night under his big Mickey Mouse duvet cover, with Happy Ted beside him, knowing we would have an hour or two at most before he came through to get us up.

We sat with a bottle of wine, watching the carol service from the Gulf. Although trying to relax, we empathised with those servicemen: for different reasons, all of our lives were equally unsettled and we surely shared innumerable anxieties for the future.

5
The Visit

Before going to bed that Christmas Eve, we put Dale's presents under the tree, ensuring the big box containing Mickey was the first thing he would see. We then opened our own gifts so the focus would be on Dale in the morning – and of course because Santa only brings presents to children.

As was his custom, Dale got up a few times that night to try to play with his cars or run around. As was my custom, I tried to teach him that this was not the done thing. I didn't put on the lights, reinforcing that it was still dark and he should go back to bed. I repeated to him, 'Daddy is sleeping; Granny Madge is sleeping; Granda George is sleeping. Because it is night-time.' Then I lay down on the floor and pretended to go to sleep. Eventually, he stopped trying to turn on lights or play and retired, this time to our bed.

We were next awakened by our little boy sitting upright between us reciting what we called his 'poetry': 'Car, tree, choo-choo, sausage.' He repeated these words for a while, before falling asleep again. Although there was little purpose to this ritual, he seemed happy and the sound of his wee voice was just lovely.

On Christmas morning, we had to waken Dale and pull him out of our bed to open his presents. He might not have been excited by Christmas, but we were. We should have known better: Dale's reaction on seeing Mickey was quite subdued. When I showed him how Mickey worked, however, things picked up.

From then on, everywhere Dale went, Mickey went too. Dale would hold on to Mickey's hand and pull him along, as if Mickey were walking with him. Sometimes when we were out, Dale would suddenly start jumping up and down excitedly, shouting, ''Key! 'Key!' I would wonder why, but then see that Dale was right – there was always a Mickey somewhere, even if it were a tiny drawing on a magazine cover in a shop window. More importantly, he was at last beginning to grasp that Mickey himself had a name, even if he could only say half of it, and I yearned for the day when he might call me 'Mum'.

I would involve Mickey in whatever activity we were pursuing, so that, just as we had hoped when making the purchase, as well as a favourite toy he became a learning tool to teach Dale imagination and any possible social skill. I treated this giant stuffed mouse as if he were Dale's friend and role model – he would be included for picnics and choose his sandwich and then he would always get to go first on the slide. Once Dale had accepted this, I would go second and so Dale gradually learned to wait his turn at the park. Learning how to take turns and similar basic social skills would take Dale months or even years, due to his literal comprehension of such things. He would have to be taught the same social rules in every single area where turn-taking was involved, before he would finally grasp the concept. As ever, all this would draw strange looks and various comments from passers-by, but I was becoming increasingly immune to this.

Finally, in January, the day came to see the speech therapist. Although deep within me I felt that a diagnosis of autism was inevitable, I was nonetheless desperately anxious, even praying the night before that I was wrong.

Jamie was keen to accompany me as he was equally concerned about the situation, but he had now changed his workplace and was travelling thirty-five miles every day to East Kilbride. I didn't want him to waste vital time off work at this stage, as I rightly suspected this was only the start of many assessments to come, and so on this occasion I went along with Dale on my own.

The speech therapist was young but very professional and made me feel at ease despite Dale's unhappiness at being there. She took a detailed history of our lives with Dale and showed great empathy and understanding. I was relieved that she spoke to me as a professional equal, rather than an over-anxious mother, and she did comment on how well I had adapted to Dale's communication problems. I later discovered that she noted in her records, 'Mum has been slogging away with him and the results are non-existent.' Unfortunately, her concluding note summed up the appointment: 'There was no way I could assess him – he kept up a whine/cry throughout most of the session.' She did, however, recommend that Dale be assessed by the pre-school language unit (PSLU) based at a local primary school, Highlanders Academy.

That night, although the speech therapist had acknowledged that there seemed to be a serious problem, I reassured Jamie that at least a diagnosis, support and appropriate education would now be forthcoming. It gave us both a great sense of relief that Dale was now 'in the system'.

Thankfully, when I took Dale along to the PSLU at Highlanders, he was in a nice, calm, passive mood and seemed to cooperate quite well with the two speech therapists there. Again I was nervous about the implications of this visit, but ran through the history as best I could. This time, however, I gained the distinct impression that the therapists were not really acknowledging what I was telling them, especially in relation to my efforts to help Dale communicate. My suspicions were confirmed when one of them concluded, 'We'll see you again in four weeks' time. Meanwhile, you should try to expand on the words that he has.' I had been doing what they were asking for many months, yet despite my explanations they didn't seem able to grasp just what had gone into getting the six words Dale now had. I had worked with stroke patients with both expressive and receptive communication problems and did therefore have a good understanding of how to facilitate basic communication. These skills failed me now, however, and I was left quietly stunned by the therapists' advice. The irony that I should be rendered speechless by a couple of speech therapists was not lost on me.

When I explained to Jamie what had happened, he was equally annoyed and frustrated, but we resolved that in the grand scheme of things four weeks wasn't too long to wait. Besides, I didn't want to step on anyone's toes because I was medically qualified, or worse, be labelled a trouble-maker at this crucial stage.

I pressed on as before, but Dale's behaviour spiralled further out of control and every moment from the start of my day right up to bedtime battles was a challenge. Handling him on my own became virtually impossible. Many a time I would have to make an emergency stop at my mum's flat, which thankfully was right in the centre of Greenock's shopping area. As well as some much-needed TLC, I was afforded some privacy there, which given that Dale was not toilet-trained was invaluable when I needed to attend to him. Despite my having tried all the normal techniques for toilet-training, Dale had no comprehension whatsoever of the process, so this aspect of our lives had to remain low priority; my survival bag continued to bulge with a ready supply of nappies.

Any attempt to touch or even approach Dale seemed to terrify him. I tried to reduce his anxiety and confusion by putting his clothes on in the same way and order each time – for example, always putting on the right side first. I knew dressing him in this way should help to teach him sequencing and give him more confidence in the process, but he would nonetheless go rigid as I tried to get his clothes on, so much so on occasion that I was frightened I might break one of his limbs if I persisted. When I was at last successful, he would often simply strip off again and make it perfectly obvious he would like to remain naked. I never allowed this and would repeatedly have to restart the whole process from scratch.

I finally clicked that Dale might be sensitive to certain fabrics, and things did improve a little when I ensured that his clothes were cotton rather than wool, soft rather than coarse. I also realised that if there was a particular item that he seemed happy to wear, it made sense to buy it in several sizes, so that when he grew out of one, I could put him straight into the next size, once I had washed it to disguise its newness. He would also wear anything that had his hero, Mickey, on, so a lot of his clothes were dominated by the mouse. I'm sure people thought it strange that my son seemed to wear the same clothes for years, but it worked and that was what mattered. What I couldn't control, however, was the nightmare of getting Dale new shoes as his feet grew and styles and seasons changed. Even though I went to the same shop and would phone in advance to see if it was quiet, this was my greatest challenge and the resulting tantrums were horrific. I would always have a reward for him, though, once the shoes were eventually bought.

One afternoon after I'd been shopping for Dale while Mum looked after him at the Wellpark, Jamie came home to find me manically jumping on the new, bigger coat that I'd bought for our son. He thought I'd gone mad as I proceeded to kick it around the entire flat to disguise its newness – and perhaps also to vent my frustrations. Then he tackled me for it and we ended up racing round the flat kicking it to one another, giggling and shrieking like kids. By that point, such light-hearted moments were rare.

Those four weeks seemed like an eternity, but finally the day came for Dale's next assessment. We saw the same two speech therapists as before. When they realised nothing had changed, they suggested that Dale see an educational psychologist. We would receive an appointment in due course.

Six days after seeing the speech therapists, Dale's behaviour yet again changed for the worse. He flew into a tantrum, which this time, to my horror, manifested in him banging his head off the walls or floor at every opportunity. Then, as I sat astride his chest trying to protect his head, he would sink his teeth into his hands or arms – or mine – and pull at his face as though he were trying to rip the skin from it. He seemed to feel no pain, only torment. To watch a child I loved so much suffering in this way, quite unable to communicate his problems, was more than I could bear.

In deep distress, I phoned my mum. Then I piled Dale into a taxi, still screaming. The driver was cringing at first, but his attitude changed as I begged him in tears, 'Please could you just get me to my mum's? There's something very wrong with my son and I need to get help.' He got us there in double time and helped me get Dale out of the car as my parents came out to greet us.

Mum and Dad were as upset as me at the state Dale was in. As the head-banging continued, we all agreed that it was time to insist on real help. I called one of the speech therapists and the meeting with the educational psychologist was arranged as a matter of urgency – though I was later to discover that my cry for help was recorded by the speech therapist as 'not coping'. This term is commonly and in my view often inappropriately used within the health profession, and I was offended to find it was used in my case. As if anyone should *have* to cope with watching their child trying to self-destruct in front of them. And surely had I continued to try to 'cope', I would have been guilty of gross neglect in *not* seeking professional help.

On Wednesday, 27 February 1991, at the Highlanders PSLU, an assistant took Dale into the nursery and Jamie and I sat down with a speech therapist, Grace, and an educational psychologist called Mary Smith. They allowed us to express our concerns about our son and both acknowledged the distress we felt.

Suddenly, I could contain my fears no longer and cut straight to the chase, asking Mary Smith, 'Is Dale autistic?'

There was a pause before she replied, 'We are thinking along those lines, yes.'

Something inside me died. I had told myself to expect the worst, but nothing could have prepared me for the moment when I actually heard a professional confirm my deepest fears. In a strange way, as well, I felt a degree of relief because at last the inevitable had been acknowledged. I remember commenting on how important it was to get a formal diagnosis and how confused I felt when they replied, 'We don't like to label children.' They went on to describe how Dale had 'communication difficulties' and that some of his behaviour would 'come under the autistic umbrella'. I kept my grief under wraps, but I could see Jamie struggling. He now had to face the word he had been so desperately hoping not to hear.

Despite what the professionals had said about labels, we both knew it was vital to get Dale properly diagnosed so that his educational needs could be met. We therefore asked for a referral to Yorkhill Hospital, which at that time was the only place where such a diagnosis could be made. The psychologist agreed to this and went on to explain that there was currently no formal 'provision' for children like Dale. It had recently been decided, however, to start a separate little group at Highlanders for three pre-school children with 'autistic-type features', with the aim of trying to bring them to a level where they could be integrated into the existing, larger PSLU, where the children had less-serious language problems. This had never been attempted before, but because there were three children of the same age with autism, the head teacher was willing to try and see if it was possible.

Thankfully, Dale was invited to join this 'Monday Class', as it became known. We were nevertheless frustrated that he would have only an hour and a quarter there in an entire week, and also that he would miss vital hours of input because we had so many public holidays on a Monday. Dale obviously needed more time than this, as well as a nursery place to help him practise with his peers in a suitable environment, but Jamie and I were simply informed, 'We don't have the places.'

We were then introduced to the head teacher of the PSLU nursery, who was very pleasant and showed genuine empathy in light of the devastating news we had just received. She took us through to collect Dale, and as I talked to the teacher who had been looking after him, I looked uncomfortably across at Jamie. He was standing gazing out of the window – frozen, numb.

Before we left the meeting that day, Mary Smith advised us that it would be helpful to contact a man named Jim Taylor, the head teacher at Struan House School for Autistic Children in Alloa. Run by the Scottish Society for Autistic Children (SSAC), this was at the time the only school of its type in Scotland.

We couldn't bear the idea of being alone after the meeting and so the three of us headed down to my mum and dad's. I remember the drive, both of us silent, in shock.

In the back, even Dale was so quiet you could forget he was there.

At my parents' flat, I fell into my mum's arms, sobbing, 'It's autism. He's autistic.'

In her usual indomitable way, she replied, 'Is that the fancy name for it? Never mind, he's still our Dale and we'll do whatever it takes to help him.'

We were quiet again on the journey home and I was worried that Jamie still hadn't taken in what had happened. Later, I heard strange sounds coming from Dale's bedroom and found Jamie there, lying on the bed in the foetal position, clasping Mickey and crying his heart out. Humbled by seeing him this way, I hugged him, promising over and over that we'd get through this.

'We're not going to give up,' I reassured him. 'We're going to get our boy back to us whatever it takes.'

Later, while Dale 'played' quietly, lining up his cars, I sat with Jamie in the lounge over a cup of tea, both of us now calm, absorbing all that had gone on earlier. For me, it was also a chance to reflect on something I had never previously appreciated, but which now seemed to make perfect sense. I vividly remembered how Mum and Dad used to take us to visit Mum's family in Dublin when we were young. Her brother Tommy grew up with a whole system of routines and rituals, which the whole family had to adhere to. He never spoke to anyone, and looking back, it was obvious that he was severely autistic.

Dale's behaviour echoed my uncle Tommy's in so many ways, but Tommy was from a different era, when autism remained largely undiagnosed, and there was no way that I was going to let my son grow up like my uncle had been forced to then. Jamie was uplifted by my determination that Dale was not going to be dismissed in the same way we suspected other children had been in the past.

My husband knew I had a tendency to go the extra mile and reminded me of a time when I had worked on the labour ward at St Luke's Maternity Hospital. Unfortunately, dealing with miscarriage and stillbirths was a fairly regular occurrence, but one such incident had a profound effect on me. While I was pregnant, with a small but just noticeable bump, I was assigned to a young woman in advanced labour who was sedated because her full-term baby had died inside her. Sadly, it was in her best interests to have a normal delivery if possible and so she needed an experienced midwife at her side. Hoping she would not notice it, I didn't mention my pregnancy and was able to gain her trust and nurse her through her grief to the eventual birth of her dead baby, well after my shift had ended. She said she did not want to see her baby and in any event was so sedated and exhausted from pushing she wasn't really awake enough to do so. I told her I would see her again and she fell asleep, relieved that it was all over.

After my next shift had ended the following day, I went to visit her. She was sitting alone in the side room she had been allocated, curtains drawn, numb with grief. She immediately knew me as her midwife from the labour ward because she had, after all, noticed I was pregnant. I dismissed my feelings of awkwardness at this, instead trying to comfort her, though words were hard to find. Then I asked if she had managed to say goodbye to her baby yet.

'I'm too scared,' she whispered. 'And it's too late now, anyway.'

I reassured her that she had nothing to be scared of; I had prepared her baby for the mortuary and it was perfect and beautiful. I told her she deserved the chance to see this for herself.

When I went to the back of the hospital to collect the baby from the mortuary, I met up with a porter, who commented, 'I haven't done this before.' I bathed the baby in really warm water and dressed it in a plain cotton gown and matching hat before placing it in a standard hospital cot and wheeling it to the mum's room. I offered to baptise the baby if she wished – as a midwife, I could do so – but she shook her head and said, 'I just want to see my baby.'

The moment I put her baby into her arms, she broke down, tears flowing freely. I helped her to see how beautiful the baby was and she commented that it smelled lovely, noticing I had bathed it. She kissed the baby on its head and said goodbye, before saying how glad she was to have had this chance. She was immensely reassured to know there was nothing 'wrong' with her baby and nothing she could have done to prevent what happened. She thanked me as I gave her a comforting hug, tears in my own eyes, and I in turn thanked her for letting me be a special part of her beautiful baby's short life. As I said my goodbyes, she wished me well with my pregnancy.

If I hadn't done what I did, that young mother would have missed the chance to hold and say goodbye to her baby. I say this not immodestly, but because it taught me the invaluable lesson that sometimes as a professional you have to stick your neck out. You may have a major impact on your patient's life, and the consequences of your actions, or lack of them, live with that patient for ever. I also learned that no matter what life was to throw at me, nothing could compare with the loss of a child.

That evening, still very upset, Jamie went round to see our friend, John Turner, with whom he normally travelled to work, to tell him he wouldn't be going in the next day and why. John was very supportive and took the initiative of letting our other friends know, which was a huge help as neither of us could bear the idea of phoning around and repeatedly explaining the situation.

Despite my apparent determination when reassuring Jamie earlier, I felt as weak and devastated as he did. The next day, I called the health visitor, who, although sympathetic, said she didn't know much about autism and couldn't put us in touch with any other family locally that was affected by the condition. Feeling completely at sea and having cried for a whole night, I asked my GP for some sleeping tablets. They didn't work and I didn't sleep properly for weeks.

Aware of how upset we were, Jamie's brother-in-law, Peter, contacted Jim Taylor from Struan House School on our behalf and he came to see us at home the following Saturday afternoon. In those days, there was no outreach service available through the Scottish Society for Autistic Children and so Jim would customarily make home visits in his free time to parents, no matter where in Scotland they lived.

In spite of our situation, Jim made us feel very comfortable as he gave us a general view of autism. People with the condition experience difficulties relating to a triad of impairments – that is, problems with social interaction, communication and imagination. Some may also have an accompanying learning disability.

With regard to social interaction, the person may appear aloof and indifferent to other people. Difficulties with communication are both verbal and non-verbal, so there are problems interpreting gestures, facial expressions and tone of voice, as well as simply the words themselves. Flexibility of thought and the range of imaginative activities are limited, which is often evident through a lack of development in play.

Jim was in no doubt about the importance of a formal diagnosis of autism so that these impairments could be treated. We asked what was meant by the term 'autistic umbrella' and Jim told us he thought that many professionals used this term or others like 'autistic features', 'autistic tendencies', 'autistic traits', 'autistic nature', 'communication disorder' or 'a tinge of autism' as a way of not fully acknowledging the condition.

With a healthy dose of hindsight, I would say now quite simply that a person either is or is not autistic. There may be degrees of severity, but if the triad of impairments is present, then so is autism. In my view, these woolly terms adopted by some professionals can compromise the individual's treatment, as we were to discover later in Dale's life.

6

The Summer From Hell

Four weeks later, on 27 March 1991, Jamie and I put on our smart suits, struggled to get Dale into some decent clothes and set off for Yorkhill Hospital in Glasgow. I thought we should make an effort to look smart as I wanted the doctors to see that we were professionals ourselves; I suppose I had a nagging doubt that we might be patronised again.

During the first part of his assessment, Dale ignored the task the psychologist was trying to set him and went to a sink in the corner of the room, where he turned the taps on at full force. I turned them off and stood by the sink repeatedly saying, 'No,' as he tried to turn them back on again. Eventually, these efforts paid off and Dale was persuaded to return to the task in hand. The psychologist commented on how well I had managed the situation and how good I was with Dale.

We then moved on to a consultant paediatrician, who also did various tests. These included assessing how Dale responded to my efforts to communicate with him. The doctor was struck by the fact that only once did Dale turn round to acknowledge me talking to him. She asked us to take a break while she spoke with her colleague.

We were called back in again later and the doctor drew a bar graph to illustrate how Dale was functioning in various areas at different developmental levels, but that overall there was a general delay. She added that there was no evidence of autistic behaviour 'as such' and concluded that they would like to see Dale again in a year's time.

By the end of the visit, my mind was a jumble of emotions. I felt relieved, confused, unconvinced and not least bewildered as to how I was supposed to continue with Dale for another year without some sort of help. It was initially such a relief to hear the doctor say that Dale was not autistic, but how could all those books I had read, which described Dale so chillingly well, be wrong?

We were heartened when the psychologist said she would recommend 'the importance of maximum support from nursery provision'. Little did we know at the time that this request was futile because the consultant paediatrician then informed Mary Smith, the educational psychologist, following this visit that 'I believe he is getting some time at the language unit, which would seem appropriate.' This was regardless of the fact that this time was only an hour and a quarter a week. The whole purpose of our visit had been to get a diagnosis and adequate provision for Dale, but neither was forthcoming.

I asked for a referral to see a geneticist, as I was worried about the implications for any future children we might have. A referral was made, but the appointment would not be provided for over a year.

Some of the earlier writers on autism – for example, Dr Bruno Bettelheim in around 1950 – sought to attribute the condition to a mother's failure to bond with her child. He used words like 'cold and detached', and a term I came across in other texts was 'refrigerator mothers'. Although this theory was subsequently discredited by Dr Bernard

Rimland and Professor Nancy Minshew, I was appalled to discover that, some forty years later, the attitude still prevailed in some quarters of the medical profession. I didn't know it at the time, but the doctor at Yorkhill Hospital had recorded in her notes, 'The psychologist and I were both quite struck by Mrs Gardner's rather cold, detached description of Dale and his difficulties.' Elsewhere, she stated, 'Father seemed much warmer in relating to and handling Dale.'

When I learned of this, years later, I was devastated. Given the circumstances of Dale's birth and the time he spent in the neonatal unit, which would normally interrupt the bonding process, I felt I had nonetheless managed to bond with him, especially as I had successfully breastfed my premature baby for nine months. Yet in spite of this and the extraordinary lengths I had gone to to break through the wall surrounding Dale, it seemed that by trying to talk to the professionals on their level, I had been condemned. No doubt if I had displayed more emotion, I would have been written off as an over-anxious mother.

Either way, Jamie and I were angry and mortified to discover that the upshot of this vital visit to Yorkhill was that both professionals felt that 'a conflict between parents and child is causing behavioural difficulties' – that is, that we ourselves were the cause of Dale's problems. The visit we had thought would end our plight had done the exact opposite, with almost dire consequences.

I made the same mistake again when Dale started in the Monday Class at PSLU. I went along one day to see the work they were doing, which was basically very similar to what Granny Madge and I had been doing, though I noted that the school worked at a slower pace, with care being taken not to overload Dale with too much detail. While this was all to the good, I had to bite my lip a couple of times when I was given advice such as 'Try to interact with Dale with a toy' or 'Don't give him too much choice.' I then chatted to the educational psychologist about Dale's problems and the type of educational approach that was required. I later learned that the psychologist's view of me was that 'She comes across as rather clinical and detached.' It is a fact of my life that I am medically trained and yet it seemed to count against me if I talked about my son's medical condition in a technical or professional way.

When we had met Jim Taylor, he had invited us to come to Struan House School to see the work being done with the children there. Unconvinced by what we had now been told at Yorkhill Hospital and desperate to find ways of dealing with Dale, we decided to take Jim up on his invitation.

On our arrival, one of the teachers took Dale off to play with some toy trains and we chatted to Jim. Although Jim told us he was not qualified to make a diagnosis of autism, he nevertheless talked to us throughout our visit as though Dale *was* autistic and the advice he gave us was invaluable. We told him how much of Dale's behaviour was obsessive – for example, in the way he lined up his toy cars, or became fixated on one particular video, or, most recently, trains.

'Don't worry about his obsessions,' Jim advised. 'Use them.'

He told us that we shouldn't try to break the behaviour as some parents did, but should use the obsession as a learning tool and a means of breaking into the autism. I told him of the way we had used the tree in the Wellpark.

'That's it,' he said. 'That's exactly what I'm getting at.'

It was music to my ears to hear from someone as experienced as Jim that we were actually doing something right.

Jim also told us that autistic children need some time to be themselves in their own world as it helps reduce anxiety and avoids overloading them. We told him that at Jamie's parents' house Dale would play in the garden with his toy tractor and just run around for a while. He would rarely have a tantrum there as he was happy with this routine.

'That's good,' said Jim. 'You should let him have time like that – it'll be beneficial in the long run.'

'But we can't leave him in his own world all the time, can we?' queried Jamie.

'He'd be happy if you did,' Jim replied, 'but he'd never learn how to look after himself. If he's going to survive in our world, you've got to break in, challenge the autism.'

Jim suggested we use visual aids such as the Makaton sign system, matchstick-men drawings, picture cards like Do2Learn or simple photographs to help Dale's under-standing – for example, using a single picture of a tree to show we were going to the park. I realised immediately that this would be an excellent way of ensuring Dale always knew what was going to happen next, and I was already mentally designing activity charts and pictures to achieve this. It was better to over-prepare than under-prepare!

We sat in on a speech therapy session with one young boy and saw how to teach the basic pragmatics of language. It immediately clicked with me and I realised how I would have to break down the basic components of daily language for Dale. Jamie didn't quite get it, but I did and felt inspired by what I had seen. Then we all went to a large sitting room where the pupils were having a break, which in its own way was an opportunity for learning. The teachers would pass a plate round, reinforcing each child's name – 'Martin, some orange' – so that each one knew he was being spoken to. The plate would be passed almost at eye level, to give the best chance of catching some eye contact, which is not generally given naturally or willingly by an autistic child. With Dale, I had already discovered that my best chance of achieving this was always to kneel down when I spoke to him, so that I was in his eye line.

I was so impressed by how comfortable the children seemed in this environment, though paradoxically our wee boy lay under the dining table throughout, grunting and unhappy. No one in the room paid this the slightest attention.

Jim told us, 'Unless he's hurting himself, leave him.' It was better to ignore inappropriate behaviour, rewarding what was appropriate with positive attention.

I virtually interrogated Jim and the teachers that day and felt I had seen and learned so much; it all made sense and I was quite excited about applying it to Dale.

We did wonder whether perhaps Dale should go to Struan House School, but I wanted a chance to apply my newfound knowledge and Jim agreed that this was the best option for now, working in parallel with the PSLU at Highlanders. This visit was ultimately to change Dale's future. We left brimming with respect for both Jim Taylor and the extraordinary work of the Scottish Society for Autistic Children.

I also felt empowered. No matter what, I was staying on this path and would ensure that Dale got the right help and education to meet his very different needs. Whatever the medical and educational people's views, Dale was first and foremost our son, and this wall of autism wasn't going to take him away from us.

When Jamie and I discussed the day's visit back at home, we agreed that to minimise disruption to Dale, I would work on every Friday night from now on. In this way, while I caught up on sleep on the Saturday, Jamie could spend some quality time with Dale and take him out to the park or into town. We thought Dale would particularly enjoy this because it was true that he seemed to have a more relaxed relationship with his dad than with me. Although it sometimes pained me to observe this, I think it was just because I spent so much more time with Dale and had to make him do things he didn't want to do, like get dressed in the morning.

So Jamie and Dale developed their Saturday routine, which would end with a trip to Burger King. Every week, Jamie asked Dale what he would like to eat and every week got no response. He therefore ordered chicken nuggets and chips because he knew this was the type of food Dale liked.

Then, one Saturday, Jamie burst into the flat in a state of high excitement. 'Nuala!' he shouted, waking me with a start.

'What's wrong?' I gasped, thinking something terrible had happened.

'I asked him if he wanted chicken nuggets at Burger King.'

I started to protest that this was hardly earth-shattering news, but Jamie shushed me impatiently.

'He replied! For the first time ever, he actually replied.'

And what a reply it was. Our son had apparently intoned, 'No, Dad, burger.'

This was also the first time Dale had ever called Jamie 'Dad'. From then on, his use of the word was always on his terms and we could never get anything on ours, like 'Goodnight, Dad'; but we were nonetheless overwhelmed to realise Dale at least knew who Jamie was. Although delighted for Jamie, I still couldn't help but wonder if the day would ever come when I would be called 'Mum'.

Dale's vocabulary continued to expand, though not always as one might have hoped. A letter arrived one day from a midwife friend, Caroline Jones, inviting us all to her daughter's christening. We were a bit apprehensive about taking Dale to such a function, but Caroline and her husband, Maurice, were aware of Dale's problems and the setting was the lovely country village of Balfron, so we thought it would do us good to get away.

On the journey there, Dale was his usual quiet, 'invisible' self in the back of the car. We always positioned his seat in the middle so that he could see both of us and we could see him in the mirror, to try for any possible kind of interaction. We'd also put on a musical tape with songs like 'The Wheels on the Bus', to try and give him some stimulus.

Jamie was driving through the winding country roads and just as he had managed to pick up some speed on a clear run, a massive combine-harvester suddenly pulled out from nowhere, right in front of us. Jamie stood on the brake, narrowly avoiding a collision, but in the stress of the moment his customary laid-back manner deserted him and the word 'Fuck!' escaped rather loudly from his mouth. Dale seemed not even to have noticed the incident and didn't stir from his trance-like state.

In the church, the usher asked us to move nearer the front, but we stayed at the back in case we needed to make a quick exit. Our fears were unfounded, however, as Dale settled down surprisingly easily and sat there as quiet as a church mouse. The ceremony began and all was well. Our son seemed to be paying studious attention to the minister's words and we actually felt like a normal family – right up until the moment that the minister began to anoint the baby's head. Dale suddenly found his voice, and a new word, which he tried out at full volume: 'Fuck!' It seemed once was not enough and my darling boy kept on shouting, 'Fuck! Fuck!' with no evident intention of stopping. Jamie hurried outside with Dale and I bowed my head with embarrassment, though couldn't resist a discreet smile to myself. In the graveyard, Jamie tried to divert Dale with a tree, but he loved his new word and inside, as the minister continued, a distant, repetitive 'Fuck!' could clearly be heard. At Caroline and Maurice's house after the service, perhaps in a quaintly British way, no one mentioned the incident.

So we survived the day and for once enjoyed a laugh in the process. We also realised that Dale had in fact demon-strated another common trait of autism, known as echo-lalia. Sometimes he would echo a word or phrase he heard right away, or it might crop up weeks later, either in or out of context, but always in the same tone it was originally spoken.

*   *   *

At Dale's Monday Class, his interest in cars and trains had helped him to settle in and the staff suggested that he try Tuesday mornings as well. Unfortunately, however, this was a step too far and the staff noted on his records that he found the nursery 'overwhelming' because he was so young and his comprehension 'very limited'. It was decided, however, that after the summer holidays, when he would be a little older, he should attend the PSLU for four mornings a week during an assessment period. Meanwhile, there was no offer of an alternative nursery place while the unit was closed from the end of June until mid-August. This was despite my constant pleas, as well as the fact that the educational psychologist had acknowledged in her notes the risk that Dale might regress if he did not continue to receive input. I was equally aware of this, which is why I desperately wanted some sort of support to continue.

I also needed respite myself. Since being placed in the system in January, Dale had received approximately ten hours of educational input from the PSLU, which had allowed me brief periods of peace; yet now I was to be left with no help at all during the long summer break.

I struggled on day and night, trying to put what I'd learned at Struan House School into practice, but Dale's responses were slow to non-existent. I knew I could never provide the learning benefits that Dale would receive in a nursery environment among his peers. I had reached saturation point with him on a one-to-one basis and felt my efforts were becoming futile. Worse still, the lack of nursery support during those summer months meant I was slowly and surely becoming physically, mentally and emotionally exhausted. If I hadn't chosen to carry on working, to let me get some sleep and a break from Dale, I probably would not have survived what Jamie and I still refer to as 'the summer from hell'.

Perhaps our problems were compounded by the fact that we were also on the move. We had finally found a buyer for our flat on Roxburgh Street and it was with some relief that we bade farewell to the Eiger stairs. We bought the upper right quarter of a large, traditional villa in Gourock. It was located on Ashton Road, which was a busy main road, but we thought the bus stop right opposite would be handy for travel. By far the biggest attraction of this location, however, was the amazing views – the vast Clyde lay just across the road and somehow the height of our property made us feel as though we lived right beside the river. Dale loved to run along the beach, tossing pebbles into the water.

On the day of the move, Jamie's parents took Dale for the day and Granny Madge and Granda George gave us a hand with our possessions. We organised the living area quite quickly and – apart from black bags and cardboard boxes everywhere – we were in.

When Jamie's parents brought Dale home that evening, he ran into the lounge and straight to one of two big windows. True to form, he adopted this as 'his' window, as it framed the Clyde before it. There were countless yachts and the Cal Mac ferry to Dunoon passed by every half-hour, top-heavy with cars, trucks and even the occasional ambulance. It was such a special way for Dale to see all these different vehicles.

Later, while I saw Jimmy and Dorothy to the door, I asked Jamie to check on Dale. He came back shaking his head in both amusement and disbelief.

'What's so funny?' I enquired.

'Go upstairs and take a look,' he smiled, and then followed as I crept up to see what was going on.

There in front of me on the landing was a long row of cars, stretching from the front to the back of the house. Dale had also found something different to add to his line-up, in a bag which had spilled open during the move. He was using my diaphragm cap as a tunnel, with the accompanying tube of gel as a train. I shared a chuckle with Jamie, and as I turned to go, he observed wryly to Dale, 'You might as well have fun with it, son, because we don't.'

While Jamie's one-liner was as witty as ever, and it was great to witness Dale's symbolic play improve as he chanted, 'Choo-choo,' sadly there was a serious subtext. With everything going on in our lives and the exhaustion that brought, it was true that there simply wasn't any time for 'us' any more. In an ironic way, I was reassured that Jamie was equally aware of how Dale was dominating every aspect of our marriage.

Dale loved standing looking out of his window, but knowing our son as we did, Jamie's first priority was to get sturdy locks fitted to all windows and doors. Granda Jimmy duly arrived with his toolkit and usual expertise and made the house safe and secure for Dale. The rest of the house needed work, but we lived in it as best we could while carrying out the refurbishments. Our efforts would periodically be interrupted by young screams of delight and we would know that *The Waverley* paddle-steamer was passing by on the river. I always made sure I joined in Dale's appreciation at this moment and the two of us would jump up and down excitedly, waving at the boat. How could I ignore such a wonderful invitation from Dale?

All in all, we felt we had made the right move in coming to Gourock, but we were not to know in those early days how the geography of the area was shortly to affect our lives.

There was a small shop about 200 metres along the road from the house, selling the usual essential groceries and newspapers. I would take Dale with me sometimes, although he wouldn't let me hold his hand. At least he knew we were heading for the shop, but a leisurely walk was out of the question and he would dash in its direction, with me running along behind him. We would make our purchases – so far, so good – and then Dale would refuse to retrace his steps, leaving me to carry him home in a screaming tantrum.

One day, I asked Jamie to take Dale with him to buy a newspaper and fresh bread. After a while, I became worried; it was two hours before they came home.

On leaving the shop, Dale had insisted on turning right as opposed to left and then going into Hillside Road, which climbed up steeply to the top of Gourock. That was the first mile. The road that led behind our house was the second mile, and then they descended the very steep Victoria Road back on to Ashton Road for the last half-mile. This circular route became the only one that Dale was happy to follow when we went out, and failure to conform would result in a tantrum of epic proportions, so life was becoming impossible.

To avoid the circular route, I had to avoid the shop, which meant crossing the busy road beforehand. I would take tight hold of Dale's hand or even carry him, along with Mickey and my survival bag, which was increasingly heavy these days as Dale would load it up with toy cars in addition to our other essentials. I freely admit there were times when I couldn't hold on and Dale broke free – which also happened with Jamie and his mum – and it seemed as though my son had more lives than a cat as he ran across that busy road. I vividly remember one day when Dorothy was bringing him home and we heard a loud screech as a car braked suddenly. This time, if it hadn't been for the driver's skill, I fear Dale's luck would have run out.

The last time I was to take Dale out on my own during this never-ending summer started innocently enough at home. The weather was lovely and I thought I would walk Dale to the station in Gourock to look at the trains, take him to the Wellpark and then round off the day with a visit to my mum's. It took the usual hour or so to get Dale ready and then we set off with Mickey and the survival bag.

I definitely did not want to get involved in the circular route and so decided to cross the road. Dale was holding Mickey and allowed me to take his free hand, which gave me hope that I could get across without having to pick him up. As we stood at the roadside, I spoke crisply: 'Dale, we look, we look . . . No cars . . . Walk!' We started to cross, but when we reached the white line in the middle of the road, Dale screamed and tried to pull me back; he had dropped Mickey at the kerb. Before I could react, he threw himself down, crashing his head off the concrete in full fury. To lessen the obstructions for the oncoming traffic, I hurled my survival bag to the pavement like a shot-putter and tried to lift Dale. But it was impossible. All I could do was sit astride him for what seemed like an eternity, cupping my hands behind his head as he tried to smash it against the concrete; I was powerless to stop him pulling my hair, clawing at my face and kicking wildly. Cars hooted angrily and pulled out round us, and a small group of passers-by gathered at the kerbside.

Eventually, the newsagent who owned the shop ran to my rescue. He intervened with the onlookers, retrieved Mickey and handed him back to Dale. Then he helped me get Dale up and a kind lady gave me back my bag. This process was accompanied by comments from the onlookers, such as 'That kid needs a damn good smacking' or 'Disgusting behaviour'. For once, I couldn't ignore it and rounded on them furiously: 'The only thing that's disgusting is the way you're all gawping at a handicapped child.'

I hate using the term 'handicapped', but it seemed the only way I could get the message across to the public and occasionally elicit some sympathy and help from them. Even so, on other occasions, the word would draw the response 'He doesn't look handicapped to me.' Autism is often referred to as 'the unseen handicap' because there are no visible physical features that betray the condition. Sometimes I tried saying that Dale had a 'communication problem', but this would produce blank expressions or replies such as 'He's got no problem communicating now, has he?' Mainly, though, as far as the public were concerned, my son was just 'a wee spoiled brat'.

In the face of all this, the debate about Dale's diagnosis caused me even more stress and grief as even though I knew emphatically that he had severe classical autism, I felt I couldn't actually say this to anyone because it wasn't official. In the end, however, following many futile attempts to explain his behaviour, I decided simply to tell people Dale was autistic.

Although to many people this word still didn't mean much, the very sound of it had the desired effect. Some would show empathy and move on, while others wanted me to explain what autism was, even if Dale was in the middle of a challenging tantrum.

After I'd hit out at the onlookers that day, the newsagent took Dale and me into his shop and closed the door to customers. Then he and his assistant helped me to calm Dale down, notably with the aid of a big bar of chocolate, which Dale devoured despite his distressed state. Once Dale was finally quiet, the newsagent helped me take him home and wished me well. When I thanked him for all he had done, he replied, 'You're welcome; but you really must get help.' I will never forget his kindness – either on that day or the many other occasions afterwards when he would witness Dale in full flow and always show empathy and understanding.

After the newsagent had gone, I locked all the doors and cried – deep, racking sobs, wishing I could find a way out of this hell . . . wishing I was dead. I loved Dale so much, but while I respected his disability, I hated his autism.

I let Dale watch his videos; I let him stay in 'Daleyworld'; I let the autism win. I had no will to challenge or break into it. I was just dying inside, wanting it all to end. I watched Dale as he sat on the floor holding a car, rocking back and forth whining, and my tears escalated. He got up and stood in front of me, laughing out loud as I cried, such was his lack of empathy and low comprehension of emotions. I felt that day that despite all our efforts, autism was now engulfing him – and no matter what, I was losing him to it.

I phoned my mum in deep distress and she and Dad came to see me. She reassured me that she would find a way round this latest problem and that both of them would continue to support me in any way they could. I would never have managed for as long as I did without my parents' dedication – to me and, especially, to Dale.

7
The War: Part I

At last that long summer began to draw to a close. On 20 August, Dale, who was now almost three years and two months old, returned to the PSLU at Highlanders. The assessment period during which he would attend four mornings a week was to be six weeks long. It had to be mornings as that was the time allocated for the Gourock area.

Getting Dale ready for the special PSLU bus every morning was a nightmare. No matter how late he had gone to sleep – rarely before midnight – or how many times he had been up during the night, he was always fast asleep at around 7.30 a.m. when I needed to get him up. So I would have to rouse him, thereby prompting a tantrum, which obviously did nothing to facilitate the ensuing tasks of changing his nappy, washing, dressing and trying to feed him. Many a morning he was handed over to the helpers on the bus, at eight forty-five, half dressed or minus his shoes and still in full-blown tantrum. Some days, the helpers, Liz and Isobel, would come into the house to try to help get Dale to the bus and they were impressively calm and patient with him. During his calmer moments, it was clear he liked them and I acknowledged their support gratefully. All they could say in reply was that they understood how hard it was dealing with him. Just knowing that they appreciated how difficult my life had become meant a lot to me.

By noon, Dale was back and I would have to find ways to amuse him until Jamie came home from East Kilbride at around six o'clock. While Jamie would always muck in to help when he got back, he once confided to me that he would sometimes sit outside in the car for a few moments, taking long, deep breaths, steeling himself for whatever dramas lay ahead on entering the house.

In spite of our ongoing battles with Dale at home, he settled quite well into the new routine at the language unit and I was pleased to learn that he was showing early signs of interacting with the other children, as well as the beginnings of some constructive play. Nonetheless, although the unit was now giving him two hours of input, four days a week, this still only totalled eight hours a week, and I used to feel really annoyed that the staff never acknowledged my efforts and would talk to me as if I knew and did nothing. There were another 160 hours in the week, during which Jamie, our parents and I would do our utmost to teach Dale, day and night, trying to break in – just as we had been doing since that fateful day of the tree. Yet continually in their notes the staff would ignore our input, referring to the situation at home only in terms of how I was 'coping' or 'surviving' with Dale. I wonder how they would have coped if they had had to spend more than just two hours a day with him, having to do all the things he hated to do.

I was literally a prisoner in my own home with Dale and so, at the end of August, I asked the speech therapist at the PSLU for a nursery place for him in the afternoons, emphasising how horrendous the summer had been. I was stunned by her response: 'We feel that our initial fears that he might be autistic are unfounded.'

'What makes you say that?' I enquired, as calmly as I could.

'Dale is making progress in the unit,' she said simply.

'I'm delighted he is,' I countered, 'but it's such a small amount. Surely it's not enough to rule out autism?'

Although she conceded that his overall abilities were 'low', her opinion about autism remained unchanged.

Soon afterwards, the opportunity arose for both Jamie and me to speak with the speech therapist again, this time together with the educational psychologist. We tried to convince them how important it was to recognise Dale's autism and the implications this would have for his future education. Jamie and I will never forget the educational psychologist's reply: 'Mrs Gardner, I think you *want* your son to be autistic.' We often felt patronised by other comments, such as 'We know like any parent you want the best for your child.' Through time I learned to answer this with, 'Actually, you're wrong. I don't want the best for my child; I just want Dale to have the same chances and opportunities as any other child.'

I could do no more to get Dale diagnosed, and Jamie and I became increasingly frustrated and angered by the professionals' continuing denial of his condition when we realised that their educational approach with him in fact mirrored that for a child with autism. At a review in November 1991 with all the PSLU staff, when Dale was three years and five months, we were told that the future aims for his education were to improve eye contact, develop pointing and increase his minimal vocabulary. Additional goals were to improve Dale's ability to interact with adults and children, as well as his ability to play constructively. In other words, the educational approach would effectively be to address the triad of impairments.

At this same meeting, one of the staff commented on the fact that Jamie's face was badly scratched on both cheeks. He looked as though he had been attacked by a wild animal. When Jamie explained that the culprit was in fact Dale, during a particularly challenging tantrum, the staff seemed unable or unwilling to accept this. For once, I was relieved that I was a compulsive nail-biter – it was plainly evident that the tips of my fingers were not up to inflicting such damage.

The situation led to numerous arguments between Jamie and me, as well as with the professionals. 'I don't understand why you're so hung about what label they put on it,' he would say. 'Surely the main thing is that he's getting help.'

'But he could end up with the wrong label and get the wrong kind of help.' I tried to explain my fears that if this happened, he would inevitably be sent full-time to another nursery and be treated as a child with severe learning difficulties. It would then be routine for him to end up eventually in a special school with children who had a diverse range of severe disabilities.

I felt alone, despairing that no one was listening to me and terrified that if Dale didn't improve, then his future would slip beyond my control. For me, it was paramount that in addition to the two-hour input he had at the PSLU, four days a week, he should spend time in a nursery in the afternoon, mixing with mainstream children who did not have communication problems. He would be in a safe, controlled environment where what he was learning at the PSLU could be put into practice, and also the children themselves could be role models for him. Unfortunately, despite Dale's progress, the PSLU didn't see it this way.

Outside of Dale's two hours at the PSLU and one-hour total journey time, I was left alone to deal with him for the remaining twenty-one hours of the day. Despite my constant phone calls and pleas for a nursery place, I was continually told, 'We don't have the places or the resources.' Finally, however, my badgering gained a result of sorts: I was to be allowed a home teacher, who would visit one afternoon a fortnight, 'to help mother cope and play with Dale at an appropriate level'. At first, I found this demeaning: I knew how to work and play with Dale; what I needed was a nursery place for him. But as this clearly was not to be forthcoming, I would try to embrace the help that was being offered. Thankfully, this was in the form of an amazing professional named Terri, a qualified primary teacher with knowledge of special-needs disabilities and autism. I thought if she could witness the horrendous time I had with Dale, this would strengthen my case to get a nursery place. It would also give Dale another person to relate to, as well as the one-to-one education he so definitely needed. Terri was to become an understanding and supportive visitor; of all the health professionals I had encountered so far, she alone was my lifeline and saviour.

Her fortnightly visits were all too infrequent, however, and I still felt as though my day-to-day existence was a kind of living hell. Then, in the midst of all this, one extraordinarily good thing happened. I was vacuuming the hall, while Dale sat watching from a safe distance at the top of the stairs. I suddenly heard a loud shout above the noise: 'Mum!'

In utter shock and delight, I turned off the machine, looked my son in the eye and said animatedly, 'Dale, Mum's hoovering.'

He made no reply, so in trepidation I switched the vacuum-cleaner back on. The same thing happened: 'Mum!' and I turned off the hoover, this time showing even more excitement at him calling me 'Mum'.

This process went on for half an hour, with me vacuuming the same metre of carpet over and over again and Dale giggling in delight every time he interrupted me with a 'Mum'. I eventually went to the top of the stairs, where, unusually, he let me cuddle him. I told him, 'Yes, Dale, I am your mum, and you are my Dale.' We ended with his favourite tickling game.

After that, he would only occasionally call me 'Mum' and, as with Jamie and 'Dad', it was always on Dale's terms. We yearned for the day when we could say goodnight to him and have him reply, 'Goodnight, Mum. Goodnight, Dad.' While it was wonderful finally to be called 'Mummy', there was still no denying Dale's lack of empathy or love for me: he would say, 'Poor Mummy', at the same time as he was hitting out angrily at me. To put this in context, Dale would many a time address inanimate objects in the same way as he would us. One day when we came into the hall, he greeted the vacuum-cleaner with, 'How you doing, Hoover?'

By this time, it was almost impossible to take Dale out anywhere. A trip into town seemed to terrify him, and shops, cafés and supermarkets all became no-go areas for us. A seemingly simple task like buying a new pair of shoes was a complete nightmare. The only place I could take him now was the Forum Shopping Centre in Greenock. Even then I wouldn't attempt this on my own. The only way the outing could work was if Jamie or Mum was there to take Dale endlessly up and down the escalators while I grabbed some shopping. Due to my mum's astuteness, however, all this was about to change.

One day, after I had snatched a few hours' sleep following a night shift, I met up with Granny Madge and Granda George at the Wellpark. There next to them was a big old-fashioned pram that my sister Linda had used for her children when they were small.

'What on earth is that doing here?' I asked my mum.

'This is Dale's new transport system,' she replied with a wink. 'We've been everywhere in the town with it today – he loves it.'

Although he could barely fit into the pram, I think it just made Dale feel safe and secure – like a cocoon. It was also a considerable improvement over the PSLU staff's offer to provide an invalid buggy and safety helmet, which would have lasted him 'for years'. I had baulked at this because I did not want to think of him travelling like this for years; whereas with the pram, he would naturally grow out of it and be able to continue developing. I was to discover that as long as I carefully prepared him for what we were doing, I could take him pretty much anywhere in the pram, although it was too big to keep at home and so had to be left at Mum's. Even with the benefits reaped by the pram, however, life was still hell.

We had a back garden at Ashton Road, which was fenced off with heavy-duty wire, about a metre high, and accessed by a lockable gate. Sometimes I would sit at the kitchen window with a much-needed cup of tea and watch Dale play, deep in Daleyworld, and sometimes I would join him. He would dig up the earth in the flowerbed in a repetitive and obsessive manner, then stop and simply gaze at his hands, held closely in front of his face, while chanting his poetry: 'Car, tree, train, sausage.'

I was feeling very lonely and trapped in the house with Dale that one day. Then, suddenly, the phone rang. Instead of letting it go into answer mode, I took the call – I was desperate to speak to someone. It was my good friend Eleanor and it was great to chat to her. Then, aware that time had passed, I said I'd better go and check on Dale. When I went into the garden, he was nowhere to be found. I screamed his name and searched frantically, then to my horror noticed a big bend in the wire fence where he must have scaled it. Heart racing and stomach churning, I searched the adjacent two neighbours' gardens, looking everywhere I could think he might be. In the third garden, and just as I was about to give up and call the police, I spotted a shed right at the back and went to look behind it. There was Dale, standing laughing with delight at the 'prize' of being found. I grabbed him, shaking with relief, and he continued to laugh as we negotiated the obstacle course back to our house.

That night when Jamie came home, I told him we would have to spend thousands on fencing. As we talked about what had happened and everything that had gone before, I realised I hated living in this house – it obviously wasn't the

right place for Dale and his autism. We decided to sell up
and move on as soon as we could.

Following that horrific day, Dale would regularly engage
in disappearing acts, even though he was unaware of the
concept of being lost – he just thought we should know
exactly where he was to be found. One night, Jamie and I
realised he'd disappeared and searched the house in vain for
about a quarter of an hour, this time at least reassured by
the fact that he couldn't be far away: although we couldn't
see him, we could smell him. The need for a nappy change
finally betrayed his position at the back of our big hall
cupboard, where he had managed to squeeze himself into a
small box.

Attending to Dale's needs became even more of a battle
as his rituals and obsessions grew increasingly rigid and
unpredictable. Just as I thought I had a handle on one and
could interpret what he meant, he would change it. And he
didn't understand that another person didn't know what he
was thinking. If he wanted a slice of bread and butter, for
example, he would drag me to the fridge and touch the
Makaton bread picture on the door. I would simply spread
the bread with butter, fold it over and give it to him – and
he was always perfectly content with this. Then, one day,
every time I tried to give him the slice of folded buttered
bread, he screamed with anger, ripped it up and threw it
away. Eventually, there were only three slices of bread left
and the floor was littered with Dale's rejects.

I took a moment to reflect on what I had learned from
Jim Taylor, the head teacher from Struan House School,
and then with some trepidation began again. This time, I
carried out each stage of the process very slowly, while Dale

carefully watched. I took the slice of bread out of the bag . . . No problem. I picked up the knife . . . scraped it over the butter . . . spread the butter on to the bread . . . all the time looking for signs of disapproval from Dale, but none came. Then I held the buttered bread in the palm of my hand and just as I was about to fold it over the way he liked it, Dale smiled. He grabbed it from me, folded it over and wandered off, at last happy. That was it – all he had wanted was to fold the bread over himself. His expectation was that I should know this. These changes to his rituals made the lonely days at home seem even longer.

Mealtimes became horrendous, as suddenly sausages were no longer allowed to touch baked beans and so on. These rituals began to dominate and literally take over Dale. Bedtime battles became all-out war. You'd think that might have exhausted him, yet still he didn't sleep, and neither did I. One morning, Jamie came down into the lounge to find me asleep on the floor behind the door, with Dale lying beside me.

My work gave me respite while Mum and Dorothy continued to look after Dale. But Jamie and I didn't want to take advantage of their kindness and so the few social outings we had been having, such as the odd drink with friends or trip to the cinema, stopped altogether. By now we were soul-destroyed, with no energy or motivation for such pursuits, anyway. We didn't even feel like eating and would survive on tins of Baxter's soup, which we came to call 'apathy soup' – perhaps just a shred of our sense of humour remaining.

I started to suffer from panic attacks and would be awake all night – when not dealing with Dale, I was just desperately anxious about what the next day would bring. Jamie witnessed this, but was powerless to help because he had to be in a fit state for work himself and by now had seen me like this so often. Things eventually reached a point where I would be ready to leave the house the very instant Jamie came home from the office – I couldn't take another second with Dale. Then sometimes I would stay at Mum and Dad's overnight at the weekend and my relationship with Jamie deteriorated further. Conversations began to focus on splitting up, and I remember one time saying to Jamie, in a bitter reversal of the usual form of custody battle, 'Fine, go. But you're taking Dale with you.'

I was so despairing that I had no idea how irrational I had become; it just felt sensible to end this hell of a life I had to bear. I remember pleading with Jamie for us to split up and he gave me his reassurance that he would look after Dale. Then I went to see my friend Lorraine.

'Great news,' I told her happily. 'Jamie and I are splitting up.' I ranted on in her kitchen about how everything would be fine now and Dale wouldn't miss me or my love because he didn't know who I was or what love was.

Lorraine took hold of me, shocked. 'Nuala, stop this, you don't know what you're saying.' She tried to give me a hug, but I shook her off.

'I'm fine, Lorraine, really,' I said manically. 'Trust me, it's for the best.'

But she persisted gently, 'Come here,' and wrapped her arms round me.

I could fight it no more and collapsed against her, sobbing uncontrollably.

I left her once I was calm, assuring her that I was all

right. Inside, though, I was numb and I went home feeling like a shell of the person I used to be. Jamie, too, was in deep despair, and we didn't resume our talks of separation – maybe we just couldn't be bothered. All we knew was that life at home for both of us was intolerable.

On the few occasions when I was out shopping, I had started to buy bottles of paracetamol and hide them when I got home. I felt desperate, angry, lonely, helpless and worthless. Only during my shifts at Ravenscraig did I feel that I bore any resemblance to the person I once was. My colleagues knew what I was going through and supported me as best they could. Even they were shocked one night, however, by the sight of me when I arrived for work. Earlier that day, while trying to restrain Dale as I got him ready for the bus, he had thrown his head back at full force, banging it against my chin and causing a tooth to pierce the corner of my lip. Seeing that it was infected, my colleagues sent me to Casualty, where I was given strong painkillers and antibiotics.

I will never forget the morning of Thursday, 14 November 1991, when I realised I literally couldn't take any more. There was no one event that triggered it. I just put Dale on the bus as usual and felt numb as it drove away. I had lost my child – not perhaps in the same way as the woman with the stillborn baby, but I had nonetheless still lost him, to severe autism. I could no longer bear it. I think on some level that is why I had extracted the promise from Jamie that he would look after Dale. I needed to know he could do that.

I went into the kitchen and took out the bottles of paracetamol I had hidden, the painkillers left over from

Casualty and a few sleeping pills that I still had from our days at Roxburgh Street. I poured a large glass of water and started to empty the tablets into a small bowl so that I could crush them into a powder. As a nurse, I knew this would enable better absorption.

As I started to crush them a few at a time between two large spoons, I tried to calculate exactly how many I should take to ensure that they really worked. I felt nothing emotionally at this point, except a strange sense of relief. Then I became more concerned about the calculation – if my plan was to be effective, I had to lessen the chances of being sick. As this dilemma got hold of me, I collapsed on to the kitchen floor, leaning against the corner units as my tears silently started to fall.

'This has to work,' I thought. 'I don't want to wake up. I have to get this right.'

But I couldn't work it out. In deep despair, I lay down fully on the floor, feeling unbearably cold, my body shaking. I curled into the foetal position to help overcome the coldness, tears still rolling down my face. My head was in turmoil – why could I not calculate a simple overdose! I decided I should get up and carry on crushing the pills, anyway.

Then I noticed in the small gap between the washing-machine and tumble-drier an object lying forgotten. I saw it was a brown wooden truck that Jimmy had made by hand, painting bold white letters on to it to identify the owner as 'Dale'. I crawled over and seized it, hugging it as if it were Dale himself, rocking back and forth, sobbing, pleading, 'Why me? Why my son? Why won't they help me? Why won't they help him? *Why?*'

As I gradually began to calm down, I was hit by the full impact of what I had nearly done and I knew that I couldn't leave Dale and Jamie to life on their own. They needed me; I needed and loved them so much. I was the best chance Dale had. All these thoughts whizzed through my head at the same time, together with, ironically, some medical information – if I didn't take enough pills, not only would my attempt obviously fail, but I could end up with permanent kidney or liver failure, or brain damage.

I remember I was boiling with anger as I cleared away the mess and pitiful display I had created on the worktop. I poured the powder down the sink and went through to the lounge to try to compose myself. Somewhere, a voice inside me, probably that of Staff Nurse Gardner, was urging me to do the right thing and phone the health visitor for help. I remember being virtually unable to form the words as I tried to speak to the health visitor, finally begging her to come and help because I couldn't take any more. She acknowledged that I was 'very upset and at the end of my tether' (her words) and started firing questions at me.

When it became clear that she was trying to establish whether I was going to hurt my son, I was taken aback, shocked. 'I'm not going to harm Dale,' I assured her. 'What's the point of that? No, I was thinking of killing myself.' I put down the phone and prepared for her arrival, weak but at least with a sense that at last the professionals would know how serious things had become and that someone was finally, *finally* going to listen.

The health visitor arrived promptly. Still in shock and with shaking hands, I attempted to make her a cup of tea.

Seeing my struggle with this basic task, she said gently, 'Nuala, let it go. It's all right.'

This was all it took for me to break down, dropping my head on my arms on the worktop in extreme distress. 'I just can't take it any more,' I sobbed. 'I love Dale, but I need help. And so does he.'

She acknowledged that I needed a break and spoke about arranging immediate weekend respite for Dale at the local hospital in the children's ward. I let her phone my doctor and arrange to have me seen later, and he told her to call the consultant paediatrician to get Dale admitted for crisis respite. I remember thinking it strange when the health visitor asked me to speak to the consultant myself. He asked me if I was going to harm Dale and again I had to explain myself, remarking, 'I wouldn't have stuck it out this long if that was my plan. The only person I intended to harm was me.' I then listened as the health visitor struggled to convince the consultant that I needed a break from Dale.

The outcome of all this was that I was to take Dale and meet the consultant at the ward for a weekend admission.

When the health visitor left, I phoned my mum and told her what had happened. She was crying as she reassured me she would come with me to the hospital. 'Whatever happens, I'm always there for you. This time, things *will* get better.'

I can still vividly recall the tiniest details of that day. I took out a small suitcase and thought meticulously about what Dale would need. Then I stood ironing two identical pairs of pyjamas and another two with Mickey Mouse on them, tears streaming down my face. It was strange that I was ironing such items for Dale because I never normally did. I remember being in turmoil as I tried to decide which cuddly toy to pack. I settled on Happy Ted, as Dale always liked to cuddle in with him, and then I snapped the case shut and we set off, as usual with Dale's friend, Mickey, in hand.

I desperately didn't want Dale to go to the hospital, as I knew it was going to be terrifying for him, but for once I had to think of my own health – I had to get myself back in order to continue helping him. I also thought that this admission would once and for all let them see Dale at his worst and finally get his autism diagnosed.

8
The War: Part II

Mum and I were equally shocked at finding ourselves on our way to the hospital in such circumstances. Dale at least was calm, helped, I think, by his granny's presence. By the time we arrived at the ward, he had switched off, retreated completely into withdrawn, passive mode. A consultant paediatrician with a young nurse at his side took Dale and me into a side room, asking Mum to wait outside. I remember thinking this was strange, but was in no fit state even to think straight, let alone challenge his decision.

I tried to explain to him how difficult life was with Dale and how Jamie and I desperately wanted a proper diagnosis. Then I froze as the consultant gestured to the nurse to take off Dale's coat and top so he could examine him with his stethoscope. My stomach heaved; I felt sick. I knew there was no need at this moment to listen to Dale's chest and from the look on the nurse's face it was obvious that the real purpose of the examination was to check for signs of physical abuse. I felt degraded, like some sort of criminal.

At least the consultant seemed to take on board my pleas for help and said he would like to talk to Jamie and me later. I managed to impress on him that I did not want Dale admitted to the ward as he would find this too distressing and so a call was made asking my GP to prescribe a strong sedative for Dale, so that we could all get some rest. Although I wasn't comfortable with the idea of having to sedate Dale, it seemed the best option in the short term; meanwhile, we would get a diagnosis for him, together with adequate nursery provision. We also felt it would be less traumatic for him than a lonely, petrifying stay in a hospital ward. I didn't want him to go away – I was just desperate for help.

While my mum looked after Dale, I collected the prescription for Dale's medication, Vallergan Forte, a strong, hypnotic syrup. I was to give him a 5-millilitre teaspoon (containing 30 milligrams of medication) and repeat the dose later if it didn't work. It didn't, and Dale needed the repeat dose. I later discovered that the consultant had suggested to the GP that if this medication proved inadequate, he 'could try him on some Temazepam, in a dose of 10–30 milligrams at bedtime'. While I suppose this was an acknowledgement of how difficult life was at home, I was still shocked that adult sleeping medication would even be considered for a child as young as Dale.

I was then informed that, with the consultant's approval, they wanted me to see a psychiatrist. As far as I was concerned, given my fragile condition, this was feasible, but I nonetheless found it horrific that these people thought it acceptable to restrain my son chemically rather than provide an afternoon nursery placement for him, which was all I had wanted. I was also later to learn that the educational psychologist wrote in her notes to the consultant, 'Child well placed at Highlanders re: structured education.' With hindsight, it appears that a decision had been taken that Dale was receiving sufficient input at

Highlanders and that the question of whether nursery resources were available was immaterial – my pleas were simply being ignored. This is further borne out by the health visitor's records. She went to the language unit a few days later to observe Dale for herself and noted that she would 'keep in close contact with nursery staff, working towards Hillend placement for child'. Why did they have to 'work towards' this? Why could it not be now? Even as I write, all these years later, I am baffled by this obstruction and disbelief in my plight. It seems all anyone concluded from my cry for help was that I would harm Dale, as noted by the consultant: 'The health visitor phoned and told me that Mrs Gardner was going to do the boy physical harm if he wasn't admitted to the ward.'

To cap it all, the health visitor also noted, 'Visited nursery to observe child at play and did not see "bizarre" behaviour as described by mother, although child does have communication problems.'

The evening of my suicide attempt, Jamie and I sat numb with shock and painfully aware of just how serious our situation had become. I hadn't called him at all during the day, as I knew my calls just left him feeling helpless because he was so far away, and he needed to work or we would lose everything. So he had been entirely unaware of everything that had happened, until I recounted my terrible story on his return that evening. He was appalled by just how fragile my health had become, and was all the more supportive because of it.

It is still painful for me to relive how harrowing it was to give Dale his medication. There was no way he was going to take it voluntarily, and we couldn't explain to him what was going on, and so we had no alternative but to phy-sically restrain him and administer it against his will.

At around 9 p.m., Dale would normally do his *Chariots of Fire* running in the lounge. During this, I prepared Dale's medicine in a plastic syringe and then Jamie had to catch him and get him down on to the floor. Once there, Jamie would kneel, cushioning Dale's head on his knees, while I sat astride him, locking his arms by his sides with my legs. The only way then to administer the sedation was to syringe it down the back of his throat and hold his mouth shut to make sure he swallowed it. Inevitably, he would scream and wail throughout, and seeing such distress, there was nothing I could do to stem my own flow of tears. To this day, Jamie and I still remember the fear in Dale's eyes as he was subjected to this appalling ordeal.

As if that were not enough, the sedation did not work instantly. My tears continued and Jamie sat with his head in his hands as we witnessed Dale staggering around the room. He became increasingly disoriented and Jamie moved closer, ever ready to lunge forward to stop him banging into furniture and injuring himself. He would eventually keel over on to the floor and fall into a deep sleep; then we could change his nappy, put on his pyjamas and slip him into his bed. He would snore like an old man, and concerned about the possible side effects of such strong medication, I ensured he was lying on his side with pillows supporting his back, so as to maintain a safe airway.

That first night, I sat with him a while, stroking his hair and face, silent grief almost choking me. Before I left, I placed a gentle kiss on his cheek and whispered, 'I'm sorry, sweetheart. I love you so much.'

When I came downstairs, Jamie had made us a cup of tea and we sat on opposite ends of the sofa cradling a mug each, too numb to speak. The complete, eerie silence between us was acutely disconcerting and I remember feeling nervous, as if perhaps I was on a first date and the conversation had dried up. We were like a couple of strangers and the need to go and check on Dale's breathing was almost a welcome interruption. His respiration was clearly depressed by the drug and I checked up on him regularly throughout the night.

At eight o'clock in the morning, I found Dale bouncing up and down on his bed as if the events of the previous night had never occurred. In fact, he was more excitable and euphoric than usual and it was impossible to get through to him in any way.

Both Jamie and I knew that there was no way we could accept this draconian treatment as a solution and vowed to get him off it as soon as possible. Quite apart from the distress it caused to all of us, if kept on the medication Dale would inevitably develop a resistance to it and need a higher dosage, thereby hindering any educational input and probably even causing him to regress. During this period, the staff at the PSLU noted he was 'not interested in activities in the nursery, not able to concentrate [. . .] Apparently, he is on Vallergan to help his sleeping problems, but this appears to be affecting him through the day.'

Three long weeks after my near suicide attempt, Dale still had not been offered an afternoon nursery place and there was no reassurance that one was to be forthcoming. In the meantime, after more consultations with the local paediatrician, I was referred to a psychiatrist, with Dale. I naïvely thought this would be to get Dale diagnosed and provide appropriate support for me. I later discovered, however, that the paediatrician's notes to the psychiatrist observed, 'Obviously, the mother is very volatile and the boy may well be at risk.'

While waiting for the appointment with the psychiatrist, we yet again had to go through the motions of Christmas. Emotionally and physically drained, I sent no cards, though Jamie insisted on sending a few to keep up appearances. Such was my despair that I worked a night shift on Christmas Day as I couldn't bear the thought of being at home. On Boxing Day afternoon, Jamie and I had an argument about the Christmas-tree lights, which weren't working. The tree looked as depressed and ridiculous as we felt. Jamie refused to fix them, saying, 'Why bother?'

'You're right, why bother?' I agreed sarcastically, as I angrily set about ripping up the cards we had received. At this, Jamie lost it. He unplugged the tree and tossed it outside the back door like a caber, still fully decorated. To this day, we still refer to that time as 'the year of the flying Christmas tree'.

The medical notes record the professionals' surprise that we had in fact survived the festive period. I can't help observing that if they'd listened to what I'd been telling them, they would have known that such 'survival' was down to Jamie being off work and me not being continuously on my own with Dale.

The New Year heralded a major breakthrough: Dale was finally allocated an afternoon place at Hillend Nursery and would at last get the full educational provision he required, which would help me to work with him and hopefully he would also start learning to integrate with his peers. However, I was later to read in the educational psychologist's notes that the place was provided solely 'in order to give Mrs Gardner some further time without Dale'.

Our second appointment at Yorkhill Hospital was as futile as the first. A whole year later, we were still being blamed for Dale's condition: 'Unfortunately, his parents have great difficulty coping with Dale and I think that he probably does get a lot of negatively distressed responses from his parents.' I don't know what it would have taken to get the doctor to understand that while we may have been 'negatively distressed' when talking to her *about* Dale, we avoided as far as was humanly possible being that way *with* him. She rounded off the encounter by noting that Dale had made significant progress in the past year and suggesting that we *wanted* him to be autistic rather than acknowledge his developmental delay. In an infuriating sense, she was correct about Dale's progress – infuriating because none of it was attributed to our efforts with him. Dale's progress in spite of the lack of nursery provision was proof that he could be helped. We realised after this visit that unless we could get a diagnosis for Dale, we didn't have a chance of helping him.

The day that I had waited a year for finally came and Dale and I visited Hillend Nursery before he was due to start properly in mid-January. We were taken into what was known as 'Room 2', where I noticed a few children with obvious disabilities, including a couple who were clearly autistic; but more importantly the majority were without disability and all socialising and integrating together. This was a perfect peer group for Dale and what I had so desperately wanted from the start.

There were plenty of staff to assist and Dale didn't seem fazed in this room at all. Here, at last, was an ideal environment to complement the work being done by the PSLU, my mum and me. Dale found a corner and played happily in his own way, allowing other children and staff beside him in the process. I was greatly relieved that it looked as though he would be able to settle here. I was offered a lift home in the nursery bus and chatted to a member of staff, happy at last, explaining my relief that all had gone so well. I will never forget her reply: 'Think yourself lucky. Some parents I know have two kids affected.'

As Dale settled into his new routine at both nurseries, I slowly started to benefit from the respite this allowed. With some free time at last, I decided to give Dale's bedroom a minimalist makeover so as not to cause him sensory overload. If there was the slightest possibility my plan would help us address the nightmare of bedtime battles, it was worth a go.

We involved Dale as much as possible in the process and offered him a choice of wallpaper from three swatches – clowns, flowers or pale blue, bold stripes. He chose the stripes, as I knew he would. We gave him one small wardrobe and a side table for a lamp and the few toys he would use at any one time. In the wardrobe, I hung only one shirt, and the drawers below contained just one pair of socks, pants and a vest. This was because if the wardrobe was full, Dale would take everything out and throw it around the room. As time passed, I would gradually increase the contents of the wardrobe as he learned to leave them alone.

Although the finished result was that Dale's room looked nice, I was struck by how sad it might appear to anyone else, with just the bare necessities and only a few toys visible. But, thankfully, it was such a success with Dale that we were able to wean him off his sedation. The battles to get him ready for bed would still be the same, but he would at least then go to his own bed, albeit very late. We had bought him a double bed to allow room for one of us to lie beside him to get him to sleep. It was frequently Jamie who did this, cradling Dale in his arms, telling him over and over that he loved him, until he finally drifted off. Another consequence of the larger bed was that Dale decided as part of his new bedtime routine to put all his toys in the bed with him, including his tricycle. In this way, he was happy to stay put until around the middle of the night, though we always woke up with him in between us. I wonder why this confused wee boy sought solace from us like this if all we had ever given him were 'negatively distressed responses'.

In February 1992, as yet another attempt to get a diagnosis, I went with Dale to see the psychiatrist at the Larkfield Unit in Greenock. Mum came, too, as moral support, and thankfully was allowed to stay in the room with us. Dale played contentedly in the corner with some small cars and farm animals. This allowed me to talk freely to the psychiatrist and give her an honest account of the challenges of living with Dale and his problems. I had thought this was the point of the visit, but it seemed that whatever I did was wrong as I was later to read the psychiatrist's observation that 'Whenever I tried to join in his play, he resisted. Neither his mother nor his grandmother made any attempts to do so and there was no real interaction between them.' Not only was I being criticised, but my poor mother, who had done so much for Dale and us, had also been dismissed by a total stranger.

When I explained to the psychiatrist my previous suicidal feelings and cry for help, her line of questioning became more probing. I could no longer bite my tongue and blurted out, 'Excuse me, are you vetting me as a child abuser? Do you have any intention at all of helping Dale or giving me a proper diagnosis?' With this, I declared the meeting at an end. The psychiatrist offered me another appointment to discuss any anxieties I might have with Dale, but I replied bluntly, 'The last thing I'm looking for is cups of tea and sympathy. I'm going to get proper provision and my son's autism diagnosed if it's the last thing I do.'

Shocked by what she had heard, Mum sprang to my defence: 'Dale can push anyone to the limit, but there's no way he's ever been in danger.' The psychiatrist seemed unconvinced and Mum tried again: 'Surely the proof is that my daughter wanted to kill herself rather than harm Dale?'

We got nowhere. The upshot of the meeting was that the psychiatrist recorded that Dale had 'severe developmental delay and communication difficulties' and, most upsettingly, noted that I was having difficulties coming to terms with him and that she had concerns over our relationship.

I was still so livid when I got home that I could barely talk to Jamie about what had happened. Once I had managed to explain, however, he was as angry and distressed as I was. We both agreed enough was enough and, as a last resort, together devised a plan of action for the meeting with the paediatrician that was due now that I had seen the psychiatrist. We wanted to see just how far they were prepared to go to try to show that it was my treatment of Dale that was wrong.

At the meeting in March 1992, Jamie deliberately went along with everything the paediatrician said. I remained slightly more reticent, as this was what would be expected of me. The paediatrician's recommendation was that Dale be admitted to hospital for a series of tests. I was horrified that the doctor was willing to try to put a cannula into Dale in order to conduct the various tests he had in mind for him. A cannula is a fine plastic intravenous drip needle that stays indefinitely in the patient's arm to allow access to a vein for blood analysis. One of the blood tests the paediatrician wanted to carry out meant that Dale would have to fast, yet he didn't seem to appreciate that the lack of food, or water alone, would be stressful for Dale. Also, there were to be X-rays of his skull and 'long bones', a process which, quite apart from leading to unnecessary exposure to radiation, would have petrified Dale. And despite all of this, the paediatrician assured us, 'There's little chance anything will be found.' He also made it perfectly clear to Jamie that I would have to stay in the hospital with Dale. I realised from the way he insisted that this would be so that the manner in which I dealt with Dale could be assessed as well, but I pretended to go along with it all.

By the doctor's own admission in his notes, the proposed tests were 'really to supplement the negative tests from Yorkhill'. It is horrifying to me to think that my son could have been harmed, mentally and physically, through these unnecessary tests.

We specifically raised with the paediatrician our concerns that Dale had autism and told him of our visit to Struan House School to see Jim Taylor. His only reply was, 'What does he know? He's only a teacher and that school isn't for autistic children, anyway.' We politely thanked him for his time and left him arranging for Dale's and my admittance. As soon as we got home, Jamie wrote to him confirming that we had no intention of going into hospital.

It saddened us greatly to have to go to these lengths, but as I read Dale's notes now, they confirm our fears were justified. A path for Dale was being prepared that could have destroyed any hope he had of a decent quality of life, as evidenced by the paediatrician's admission to a colleague following our meeting that Dale was 'a wee boy who sounds as though he has got non-specific mental retardation [. . .] You will see the various investigations I have suggested and you are free to add any others. It would be good if you could undertake putting a cannula into this wee boy because he will not be easy.'

When our appointment to see the geneticist at Yorkhill Hospital at last came up, we were both shocked and relieved to discover that Dale really had had a near miss regarding the invasive tests. After taking a thorough history, in which I mentioned my uncle Tommy and others with language problems and disabilities in the family, the geneticist commented, 'Since there is no explanation for Dale's handicap, there must be a possibility that genetic factors have been combined in Dale.' Then, crucially for us in light of what the paediatrician had wanted to do, 'There

are no tests which can be used to diagnose Dale's condition.' There were simply genetic-screening tests for other
conditions or chromosome disorders, should we be thinking of having more family in the future. In this last respect,
the geneticist felt there was only a ten per cent chance that
any further child we might have would be affected by the
type of problems Dale had.

Looking back, Jamie and I wonder how many other
children in similar circumstances might have been put
through a string of medical examinations and tests that
were as harrowing as they were pointless. We also feel I
might have been singled out as a suspect for Munchausen's
syndrome simply because of my medical training; it was as
though they thought I was using this as a smokescreen to
conceal the real problem, that it was me who wanted
attention. It was obvious from the notes that many involved
with Dale didn't believe what I said about what he was like,
either at home or outside. If I was such a potential danger
to Dale or others, though, why was I allowed to continue
working for the same health trust with a ward full of
vulnerable elderly people directly under my care?

In desperation, I wrote to Jim Taylor. A couple of weeks
later, he came to see us, with a teacher colleague, Janet
Stirling. Janet played with Dale while we brought Jim up to
date, and after observing Dale for a couple of hours, Jim
acknowledged, 'It's vital that we get a diagnosis.' He added
it was a shame we didn't live in Nottingham, as a Professor
Newson at the university Child Development Centre was a
leading expert in autism. Jamie explained that by coin-
cidence we were going to the Centre Parcs holiday village in
Sherwood Forest in two weeks' time. Jim agreed to contact

Professor Newson, and almost before we knew it, we had an appointment to see her.

Backed up by Jim and Janet's view that Dale's problems were remarkably similar to those they dealt with every day, we felt empowered. We were already members of the Scottish Society for Autistic Children, but now joined the National Autistic Society as well, as we did not want to miss out on any initiatives that might help Dale. We had also recently attended a conference and workshops on autism and so headed off to see Professor Newson as genned up as we could be.

We spent a full morning with her and talked her through Dale's history from birth to the present, while a PhD psychology student also made a detailed assessment. Finally, with Dale aged 3 years and 11 months, after sixteen months, and appointments with thirteen different professionals, a diagnosis was made: Dale had classical autism. No other condition was identified, and Professor Newson used the triad of impairments to describe Dale's autism in her report. She gave various recommendations for his treatment and more specifically mentioned that Dale had 'language disorder of a global kind, affecting gesture, facial and other body language'. The language disorder of autism is greater than would be expected merely as a result of a child's general learning difficulties. Crucially, Professor Newson expressed optimism for Dale's capacity for continual improvement, as long as 'appropriate educational and therapeutic intervention' was provided. A copy of her report was sent to the paediatrician and we never heard from him again.

At a review meeting with all the staff at Highlanders in

May 1992, we were subjected to the usual scepticism and then asked if we had any comments. At this point, I produced from my bag copies of Professor Newson's report for each of them, which vindicated us entirely.

The educational psychologist acknowledged to Jamie and me that we were more relaxed since Dale's diagnosis. I felt like yelling, 'Of course we're more relaxed. His condition has finally been recognised.'

At least we could go home knowing that, at long last, we were to be allowed the dignity of acknowledging our son's disability as autism.

9
Thomas: A Really Useful Engine

Dale's autism was now a fact we had to live with, but the daily struggle was no easier. When Terri's fortnightly visits came around, Dale would lash out at her and refuse to cooperate. She couldn't work with him like this so we would take him out instead, usually for a drive to a quiet park in Largs. This gave me the opportunity to talk to her, which I found immensely helpful. She also introduced me to an array of specialised toys and educational resources, which were to prove of vital assistance. One such toy, I recall, appeared in our lives in about August 1992, when Dale was just over four years old.

Mr Wiggly Worm's cute, smiley face was impressed on a bright-red wooden rod, which was attached to a piece of rope, about a metre long. The other end of the rope joined a flat piece of wood with numerous holes in it, which was painted in various greens to look like the grasses in a garden. Wiggly Worm could be threaded in and out of the holes . . . and that was that. Yet this simple toy became an extraordinary resource; I doubt that even a computer would have been such a useful educational tool for Dale at that age.

We would play with Mr Wiggly for hours, singing a special Wiggly song as he went up and down in his 'garden', with me holding him at eye level to try to catch some eye

contact with Dale. I used the toy for anything and everything I could think of: tickling Dale, playing tug of war or
trains, and one day the worm even became a sausage. Dale
laughed heartily as I pretended to eat Mr Wiggly with
lashings of red sauce, poured from my imaginary bottle of
ketchup. I had to say 'red sauce' because calling it 'tomato
sauce', when it was so different in appearance from an
actual tomato, would have been too complex for Dale to
understand, and confusion over something like that might
have put him off the game completely.

Despite Dale's previous unscheduled disappearances,
when unknown to him he was lost, if we specifically tried
to play hide-and-seek with him, he found the rules very
difficult – he would always hide in the same place. I tried to
help his understanding with Wiggly, leaving the long rope
trailing out to give away each place that he was hiding, but
unfortunately Dale still couldn't grasp the concept of the
game.

One afternoon, I was putting away washing upstairs,
having left Dale in the lounge watching children's TV
cartoons. Rapturous laughter suddenly erupted from his
direction, and never having heard anything quite so hearty
from him, I sneaked down to see what was giving him such
joy. There he was, stood in front of the TV screen watching
an animation of *Thomas the Tank Engine*. The engines
were of the original type with fixed faces and Ringo Starr's
narration was translated into Gaelic, but no matter – Dale
was so happy and receptive to *Thomas* that I immediately
phoned Jamie and sent him on a mission to purchase a
Thomas the Tank Engine video.

Happily, the video Jamie bought was in English and showed the new generation of trains, with different, exaggerated facial expressions. We found that by copying these expressions and relating them to the trains, Dale would respond and slowly understand what we meant by them. Granda George and Granda Jimmy would sit with him for hours drawing trains with different faces – happy, sad, surprised and so on – because we now understood that in this way there were fewer non-verbal signals for Dale to decode than with a human face.

I am not surprised to learn now, all these years later, that recent research has shown that many children with autism have a particular love of *Thomas the Tank Engine* and that the bright colours and clear facial expressions make the characters easy to relate to and identify.

Eighty per cent of our communication is non-verbal, coming from eyes, faces and body language, and it is in this area that people with autism often have the greatest difficulty. They find it extremely hard to interpret these unspoken signals or understand that behind a person's facial expression may be thoughts, feelings and emotions very different from their own. To this day, Dale still finds non-verbal communication his biggest problem as he tries to make eye contact and decode the legion of signals a human face throws at him. Even with the spoken word, it is a challenge to understand the meaning behind all the many and varied tones of voice. With the incident with the slice of buttered bread, Dale simply thought I should know what he wanted and he must have been so confused as my face and tone of voice became more stressed as I tried to work this out before I ran out of bread.

Dale predictably adopted *Thomas* as his new obsession. With Jim Taylor's words 'use the obsession' ringing in our ears, we plunged in and from that day onwards it was welcome to the world of *Thomas the Tank Engine and Friends*. Dale seemed to love *Thomas* because of the motion and sound of the trains, the rigid tracks, the predictability and repetition that the videos allowed. He inhabited the fantasy world of *Thomas* on a daily basis; it was his compromise with the real world. What was important for us was the world of learning that opened up as a result.

We started to take Dale to the Transport Museum in Glasgow, which he loved to explore in great detail, his interest helping break down the barriers between his world and ours – just as it had in the past with the Wellpark and Mickey. His favourite car there was a Rolls Royce, which he subjected to extraordinary scrutiny. We were intrigued as he would show us tiny details like the Rolls Royce emblem in the centre of the hubcap, which many might have missed. And of course he loved the trains, referring to the museum itself as 'the steam trains'. We felt he should have been given a loyalty card, we visited so often.

Over time, the *Thomas* trains helped us to teach Dale so much: primary colours; nouns – all things have names; verbs – Thomas is *climbing* the hill; adjectives – *big* Gordon and *little* Percy; prepositions – Henry is *in* his tunnel, or *under* the bridge; opposites – wet/dry, on/off, same/different. But the most difficult component of all to master was pronouns – understanding how to insert 'me', 'he', 'she', 'you' and 'I' into a conversation was Dale's greatest problem.

We used the numbers on the *Thomas* trains to help Dale with the rudiments of counting and continued to explore every other means we could think of to exploit *Thomas*'s teaching potential. To help Dale play imaginatively and constructively, for example, Jimmy built a row of engine sheds so Dale could put the engines away at night and we would reinforce the associated language as he did. The staff at the PSLU were carrying out similar work, and due to us all having a consistent approach, the results slowly started to come. It would take many months, and in some cases years, but Dale was gradually acquiring basic language and social skills.

We indulged in a little poetic licence with the *Thomas* characters, adopting our own descriptions to help Dale understand their individual personalities. Trust Thomas was train number one, a little blue engine with 'fun friends', showing Dale that having friends was good. The social rules of friendship were so complex that it would take years of playing with Dale and the trains before he would grasp this mammoth concept and understand what real friendship meant. With Trust Thomas, who could be relied on as a friend, the meaning of emotions, honesty, mutual respect, forgiveness, lying, white lies and good manners would all gradually be taught.

Number two, Elderly Edward, who was big and blue, was old and very slow. I would say things like, 'Dale, I am so tired. I feel like Elderly Edward. I have been working so hard.' Then Helpful Henry, number three, was the green engine who helped to save the forest and was Dale's favourite. So it went on, with Grand Gordon, number four, the fastest and strongest; and Jealous James, number five, who couldn't bear for another train to equal his splendid shiny red paint. Perky Percy illustrated to Dale the concept of happiness, while Clarabel, who was occasionally coupled the wrong way in the videos so she couldn't see the beautiful island of Sodor, gave him the concept of sad. Then there were Donald and Douglas, the Scottish twins, who deliberately lost their numbers and plates so people couldn't tell them apart and they could misbehave. All the while we would do really animated and exaggerated voices, which appealed greatly to Dale's sense of humour.

Bertie the Bus became Boring Bertie, as he always wanted to race Thomas to prove roads were better than rails. Given autistic people's obsessions, we felt the concept of 'boring' was particularly important to try to get across, and this would help Dale in the future in terms of engaging with other children in the playground. Harold the Helicopter gave Dale an interest in other forms of transport, and he especially liked the whirring noise of the rotor blades.

Occasionally, I would lie down on the floor, my face turned away from Dale, and he would run his toy *Thomas* trains along me as though I were the island of Sodor. In this way, I gained his trust and he gradually allowed me to join in his play.

We used the Fat Controller (as he was then) to introduce Dale to the idea of figures of authority – the Fat Controller was in charge and made sure all the trains ran on time and were 'really useful'. This helped to prepare Dale for meeting people in similar roles – for example, the way the Fat Controller led and guided the trains was similar to the way a teacher would run a class. Perhaps most importantly, we were able to teach Dale that people, like the trains, had individual personalities, with different emotions and needs, which would all come across as they socialised together. Plus, what we were doing was a great catalyst for imaginative play in the first place.

We didn't know it then, but some of the *Thomas* characters would in their own unique way open doors of opportunity for Dale later in life. We owe so much to *Thomas* that we still have him in our lives and family, and always will, even if hearing the signature tune in passing does make us shudder, having penetrated our brains on a daily basis for years. But while Thomas was indeed 'a really useful engine', we always remembered to use this obsession constructively and try to introduce other interests as well.

One evening, we all sat down to a fish and chip supper, with Dale in a seemingly passive mood. Jamie had just come back from work in East Kilbride and we were both tired. I started cutting up Dale's food for him and he suddenly started to chant, 'Steam train, steam train, steam train.' Jamie's heart sank: he knew what this meant. He tried to explain that the Transport Museum was closed, but Dale kept on repeating, 'Steam train,' ever more insistently.

'He doesn't understand the concept of "closed",' I gently reminded Jamie.

Jamie immediately realised what had to be done to solve the problem. 'I suppose I might as well spend the next couple of hours driving a happy boy up to Glasgow and back,' he observed, 'than fighting the inevitable tantrum if I don't.' So he got Dale ready for the sixty-mile round trip.

I waved the pair of them off, calling, 'Goodbye, darling,' to Dale.

He promptly echoed back, 'Goodbye, darling,' as he carried on walking to the car, not looking back at me once.

Realising I had a couple of hours to myself, I ran a bath, knowing for once I could enjoy it in peace and quiet.

Jamie told me later that Dale had been his usual self on the way up to Glasgow, saying nothing, but sometimes grabbing hold of Jamie's hand, face expressionless. I think now that this was Dale's way of showing his gratitude that Jamie was doing what he wanted.

It was dark when they pulled up in the empty car park. They walked up the stairs to the Transport Museum and Dale pulled at the door, but it didn't move. Jamie knelt down to Dale's eye level, explaining, 'You see, Dale, we can't go in. The museum is *closed*.' Dale remained quiet and Jamie continued, 'It's dark, Dale, night-time. No one is here.' Dale was still quiet, but tried the museum door again. Jamie reiterated, 'The museum is *closed*. The steam trains are resting, ready for work tomorrow.'

Seemingly happy with this explanation, Dale echoed, 'Work tomorrow,' as Jamie turned him back towards the car.

'That's right, Dale,' said Jamie nervously, wondering whether he would get away with this. 'So let's go home and rest, too, like the trains.'

Another echo from Dale – 'Like the trains' – then just as they reached the car, to Jamie's eternal relief a single word from Dale: 'Closed.' With this, they set off on the return leg of the journey.

When they arrived home, I was snug in my bathrobe, relaxing with a nice glass of my favourite red wine. 'How was it?' I asked.

'All right,' said Jamie, exhausted but pleased. 'I think he actually got the message.'

Uplifted, I reassured him, 'We can do this, you know. It's going to be so hard, but we can do it – together.'

'Aye, we can,' replied Jamie. 'But only if we have no other life.'

He was right of course: caring for Dale left no time for anything else. Nevertheless, I felt so happy for Jamie to have achieved such a breakthrough. He had been really tired and it had taken time, distance and effort, but the concept of 'closed' had been cemented for ever. Dale grew to hate the word, but we loved it because we could use it to our advantage whenever necessary.

That night, as he sometimes did, Dale clambered up on to Jamie's chest as he lay on the couch. Jamie looked over at me, observing, 'It's great that he's learned a new word, but wouldn't it be wonderful if when you asked him his name, he would answer correctly?' To prove his point, he turned to Dale and asked him, 'What's your name?'

I'll never forget the look of stunned amazement on Jamie's face when our son replied for the first time ever, 'Dale.' It was almost as if, through their extraordinary trip to the Transport Museum, Dale had made a special connection with his brilliant dad. It was another example of why I used to tell people, 'Good cop, bad cop, that's us.' Jamie was the good guy, as he did most of the fun things with Dale, whereas I was the bad cop who was more like his teacher, continually challenging his autism.

If there was a chance to teach and socialise Dale using his transport obsession, we seized it. From a Sunday-supplement advertisement, we learned that there was a working steam railway at Boness that had *Thomas the Tank Engine*-themed days, where they would attach the characters' faces to the trains. We thought this would be ideal for Dale, but as soon as we arrived, he threw a major tantrum, refusing even to set foot inside the station.

We thought Dale was simply overwhelmed and excited, as we'd seen the same distressed reaction when he had got a train set for Christmas. We had also learned by now that there is a fine line between fear and obsession, in that a fear of something can itself become an obsession later.

We tried for about thirty minutes to soothe him, even returning to the car to do this, but he remained welded to Jamie, screaming in rage. Bearing in mind how well we knew him, and somewhat to the disbelief of onlookers, we eventually decided to carry him into the station, still in this state.

As soon as he saw the two old carriages that were being used as a café, Dale calmed down and went on to enjoy the whole experience greatly – especially the trip to the clay mine on a big, black steam train, which Dale particularly took to because it looked like one of the Scottish twins from *Thomas*.

I had also recently hit on a system whereby every time I took Dale into town he was allowed to choose his next train. These cost about £5 a time, but I didn't mind; in asking for them, Dale was communicating – and bargaining – with me, and a deal was struck so that as long as we bought the train first, he would let me take him through the town for a while without fuss. This system had the added benefit that Mum and I were able to wean Dale off his previously preferred method of getting around town, the pram.

Inevitably, Dale's train collection reached saturation point. I got round his desire to buy a train every time we went into Woolworths by having two identical purses. One was my actual purse and the other was where I kept a few coins and, occasionally, a £5 note. Dale had great difficulty understanding the concept of money and so I taught him that things like a train could be bought with paper or 'big' money, like the £5 note. If I did not want to buy him a train on a given day, I would make sure the second purse contained only coins and say to Dale when we were in Woolworths, 'No toy today – we just look.' Then I would show him the purse, explaining that the coins were enough to buy a sweet treat or a comic instead. Eventually, I also used this technique to teach Dale the concept of greed.

In April 1993, we were finally able to move out of Ashton Road and into a detached house in a quiet area of Green-ock, Dresling Road. The first thing we did was to make over Dale's bedroom along the same lines as Ashton Road, only this time, mindful of the need to divert him from his *Thomas* obsession, with a maritime theme as we still took him to see the boats in Gourock and the Transport Museum. Dale helped paint the walls and loved the result. We finished it off with a wooden floor, which allowed him to run his trains around more easily.

We moved to Dresling Road because it was a new estate with houses that would need minimal work, which would allow us to concentrate on Dale. We also thought the house would be more suitable as it had four bedrooms and we wanted to give Dale a brother or sister so he wouldn't be alone in the world. Although we settled in very quickly and were surrounded by wonderful neighbours, many of whom were to become good friends, there was soon another near miss with Dale.

Shortly after we had moved in, and before all the back fences were erected, I was watching Dale playing in the garden. It was quite a windy day, but the sun was shining and I decided to give him a change of scene and take him to the local park, which he loved. I took his coat out into the garden, saying, 'Dale, let's go to the park.' Showing him the coat meant he knew he was going out.

Dale followed me into the house to the hall cupboard, where I told him, 'Dale, Mum will get her coat and then we can go to the park, OK?'

As I reached into the cupboard for my coat, Dale angrily responded, 'Don't say "OK"!' and slammed the door shut behind me.

It was a small cupboard, with no light, and I quickly felt around, only to discover there was no handle on the inside of the door. I had no way of getting out without Dale's help.

I came across Jamie's toolbox and tried to find something that would free me, but to no avail. All the while I was shouting to Dale, calmly at first, 'Dale, please open the door for Mummy.' We always kept the front door to the house locked, but then I remembered the back door was wide open: without fencing, there was a direct route out on to the street. I panicked and tried a desperate shoulder-barge on the cupboard door. The only result this produced was a very sore shoulder.

I got no response whatsoever from Dale and all was

quiet, until I heard familiar music coming from the TV in his bedroom. I would never have believed I could be so relieved to hear the *Thomas* signature tune. Time passed and when the music stopped, my anxiety levels soared again. I shouted and pleaded with Dale to open the door, but all I heard in return was a deafening silence.

I screamed, 'Help!' as loudly as I could, in the remote hope that a neighbour or passer-by might hear me. No one did. I heard a car hooting and feared that Dale was on the road. Eventually, I became a wreck, collapsing in a heap, sobbing.

After about ninety minutes and entirely without warning, the cupboard door opened and there stood my son, laughing heartily. I was so relieved that he was unharmed. Then I grabbed him, shouting, 'Don't do that to Mummy.' He didn't understand, of course, and I just hugged him, glad to be free.

Jamie came home that evening and asked, 'What's the damage today?'

'We need a handle on the inside of the cupboard door,' I promptly informed him.

Thankfully, our fences were erected the following week and Dale's outside environment was at last safe.

While it was good that Dale had a secure garden to play in, it also seemed cruel, in the sense that he became the only boy on the estate who could never leave his garden and play alongside the other kids in the street. I was very aware of the other children from neighbouring houses coming and going past our lounge window, all playing happily together while Dale played alone. Sometimes the kids would come into our garden to play, but would only stay a short time, unable to understand Dale. Still, I appreciated their efforts and always welcomed them with a few sweets to let them know they could come any time to see us. We were so lucky to have such understanding neighbours, with nice children.

Life finally became more stable, but once we had been living in Dresling Road for about a year, the reality of not conceiving became a concern for us both. Around this time, early January 1994, when Dale was five and a half, I started to feel generally unwell. I had become physically and mentally exhausted, had inexplicably put on weight and was alarmed to be showing signs of lactation, so I went to see my doctor, Craig Speirs. We discussed my failure to conceive as well as my other symptoms and Dr Speirs took various blood samples. He wanted to check my hormone levels and establish whether I was ovulating, as well as exclude a condition known as pituitary adenoma, in which raised levels of the lactation hormone prolactin are present.

When I returned for the results, while most of them were normal, I was shocked to be told that I did have raised prolactin levels, which explained my general ill health. I went home and told Jamie there was a real possibility that I had a pituitary adenoma – a type of brain tumour – and I would need to undergo a brain scan in a few weeks' time. Jamie was naturally as shocked as I was, although I did explain that Dr Speirs had also suggested that a more likely cause of my symptoms was the accumulation of the extreme stress I had been under for such a long time. He had advised me to try to reduce my stress levels by adapting my life accordingly, otherwise he felt I would not be able to conceive for some time, if at all. I sensed he was right. I was doing too much, being heavily involved in autism support groups and working extra hours. Jamie and I agreed the first thing I should do was change my work pattern from permanent night shift to part-time day shift. I would also take a break from helping run the Strathclyde Autistic Society support group.

In addition, Jamie thought it would be good for me to get away and suggested we visit his cousin David near Perth, hopefully to take my mind off my health scare. Jamie had recently spoken of Dale's problems to David and both he and his wife, Isobel, were very understanding about our situation.

This visit was to change our lives for ever.

10

Henry: A Really Useful Dog

'Puppies for sale: the only love which money can buy'
Sign on a bulletin board

As usual with such trips, we loaded up the survival bag
with what we thought we would need for the day. Dale was
allowed his favourite five trains, plus a couple of videos of
his choice. With all these essentials in place, we set off from
Greenock on the hour or so journey to Auchterarder, the
large village where David and Isobel lived. Their house was
on the edge of a new estate, with stunning views beyond the
garden wall to the Perthshire hills.

As soon as we arrived, Dale ran straight out into the back
garden and began his *Chariots of Fire* routine, running up
and down beside the wall. The four of us followed, and,
with a little effort, Isobel was able to divert Dale's attention
to a small football.

'This is one of the balls the dogs play with,' she told him.
'Shall we go and get them?'

'Them?' I queried. 'How many have you got?'

'Two,' she replied. 'Barney, the black Scottie, and Dougal, the white Scottie.'

David went into the house and liberated Barney and
Dougal, who came out in full play mode, anxious for
someone to throw their balls for them. Dale's face instantly

lit up and David and Isobel showed him the dogs' favourite game. Then Dale threw a ball himself, which Dougal returned to him, dropping it at his feet. And so it went on with both dogs. Barney retreated to the house for a nap, but Dougal was still up for fun and Dale kept going, continually repeating the command Isobel had taught him: 'Fetch!' Jamie and I were delighted because Dale was not only engaging with the dog, but also responding to the other language associated with the game, such as 'Throw it high', 'Throw it far' or 'Tell Dougal to wait.' It was all happening naturally and he seemed to understand. Quite simply, Dale was focused, switched on to Dougal's needs.

It was a dry day, though cold, and David suggested we leave Dale running around with Dougal and go inside for a cup of tea. Every so often one of us checked up on him, but he was quite happily playing with both dogs; Barney having found his second wind.

Jamie turned to David. 'I can't believe what I'm seeing,' he told him. 'If we were visiting anyone else, he'd be tuned in to a video by now.'

'Ever thought of getting a dog yourselves?' David asked innocently.

'We need a dog like we need a hole in our heads,' was Jamie's subtle rejoinder.

The two dogs having finally retired exhausted, Dale joined in with our evening meal, and then we got ready to leave. He happily waved goodbye to Barney and Dougal, before retreating into his usual silent mode in the car.

For the rest of the journey home, I was bubbling with excitement over what I had witnessed with Dale and the dogs, so much so that Jamie eventually conceded that *perhaps* this was something we should think about for the future, once my health had improved. I think he just said this to shut me up, but as he should have known, once I decide to do something, the future is not an option. Little did Jamie realise it then, but I was on a mission. The only question for me now was what type of dog!

While awaiting the brain-scan appointment, Dr Speirs ran regular blood checks to see if my change in lifestyle had reduced my stress levels. Gradually, much as he had predicted, my prolactin levels fell and ultimately the brain scan was not necessary.

In addition to the lifestyle changes I had made, a major factor in reducing my stress at around that time was that Dale was happily settled at both nurseries. One day, however, the staff at Hillend reported a new behaviour that was giving them cause for concern. After all the work by Madge, the language unit and me to get Dale to engage and make eye contact, he was now taking this to extremes, leaning in very close to people's faces and staring right into their eyes. I remember sometimes he was so close that his nose would almost touch mine. He would raise his voice and turn my head with his hand to ensure I looked right at him and that he had my full attention – just as I or his teachers would have done with him.

The staff at Hillend Nursery were trying to discourage this behaviour as they felt it was socially unacceptable, which in a sense of course it was. They wondered why he did it, though this was no mystery to me. He may have got the 'social timing' all wrong, but it was still a big breakthrough – he had not only overcome his fear of non-verbal communication, but was now confident enough to initiate eye contact himself. However, such is the complexity of autism that he still had a problem with spatial awareness and proximity, which would take months, if not years, to modify to an appropriate level.

Although Dale still had mountains to move in terms of continued progress, I was convinced that because of all that had been achieved to date, he was now at a level where he could cope with, learn from and enjoy owning a dog. And nothing was going to deter me from my quest to find the right dog for him.

After my next early shift, while Mum had Dale for the day, I went to the library to get some books on pedigree dogs. I had been brought up with mongrels, which were lovely, but due to the stressful environment our dog would be exposed to, I needed to be sure it would be able to cope with and adapt to the challenges of life with Dale. I therefore felt I should try to identify a breed with a proven set of attributes.

I was so happy to be back in the library and looking this time at a very different subject. When I got home with my selection of books, I was too excited even to take the time to change out of my uniform and sat on the sofa with a soothing cup of coffee to begin my research. I started with a book that had a table scoring various breeds out of ten for temperament, intelligence, potential health problems and, most importantly, suitability for young children.

As I studied each category, one breed shone through, scoring full marks and ticking all of the boxes. The more I read about the golden retriever, the more obvious it became that this was the dog for us. I spared no time in phoning a local vet, who gave me some numbers to call. I became despondent as I was told by various breeders that they had no pups at this time, or if they did, the pups were all spoken for, or the dogs had already grown up and so on. The last person on my list, however, although unable to help herself, told me of a local breeder called Val whose bitch had recently delivered a litter of pups. Barely able to contain either my anxiety or excitement, I phoned Val and was ecstatic to find she still had pups available. I explained fully about Dale and my intentions and she kindly invited me to visit with Dale to see how things went. She seemed impressed that I expressed more concern for the welfare of the dog than I did Dale and was reassured that I was taking the prospect of dog ownership responsibly. She said she would help in any way she could.

After the call, I became so engrossed in reading a book on golden retrievers that I didn't hear Jamie come home. I quickly tried to hide the book under a cushion, but he saw me doing this.

'What are you up to?' he enquired suspiciously.

'Nothing,' I replied nervously, as you do when you have something to hide. Trying to sound legit, I added, 'I've been to the library. Just enjoying a quiet read while Dale's at Mum's.'

'There can't be any more books on autism, surely,' said Jamie. 'And even if there are, why are you hiding them?'

Conceding I'd been rumbled, I showed Jamie the book cover with a golden retriever on it, then as his face dropped, tried to plead my case – after seeing Dale come alive with Dougal and Barney, I didn't want to wait, I wanted him to have a dog right away.

Jamie's response was tactful, sensitive and to the point: 'Are you nuts?'

My husband was convinced we had quite enough going on in our lives and that the additional responsibility of a dog was the last thing we needed. I was neither listening nor about to give up. 'You've never had a dog. It's not all responsibility. Listen . . .' And I read aloud from the book: ' "If you want a good-natured, sociable dog, then a golden retriever is ideal. Gentle, responsive, affectionate, its most attractive attribute is its generous nature; it never tires of company and is always eager to please." '

Jamie was still anything but persuaded, so I looked at him mournfully and, with a pathetic 'please' in my voice, informed him, 'I spoke to a breeder in Gourock today. She has a few puppies left.'

Defeated, Jamie uttered the fateful words: 'I suppose there's no harm in looking.'

The day came to go and see the pups, and although we tried to explain the outing to Dale, he clearly didn't understand. Thankfully, however, he was quiet and withdrawn as Val showed us into her lounge and he remained this way despite the deafening noise of dogs barking in the back room. Val left us for a moment and we took in our surroundings. The lounge was like 'Retriever World', with every available space covered with photos and ornaments of golden re-trievers, young and old alike.

Jamie panicked, saying, 'Is this what happens to you when you get a dog?'

At that moment, Val reappeared with her mum, Sheena, both holding two of the cutest bundles of fur under each arm. When they set the pups down to run around, I was enchanted, but Dale ignored them completely. Worse, he started to rock and moan as if it were all too much for him.

Picking up on this, Jamie told me quietly, 'This isn't going to work, Nuala.'

Disappointed, but not about to lose hope, I replied, 'Let him at least see the pups for a while.'

'He is seconds away from a tantrum,' hissed Jamie.

Then Dale suddenly pointed to the bookshelf beside the television, exclaimed, '*Thomas*!' and proceeded to help himself to the solitary *Thomas the Tank Engine* video he'd spotted nestling among a host of other videos and books. He gave it to Sheena to put on, kicked off his shoes and settled down to watch from the big armchair in front of the TV, now totally content.

I apologised to Val, then melted as a couple of the pups came over to me. 'They're absolutely adorable,' I told her.

'But can they play football?' piped up Jamie.

'You'd be surprised what a goldie can do,' said Val.

Even though Dale only had eyes for *Thomas*, I wasn't yet ready to give up. I knelt down and began to play with one of the pups to try to catch Dale's attention, but to no avail. I waved the pup's paw at Dale; he still ignored me. Jamie gestured to me that this was pointless and I started to think he was right – nothing was going to distract Dale now that he had *Thomas*. I asked Val if it was all right to stay until the end of the tape, to avoid a tantrum, but in a way also playing for time – I desperately didn't want to give up.

'Maybe when the video's finished . . .' I added hopefully.

But Jamie was emphatic. 'He doesn't want to know, Nuala.'

Heavily disappointed, I had to concede. Then one of the pups wandered over to Dale's chair, tried valiantly to clamber up on to it. Sheena rewarded the little chap's efforts with a helpful push, whereupon the pup turned round and snuggled in beside Dale.

'Look at that,' I told Jamie and Val, heartened. Dale was still engrossed in the video, but he was now also gently stroking the pup's back, though he hadn't so much as glanced at it.

Jamie was pleasantly surprised by this turn, but nonetheless pointed out, 'He may be all right with him here, but lots of kids with autism are terrified of dogs.'

'Does he look terrified to you?' I countered. 'He needs company, Jamie, I know he does.'

Sheena stood in front of the TV to speak to our son. 'Have you got a new friend there, Dale? This wee fellow needs a name. Can you think of a name for him, Dale?'

Dale simply leaned round her to see the TV and at that moment his favourite engine appeared on the screen. 'Henry! Henry!' Dale cried excitedly.

'Henry?' said Sheena, surprised.

'He doesn't understand,' explained Jamie.

'But why not?' I enquired. 'It's a subject he knows, and a name he loves.'

'Henry?' repeated Jamie, before muttering, 'The poor thing's doomed from the start.'

I was about to agree with Jamie that it perhaps wasn't the best choice of name, when Sheena observed, 'Well, if he loves Henry the dog as much as Henry the train, we'll have no problems there.'

So it was that this little pup was named after a cartoon

engine, and with Jamie conceding defeat, we had a new addition to our family.

After the video had ended, in order to confirm that the pup was indeed to be Dale's dog, Val lifted up a floppy ear and wrote a big 'H' on the underside using a black felt-tipped pen – much to the delight of Dale. While Jamie wrote out the cheque, I asked Val if she'd be prepared to take Henry back if his welfare started to suffer at Dale's hands and she confirmed she would.

Val said we could take the pup right away, but we needed time to prepare Dale for this big change in his life and so decided to collect Henry in a couple of weeks. I asked Val for a photo of a single puppy so that we could tell Dale this was Henry and use the image to help teach him what was to happen and remind him what Henry looked like; it would also help to create a sense of belonging in Dale.

As we left, Val informed us, 'You'll need to get a Dyson. No other vacuum will cope with the amount of fur your carpets are in for.' Then she added cheerily, 'And lock up your socks and underwear. Next to food, a goldie can't get enough of them.'

It would not be long before we learned that Val knew exactly what she was talking about.

To try to help Dale understand the timescale that was involved before Henry came to live with us, I took him on a couple of shopping trips to buy all that we would need for our dog and then I put our purchases in a large black bin bag. Jamie made a very professional countdown calendar, showing a picture of a specific dog item for each day and Dale would tick off the appropriate item on a daily basis. I would then put that item in the dog bed which now occupied a corner of our lounge. I involved Dale as much as possible during the shopping process, so he chose, for example, the colour of Henry's bed, a special quacking-duck tugger toy and a small blue collar. We were really happy during this process and I remember it felt as though we were preparing for the arrival of a new baby.

Jamie also spent time with Dale, using facial expressions, as he had done with the *Thomas* trains, to show how the dog would be feeling – happy, angry, sad and so forth. He drew simple line drawings of a dog's face to illustrate each expression, though Dale seemed to prefer his dad's own physical attempts to replicate these. He found Jamie's impression of a happy dog, involving bright eyes, panting and a waggy tail, particularly entertaining.

We used a toy cuddly puppy to reinforce our efforts and I also drew basic pictures of the house, showing Mummy, Daddy and Dale, and then adding in the dog to illustrate that he would be joining the family. Dale was used to this type of visual explanation, and although he never re-sponded, I could tell by the interest in his face that he understood.

The night before we were due to collect Henry, the puppy photo that had been on Dale's bedside cabinet throughout was put down on top of all the other para-phernalia in the dog bed, to reiterate to Dale that his dog would be arriving the next day.

The big day dawned on Friday, 18 February 1994, when Dale was five years and eight months. We arrived at Val's and as before Dale went through the door without saying a word, but he was at least in a calm, good mood. He stayed close by my side as Val left us in the lounge to go and get young Henry.

When she came back with our pup, Jamie was sat reading a newspaper, oblivious. Val told me, 'You'd better take him, Nuala, he's a big lump now,' and passed Henry over to me. He had indeed grown in the two weeks since we had seen him. As his two big front paws rested on my shoulder, with Dale contentedly stroking his back, I hugged him to me, nestling into his soft, downy coat, then placing a kiss on the top of his head. He snuggled in, and as I felt the love coming from this wee pup, I realised that here was someone who would let me love him back. Silent tears were now running down my face. I hadn't been prepared for this, but I just couldn't help it – it felt as though I had at last been handed my yearned-for second baby. Jamie gave me a small nod to show that he understood.

On the way home, I sat in the back of the car beside Dale, with Henry on my lap. Dale seemed quietly pleased as he stroked the pup, chanting, 'Henry, Henry.'

That night, Jamie and I had to go out for dinner with friends who were leaving the area and so Mum and Dad came round to watch Dale and Henry. They were used to dogs, but still had a busy evening thanks to the games that had ensued between their grandson and his new companion. I was delighted to hear that Mum and Dad had witnessed the same spark as we had seen when Dale had been with Dougal and Barney, and there was no doubting that poor Henry was as exhausted as they had been.

I looked across at our new pup, curled up in his bed, and thought how cute he looked when he was asleep. Then I noticed something different. The fleecy lining that I had bought for his bed had been thrown across the room and Henry was now lying on Dale's cot duvet with patterned trains on it. I now kept this in the lounge cupboard for the rare occasions when Dale burned out on the sofa; when Mum had tried to settle Henry down for the night, Dale had tossed away the fleece and fetched the train duvet instead. He had then proceeded to lift Henry and wrap him in the duvet, saying, 'Bedtime, Henry.' Mum and Dad had been pleasantly shocked by this unexpected communication and of course I was thrilled. Even Jamie couldn't ignore that our wee pup had made an impact already.

We woke up the next morning to two things: the surprise that there was no Dale in the middle of our bed and a lot of noise from him downstairs.

'What's all the commotion?' asked Jamie, half out of bed to go and check what Dale was up to.

'Wait,' I told him. 'That's not commotion, it's communication. Listen to all the language he's using.'

We sat in bed, mesmerised by what was going on in the lounge downstairs. Dale was saying, in an uneven, sing-song style, 'Henry puppy . . . Duck, puppy . . . That's not good, puppy . . . Stop it, Henry . . . Duck, puppy . . . Give it to Dale.' All of this was punctuated with shrieks of laughter and little yelps from Henry as the two of them engaged in boisterous play together. We'd never heard our son play so verbally or joyfully before with anyone, either human or animal.

When we finally went downstairs, we didn't care about the puddles and mess on the floor, or the new smell in the lounge. Henry had been paper-trained by Val, but he was only a little pup and accidents were to be expected in the short term.

We had a busy time keeping Dale and Henry entertained that day and then the usual bedtime battles in the evening, which thankfully didn't seem to faze Henry at all – he just took everything in his stride. We had all bonded already with this gorgeous wee bundle of joy, who had rapidly become a major part of the family. Both Jamie and I had seen a real change in Dale from the moment Henry had come into his house. He had suddenly been transformed from a lost and lonely child into a happy little boy, who at last had a friend to give him a sense of purpose. Our home had come to life in a sense we had not known before Henry crossed the threshold and began to work his special kind of magic. By the end of day two, we felt, quite simply, that we couldn't do without him.

There was another benefit we hadn't fully anticipated. Whereas Mickey, the Wellpark and the wonderful *Thomas the Tank Engine* had taught Dale so much, suddenly here was Henry, the most amazing, *living* educational resource I had been given to date – and I was certainly going to embrace the opportunities this provided.

To allow the pup to interact with Dale wherever possible, we decided to give him the run of the house: nowhere was out of bounds, not even the sofa or our beds. We wanted Henry to feel free and comfortable in our household, and with this established, we began to teach Dale about his dog. We told him the names of the different body parts and Dale would sit with Henry, studiously informing him, 'This is your nose . . . your paw. These are your ears . . . your eyes . . . and Henry has big teeth, too.'

Autistic children have problems with literal meaning. Just as Dale had thought broccoli was a tree, so he decided all animals' feet were the same – to him, a horse's hoof was a paw. It was very hard for him to understand that all animals were similar but different, but with a little time and his interest in Henry as motivation, Dale was eventually able to grasp this difficult abstract concept.

We wanted Dale to learn how to take care of his dog and ensured he was fully involved with all aspects of looking after Henry. We hoped that in addition to the benefits this would have for Henry, Dale might also learn some things about looking after himself in the process.

Dale had never previously shown any desire to wash his hands without prompting and constant supervision. Now, before we would start to feed Henry, we would wash Dale's hands, and ours, and through time Dale was happy to apply this skill on his own because he was doing something for his dog.

Dale was also a bad eater, never hungry, whereas goldens, especially our Henry, are the world's greediest dogs. As Henry grew, he quickly learned when his meals were due and would bark at 'his' cupboard to remind us it was dinnertime. Each day, I would deliberately wait for Henry to do this, saying to my son, 'Dale, what is Henry wanting at his cupboard? He is *hungry*.' This evolved to a point where Dale would tell me, 'Mum, Henry's hungry. It's time for his dinner.' Eventually, Dale learned through this the concept of his own hunger and when it was dinnertime for him. I developed the trick of telling Dale that eating his food was good for him as it would help him grow big, just like Henry.

Again through Henry, we dealt with the concept of greed. 'Henry, you've had enough to eat,' I would say. 'Don't be greedy.' Once Dale had learned this, I loved watching him tell Henry off for this very sin: 'Henry, lie down, don't be greedy,' he told his dog with real meaning, and then glowed with pride as Henry did what he had told him.

Along with many other children with autism, Dale was lacking in sequencing and organisational skills. The fact that young Henry needed three meals a day gave us plenty of opportunity to practise and I would break down the process of preparing Henry's food into minute steps. So once we had established that it was Henry's dinnertime, I would say, 'Dale, *open* Henry's cupboard door. What do we do next? We need his *bowl*,' thereby reinforcing language and the task sequence stage by stage. To help increase his comprehension, as this precedes spoken language, I would talk in a basic, concise way, always at Dale's eye level, emphasising the word I wanted him to learn. Once he appeared to understand, I would try to get him to respond. So if I had said, 'Dale is *pouring* the food into Henry's bowl,' I would then try a question: 'Now we add some . . . ?' And with luck Dale would say, 'Water.'

This entire process of getting Henry's food could take up to half an hour, not least because as well as the fact that I was trying to teach Dale to communicate, I was also hoping to develop his fine motor control. His tripod grip (the ability to hold a pencil between his thumb and first two fingers) was poor and he had only just got the hang of the more basic palmer grip, meaning he would grip the pencil in his fist, so these sessions were invaluable. Poor Henry, however, would drool so much in anticipation of his dinner that he would flood the floor and often one of us would skid as if we'd stepped on a banana skin.

Perhaps slightly unkindly, I told Dale that Henry's favourite TV programme was *Ready Steady Cook* and of course Dale took this literally. He would shout to his dog, 'Henry, come here. It's your favourite TV show,' and they would settle down to watch. If Henry had not been happy with the choice of show, it wouldn't have surprised me if he had changed the channel himself just by barking, he had eaten that many remote controls.

II

The Voice

'It is by muteness that a dog becomes for one so utterly beyond value; with him one is at peace, where words play no torturing tricks . . . Those are the moments that I think are precious to a dog – when, with his adoring soul coming through his eyes, he feels that you are really thinking of him.'

John Galsworthy

Only three weeks after Henry's arrival, staff from both the PSLU and Hillend Nursery commented on the change in Dale. The minutes of their meeting record how he had 'had a particularly happy spell recently' and was now mixing well with the other children. All of his skills were showing progress, and his key worker at Hillend had 'noticed a considerable difference in him'.

When I spoke to friends and work colleagues about the change in Dale and how Henry was helping him, their reaction was one of confusion: 'How can you use a dog to do this?' Quite naturally, they all took the ability to communicate for granted and it was very hard for me to explain the difficulties involved in communicating with a child with severe autism. But whether they understood or not, what mattered to me was that involving Dale in the minutiae of Henry's care was getting results.

Due to an occasional 'puppy-pee stench', Henry had become used to having a bath and seemed to enjoy it. One day, he and Dale had been playing in the back garden and Dale came in covered in mud from top to toe – it was in his hair, his ears, everywhere. He refused to get in the bath as it was daytime and he only had a bath when it was dark outside. A further obstacle was that he would never get in the bath until all of his trains had been placed round its perimeter, one at a time, in the precise order he wanted. Dear Henry came to the rescue again. I simply popped him in the bath first and, amazingly, Dale followed, during daylight hours and without the need for the bath to look like Clapham Junction. The two of them had a wonderful time, even if my bathroom resembled a disaster zone. On later resuming Dale's usual night-time bathing routine, with Henry sitting beside the bath rather than in it, the ring of trains reappeared. But by giving Henry a quick scrub, too, I was able to give Dale the same without the kind of battle that had always ensued in the past.

Dale's aversion to having his hair brushed was reduced by adopting the same approach. I would take the brush to Henry, saying, 'Dale, why do we have to brush Henry's fur?' I would then pause to try to prompt a response, but if none came, continue, 'To take out the tangles, like when we brush our hair.' I could eventually leave Dale grooming Henry and he could see that, far from being frightened, his dog was enjoying the experience. Henry would finally fall into a deep, contented sleep, with Dale still talking to him and brushing him lovingly. We used to get so much fur that I would laugh and say, 'Dale, we can make another puppy from this,' or, 'Look, Dale, a *tiny* Henry.' I took any opportunity to introduce a new word.

Sometimes poor Henry would even be 'attacked' with the scissors to show there was no pain in getting a haircut, although Dale still had a lot of anxieties about the process and the fact that he had to go somewhere he found terrifying for the purpose. One of his teachers in the language unit, Paula, had been playing hairdressing games with Dale, using dolls, and because his fear and autism were so severe, she had taken him out in her own time to a barber's shop. There, she had found a gentle, kind old barber called Charlie, whom Dale adopted as his personal hairdresser, refusing to let anyone else cut his hair until he was ten years old. I'm not sure we would ever have got him to that point if he hadn't first observed Henry having a trim at the dog-grooming parlour.

One time, we went to collect Henry, and the grooming lady said, 'You'll have to wait a few minutes as he's still in the drier.'

Dale became highly anxious, telling me, 'I don't want Henry to spin round and round.'

I had to show him that Henry was sat in a heated box, rather than a tumble-drier.

Another day, I remember going into Dale's room to check on him as he'd been quiet for too long. There he was in front of the mirror, getting stuck in with the scissors and laughing at all the hair on the floor. Not only was I pleased his anxiety had been cured, but also immensely relieved to have caught him just before the point where the electric hair trimmers would have been needed.

We brushed Henry's teeth and, together with the fact

that the vet would also examine Henry's teeth, this helped to reduce Dale's fear of visiting the dentist and give him independence in caring for his own teeth. I remember many times over-reacting to Henry's halitosis, which gave lots of scope for fun and interaction with Dale. All future visits to the dentist or doctor were to prove straightforward as long as Dale had his Helpful Henry train in his hand and the real Helpful Henry waiting in the car.

Introducing Dale to dog stories and videos helped to lessen his need for *Thomas*, and his growing love of all things canine eventually led to a significant expansion of his social world in the form of his first ever trip to the cinema.

Given Dale's fear of the unknown, previous attempts to take him to the movies had resulted in tantrums before we even got beyond the foyer, and we had thought it would take years to overcome this. However, with the release of the new film *Beethoven*, about a large St Bernard dog, we devised a plan, aided and abetted by my brother-in-law, Gerry, who fortuitously worked as the projectionist (booth manager) in the local cinema. So, with a cuddly toy St Bernard under his arm, Henry in the car and a bag of sweets from the kiosk, as well as enticing *Beethoven* posters everywhere, Dale visited the empty cinema to see the giant television screen and sit in a seat. Gerry demonstrated the lights going out and also showed Dale the 'giant video machine' in the booth. He then reserved two seats at the back near the door for us for the day in question.

When the momentous occasion arrived, with all neces-sary preparation taken care of and Dale entering the cinema only at the start of the film, we watched in anticipation as he took his seat. He promptly shouted, 'Gerry, switch off the lights!' and then sat through the story of *Beethoven*, generally happy, although a little anxious at times. By using the new obsession, we had managed to open another door and Dale became a regular cinema attendee thereafter.

When Henry grew out of his first puppy collar, Dale chose a new one – in 'Thomas blue' of course – and Paula, his teacher, was able to remind him of this when she took him out to buy new shoes 'to go walking with Henry'. She told him, 'Your feet have grown, just as Henry has grown. And Henry didn't mind his new collar, did he?' The result was so successful that Dale insisted on taking his new shoes to bed with him.

A whole new world opened up as we visited dog shows and went for regular walks with Henry. When people stopped to pat Henry and comment on him, this only served to increase Dale's interest in his dog, as well as dramatically improve his socialisation skills.

One day towards the end of May, Dale was being assessed in the PSLU for starting school. It came to the point where he was to demonstrate his pencil control and imagination and Paula gave him a blue felt-tipped pen. Aware that he would have difficulty as he still used a palmer grip, she asked him, 'Dale, can you try to draw me a good picture?' She left him to do his best and when she returned was amazed by the result. She sent home the little picture, with a note in his diary: 'Nuala, I think getting Dale the dog is going to be really good for him. Please see the enclosed drawing – his first ever attempt to recreate an image.' I carefully took out the piece of paper and there was the image, a definite picture of a 'Henry dog', with a big, happy grin, fan-shaped tail and water and food bowls.

I showed the drawing to my mum and we gazed at it with immense pleasure. Everyone had been working on the tripod grip, facial expressions and imagination for years and had thought it would take several more before Dale acquired the requisite skills. Yet here at last was proof that he had understood what we had all been striving for so long to teach him, as well as real, tangible evidence of the impact Henry had had on his life in just a few short months.

This basic drawing, after years of nothing but the blobs and daubs of a toddler, acted as a catalyst for similar drawings over the next few weeks. Paula again sent home a very mature picture of a woman's face, clearly Granny Dorothy, with hair, earrings and more importantly a definite facial expression. Dale also drew a whole person, complete with arms and legs, and of course endless pictures of characters from *Thomas the Tank Engine* with various facial expressions, confirming he did at last understand them.

Progress such as this was especially heartening given that Dale was due to start school in August, although a particular worry remained: at almost six years of age, he was still not fully toilet-trained.

For years, I had continued to do all the usual things to try to get Dale out of nappies, but he simply didn't understand, added to which he seemed terrified of using the toilet. I didn't realise until much later that he had a real phobia of the toilet process itself, in terms of the actual environment and the personal element involved.

An obvious downside to owning a puppy, apart from the constant chewing, has to be toilet-training. You need patience and vigilance to be able to catch the precise moment to put the pup outside, and it helps if you can tolerate the fact that your house will smell like a public toilet for a while. We went through the normal house-training routine with Henry and as ever Dale was involved. So when Henry had an accident in the house, I would say as I cleaned up, 'Dale, we don't want to make the house all dirty and smelly.' When Henry got it right and performed in the garden, he would be rewarded with a choccy drop as Dale looked on.

One day, after a successful pee from Henry in the garden, followed by his reward, Dale and I went back into the house. A few minutes later, I was astonished to be informed by my little lad, 'I need a wee. Don't want to make the house all dirty and smelly.' He did the necessary in the toilet and put out his hand, demanding, 'Choccy drop.' I quickly found him a treat from his *Thomas* sweetie tin.

I never put a nappy on Dale again, as I felt that the occasional accident was better than confusing him now that he had at last understood the concept. I felt confident to do this because once the breakthrough had been made, Paula had similar success at the nursery. It still took months for Dale to overcome his fear of sitting on the toilet and it used to worry me how he would hold on to a full bladder for as long as ten hours at a time, but eventually, with *Thomas the Tank Engine* posters in Dale's 'own' little toilet and Henry the dog and Helpful Henry the train beside him, his confidence and independence increased.

Like all retrievers, Henry was a very sociable dog; if he wasn't getting in our faces, then he would be in Dale's instead. He was always looking for a biscuit or, with great excitement – duck toy in mouth, tail and whole back end wagging – nudging Dale for a game. On many occasions he would break into Daleyworld, or interrupt Dale's autistic mannerisms such as staring or flapping his hands, and Dale didn't mind. On the contrary, he would sit with Henry and show him his favourite trains – 'Thomas train . . . Henry train . . .' – something he would never do with us.

Cutest of all was when Henry wanted just to snuggle up to Dale; being a true goldie, he could never get too much attention. His affectionate, outgoing nature was all too apparent when he gave what we came to call the 'five-minute, five-year response'. That is, like most dogs – but especially retrievers – if you left him alone in the house for as little as five minutes, the welcome on your return was as though you had abandoned him for five years. This response made Dale really happy and worked wonders for his confidence and self-esteem.

Dale and Henry's favourite activity together was the boisterous game of tugger, and the longer this game continued, the more their excitement would escalate. As Henry tugged away at the toy, Dale would maintain complete eye contact with him without even realising it. We also noticed that he was not afraid to look at the puppy's unthreatening eyes when talking to him, which was something we encouraged in the hope that one day he would be comfortable enough to look at us and others in a similar way.

It was ironic that adults and professionals found it hard to understand Dale's autism and problem with eye contact, whereas children sometimes took it more in their stride. A very nice five-year-old boy from the language unit, who had Asperger's syndrome, part of the autistic spectrum of disorders, had the insight to recognise Dale's problems with eye contact when he told his mum that he thought Dale was blind. This was because he had noticed Dale's eyes were always cast down to the floor, instead of looking at people. When I bumped into the mum in town one day, she eagerly told me her son's latest observation: 'Now that Dale is not blind any more, it's good they let him keep his guide dog.'

Jamie and I decided Dale should go to St Anthony's, a mainstream primary school about fifteen miles away which had a new unit for children with autistic-spectrum disorders. There would be about six pupils in both of the two classes in the unit, with a ratio of one member of staff to two children. This was the exact provision Professor Newsome, the specialist who had diagnosed Dale with autism, had recommended in her report. The objective of the unit was to address the children's deficits and, once they were able to cope, allow them to integrate with the mainstream pupils. Although this meant Dale making the thirty-mile round trip by taxi every day, we thought it was worthwhile, as the unit ultimately aimed to get the children to a level where they would be able to attend their own local school.

Dale did not even like small changes to his routine, and as a new school would be a total life change for him, a great deal of work was required to prepare him for the move to St Anthony's. With this in mind, Paula and a teacher from the new unit drew up a transition plan, which involved the new teacher making many visits to the language unit and Dale making a similar number to St Anthony's. This introduced him to the concept of wearing a uniform, which he would now have to do, as well as travelling in a taxi. These measures would be taken for weeks on end; meanwhile, aware of Henry's impact, Paula came up with a great idea. With our help in providing the appropriate photographs, she prepared a picture book to show the various stages involved in Dale going to his new school – there was Henry waving goodbye with his paw, a nice shiny taxi, a photo of St Anthony's and a picture of Henry welcoming Dale home again. When it came to the big day that Dale started school, with a few *Thomas* stickers on his little bag helping to boost his confidence, everything happened exactly as shown in the book and all was well.

The picture book made such an impression that when we decided to take Dale back to the language unit with some gifts to say thank you to Paula and the other staff members, he refused to go through the entrance doors because this was no longer his school. As we knew that if we forced him he would have a full-blown tantrum, Paula had to come down to the main entrance and our farewells were said in the street.

Despite the difficulties encountered before Dale was

formally diagnosed, I will for ever be grateful to Paula for all her help with him, especially because he was the first child with severe autism in the unit and she took a real chance taking him.

With Dale having survived the huge change of a new school, life seemed to be going well for the first time in years. Now that he was toilet-trained, he was also able to go to Sunday school and was happy to do so as long as Jimmy and Dorothy took him. He rang the church bell and all there were quite taken with him, despite the fact that he adopted the bell as his own and refused to let other children have a go.

For this latest venture to succeed, there had again been careful preparation in that Dorothy had told the woman who ran the Sunday school about Dale's difficulties and she had enlisted the help of her daughter to support him while he was there. For us, this was another invaluable way for Dale to integrate and socialise with his own peer group, something that could not happen while he was in the special unit at St Anthony's. Nonetheless, he had settled in well at St Anthony's and we were all happier than we had been in a very long time.

One day in September, I was standing at the window watching Henry playing with Dale when I noticed something wasn't right – with Henry, that is. With growing concern, I watched him chase around the garden, displaying a slight but definite limp, favouring his right front paw. Over the next few days the limp became more pronounced, until Henry finally refused to go out for a walk, or even into the garden; to get him to go to the toilet, Jamie had to physically lift him and take him outside. Our poor dog seemed miserable, even depressed and, most worrying of all, was not interested in food. I immediately took him to the vet, Nigel Martin, and was appalled to learn that Henry was very ill – lame in all four legs and in a lot of pain. Nigel suspected he had either a very serious condition with a long Latin name that I cannot remember or something called panosteitis whereby his bones and joints had grown too fast, making them weak and inflamed. The only way to reach a diagnosis would be by X-ray, but for this Henry would need a general anaesthetic, which Nigel could not recommend because of his poor condition. In any event, with or without the X-ray, the treatment would be the same and so high-dose steroids were prescribed for the next month. I was devastated to learn that in cases where the treatment was not successful, it was usually kinder to put the dog to sleep.

Nigel was so understanding as I tearfully tried to explain what this dog had done for Dale and how much he meant to us. 'This isn't just a dog,' I kept saying. 'This isn't just a dog.' He did his best to reassure me and said all we could do was wait and see how Henry responded to the treatment.

Because we couldn't take Henry out for walks and were giving him medication, we couldn't hide from Dale the fact that his dog was ill, but we did our best to shield him from our true feelings. I will never forget how he adapted to the situation and cared for Henry as he rested in his bed, showing him understanding and kindness, gently stroking his fur and talking to him. He was behaving towards his dog as we would towards him if he was ill.

Once, when Jamie had lifted Henry on to the sofa, where he had fallen asleep, Dale fetched his train cot duvet and wrapped it round him. Then he gathered his collection of trains from upstairs and placed them round Henry. He would in his own immature way tell Henry stories from his *Thomas the Tank Engine* comics. He was not of course actually reading, but re-enacting videos, mostly picking out stories concerning Henry the train.

Throughout this time, Jamie and I sat nursing the dog in deep despair, with me repeatedly asking, 'Why us, after all we've been through?' I just couldn't take in that this could possibly be happening to our dog, but Jamie tried to comfort me through this ordeal.

After a couple of days, I served Henry one of his favourite dog foods and was overjoyed when, instead of sniffing at it and turning his head away, he started to eat with something resembling his usual appetite. The steroids had started to do their work. From then on, he began to rally and became more and more his old self again. When I was sitting on the bed one day, the real breakthrough came when Henry walked in holding a squeaky toy in his mouth – I was pleased enough to hear the noise of him squeaking the toy, but was absolutely delighted when he actually jumped up on the bed beside me. I clasped him round the neck and said, 'Henry, good dog. I love you!' Dale came in and saw what was happening, and was even more thrilled than me, if possible, to see his dog so well.

After a month, Henry was totally back to normal and enjoying his evening walks with Jamie and Dale. I felt so thankful that he had recovered, and could not have been more delighted once again to be eaten out of house and home.

*   *   *

Birthdays were a real source of stress. Just as Dale didn't like the appearance of the house to change at Christmas, so he didn't like the number of his age to change on his birthday. If only I could have explained to him that neither did the rest of us but we learned to put up with it! As it was, we had to deal with tantrums at birthday parties, rather than celebrations.

Henry's first birthday was on 17 December, and as the day approached, we thought we'd try to use the occasion to help Dale. We involved him in the whole process, from buying a new toy and birthday cake, candle and all, to taking him with Henry to the butcher's shop to choose a nice, juicy steak. Dale made Henry a card and even helped to cook his steak, then laughed happily as he watched Henry devour it. We would have to wait and see whether all this had any effect when Dale's birthday came round the following June.

For the first time in ages, I was really looking forward to Christmas, all the more so because I was convinced I was pregnant. We'd had a few false alarms before, but this time I was three weeks late. We were all going to go to the garden centre once Jamie came home from work, to choose a real Christmas tree, but just before he arrived I discovered to my extreme disappointment that I wasn't pregnant – it had been another false alarm.

Jamie turned up, full of the joys of the season, and shouted, 'Come on, Dale, get in the car. We're going to get the Christmas tree.' He then called to me, too, to chivvy me along. Because of my news, I was not exactly in a festive mood and Jamie called again: 'Come on, Nuala, let's go.'

I didn't want to get into the whole thing at that point and

told him to go and get the tree, I wasn't feeling too well. Jamie didn't get the message and hustled me again. Not realising that Dale was by now just behind him, I lost patience, snapping, 'Look, just go and get the fucking Christmas tree.' So off they all went, with Jamie feeling understandably miffed by my outburst.

That night, after Jamie had decorated the tree with the help of the dog, he came up to see what was happening. At the top of the stairs, he found Dale playing with his trains. Nothing unusual about this . . . except that he was using my tampons as trucks. Jamie immediately realised what was wrong with me and found me in the bedroom tending to my tear-streaked face. He was very comforting and tried to reassure me that things would work out eventually. After we'd talked it through some more, we decided that we would carry on as we were for a while, but might ultimately need to seek medical help, because we did not want Dale to be an only child.

Christmas Day came and Henry, delighted with the whole concept and proudly wearing tinsel round his neck, was presented with his gift, a new toy, which Dale had chosen and wrapped. Then Dale helped dish out Henry's turkey dinner with all the trimmings and served it to him. It lasted about five seconds.

Dale's uncle Peter and aunt Carol were with us this year, and after Henry had been fed, we all sat round the dining table for our own Christmas meal. We pulled crackers as usual and fired off party poppers, Dale's whizzing off in the direction of Uncle Peter, multicoloured streamers raining down on his head. Dale observed cheerily, 'Funny Uncle Peter, he looks like a fucking Christmas tree.'

In the New Year, Dale took an interest in a Charlie Chaplin video that Jimmy had given him. I think he particularly loved this because it was non-verbal, with the over-animated slapstick humour being easier to interpret than a bombardment of language.

Another thing he liked to watch at the time was 999, which showed re-enactments of accidents and how they were dealt with by the emergency services. One day, when he was sat in front of the TV with Henry, we heard him say, 'Oh, that's terrible, that's not nice.' We immediately stopped what we were doing in the kitchen and hurried through to the lounge, not quite believing that our son was actually sounding as though he felt sorry for someone. On the screen, there was a badly injured woman in a mangled car. We eavesdropped as Dale went on, 'Oh, dear, Henry, that's a shame.' Jamie and I looked at each other in amazement – at long last our son was showing empathy – but with impeccable timing came Dale's punchline: 'It's all broke, Henry. Poor car.' We resigned ourselves to a slightly longer wait for empathy.

Despite our continued efforts to engage with Dale when he was in 'his' world, he often refused to let us near. We would try to play with his trains with him, although sometimes just picking up or even touching a train would bring on an enraged tantrum. With Henry, however, it was a different story. If he helped himself to a train, such as Grand Gordon, Dale would simply prise open his jaws and take it back, saying, 'That's not good, Henry. You've got my Gordon and you don't do that to Dale.'

I remember observing one such incident and saying to Jamie, 'He's let Henry in. That dog is totally a part of his world. But we're still just objects, there to meet his needs.'

'I get more response from Henry than I ever do from Dale,' Jamie agreed.

At that moment I was really feeling the lack of that crucial emotional bond which most mothers are able to take for granted with their children.

Jamie understood, but reminded me this was autism we were dealing with. 'He may never love you, Nuala. He doesn't know what love is. You just have to accept that.'

'How can I accept it?' I retorted. 'I'm his mother.' No matter how much my son was to progress, I knew that deep down it was words of love and affection I so desperately needed to hear.

Back in the real world, Dale was at least becoming more sociable with anyone who took an interest in his dog. Jamie was out in the front garden with Dale and Henry one day when a lady walking by stopped and said to Dale, 'What a lovely puppy you have.'

'This is my dog,' Dale began. 'His name is Henry. He's just a puppy. He's going to grow to be a big dog.'

Jamie came rushing into the house, brimming with the news. 'He's just made a speech to a total stranger!'

Wonderful stuff, although apparently after that things had gone downhill in that Dale had leaned towards the woman and sniffed her. Autistic children are very sensitive to people they meet and I think they work out in their own way whether a particular person 'understands' them. I think if Dale felt comfortable with someone, or 'liked' them, he would smell them perhaps to get to know them better.

*   *   *

By the spring of 1995, we had come to accept that it was going to take years before Dale would be ready to let us into his life in the same way as he had embraced Henry. In spite of all the speech therapy, specific programmes at school and our own input, it also seemed that it would be a very long time before he would learn to integrate and socialise appropriately. He still had great difficulties with interpreting facial expressions and non-verbal communication generally, as well as problems with intonation. Not only would he speak in the wrong tone and laugh inappropriately, but also hearing certain words caused him particular distress. If we said 'OK' or another word he didn't like to hear, such as 'school', he could fly into a fit of rage.

Although we were aware of this, they were common words and it was impossible not to let them slip sometimes. Having to mind every word we said in case we inadvertently prompted a tantrum was extraordinarily difficult, but we could never have foreseen how, because of this very problem, our life with Dale and Henry was to take an incredible twist.

One seemingly normal day, while Dale drew happily in the dining room with Henry at his side, I checked his schoolbag to see if there was a note from his teachers about homework. I found his jotter and, noting that his handwriting was much improved, went over to him to show him the page I was so pleased with.

'Dale,' I told him, 'your writing is very good. I'm so proud of you.'

Dale immediately took great exception to this and I remembered too late that the word 'proud' was one of the ones he couldn't bear to hear.

He stormed around the room, shouting, 'Don't say "proud",' all the while clutching at his head.

I tried to reassure him, saying, 'It's a good thing that I'm proud of you. It's OK.'

If it hadn't been for the stress of the moment, I might have avoided the word 'OK', but again it was too late and my wee boy's distress escalated.

'Don't say "OK",' he screamed and I knew he was heading into a full-blown tantrum as he started to bang his head furiously against the wall. I had no option but to restrain him the way I always had to in the past.

I sat on top of him, cradling his head as I tried to reassure him. Henry was by now used to seeing Dale like this and just lay by his side, watching him. Such was the force of Dale's anger that I had to sit with him like this for over forty minutes, during which he ripped the sleeve off my blouse. This was the scene that greeted Jamie on his return home from work. Hugely relieved to see him, I said to my still struggling, wailing son, 'Dale, look who it is – it's Dad.'

Also trying to reassure him, Jamie said, 'Dale, I was hoping we could go for a run in the garden. Would you like that?' But even this was to no avail and Dale remained crimson-faced, eyes popping out of his head with rage.

I remember muttering to Jamie, 'This is terrible, even the dog looks worried now.'

For some reason, this produced in Jamie a moment of divine inspiration. He suddenly adopted a deep, refined voice and told our son, 'Dale, this is Henry speaking. I hate it when you cry. I'm so worried. Could you please stop this?'

On hearing this, Dale immediately calmed down and composed himself, telling his dog, 'All right, Henry. I'm sorry.'

Jamie and I looked at each other in slightly bewildered relief, and then Jamie said in the same deep voice, 'So, Dale, shall we go for a run, then?'

At these words, my wee boy sat up, practically threw me off him and said, 'All right, Henry, let's go.' Out into the garden they went, Dale pulling Henry by his collar.

Later that night, with neither of us yet fully appreciating what had happened earlier, we steeled ourselves for the forthcoming bedtime battles.

Jamie first broached the subject, suggesting, 'Dale, pyjamas, it's bedtime.'

Henry was lying in front of the fire, deep in a contented sleep. Dale looked at his dog, then went over to Jamie, shaking his jumper, though not looking at his face, and said, 'No, Dad, speak like Henry.'

Again, Jamie and I exchanged a look, then I nodded towards the dog and gestured that Jamie should do as Dale had asked. He cottoned on and, in what would become a very familiar voice, said, 'Dale, this is Henry speaking. Please get your pyjamas. It's bedtime. I'm tired. I'm going to my bed.'

At this, Dale responded contentedly, 'All right, Henry,' and off he trotted to his bedroom.

We sat bemused, thinking there was still a battle ahead of us, but Dale came back down actually dressed in his pyjamas – something he had never done before. He had even attempted to do up the buttons, although they were endearingly misaligned. He looked at his dog a moment, then said firmly, 'Henry, bedtime. Come to bed.'

Jamie and I sat there, stunned, and then Jamie found his voice – his own this time. 'Goodnight, son.'

Another all-time first followed when Dale said, 'Goodnight, Dad' – finally responding on our terms.

This was so good to hear that I took a chance myself, saying, 'Goodnight, Dale.'

The resulting 'Goodnight, Mum' was the sweetest music ever to reach my ears.

12
The Kick

From that memorable day when Henry found his voice, his power seemed almost miraculous: Dale would do virtually anything his dog 'asked'.

The very next morning after we had discovered the voice, I seized the opportunity myself, anxious to see whether Dale would respond to me using it. As usual, Dale was running late and his school taxi was about to arrive. Normally if I tried to interrupt and hurry him along, he would get angry, so instead on this morning Henry asked him, 'Dale, put on your shoes and coat – I can hear the taxi coming.' I did my best to emulate the same deep and refined tone that Jamie had used and was astonished to find that Dale immediately got himself ready and was waiting with Henry at the door by the time the taxi pulled up outside.

When Dale arrived home, I checked his school diary as usual to see what he had done that day. I did this to try to encourage him to tell me himself, but most times I got one-word answers or he would take great exception, exclaiming crossly, 'Don't say "school".'

Today, however, once Dale had settled down to play, with Henry at his side, I cautiously approached with the diary in my hand and asked in Henry's voice, 'Dale, what did you do at school today?'

Without missing a beat, Dale replied definitely, 'Drama, Henry.'

'Dale, what's drama?' Henry continued, on a roll now. 'Is it fun?'

'Yes, Henry, it's good fun. We go to islands in a boat.'

'Dale, did you not get wet?'

'No, funny Henry, it was pretend. We play at pretend at drama.'

I found that as long as I followed the usual rules for talking to Dale – for example, keeping things simple – with Henry's help I could have very basic little three-way conversations like this. Despite my excitement at this development, however, I was concerned about whether or not this was an appropriate way to communicate with Dale. When Jamie came home, I told him how well Dale had connected to the voice, but we both agreed it would be sensible to get advice before we continued to use it.

Fortunately, a speech therapist called Christine Cuthbert, who worked with Dale at St Anthony's, was due to make a home visit. She was brilliant at her job and had implemented an Odyssey drama programme at the school which really did relate to all the children. She was also using a speech therapy programme called Social Use Language Programme (SULP) that was specifically designed for autistic children, where phonic and picture characters were used to illustrate the rules of social language. With character names like Listening Lizzie, Butting-in Betty and Looking Luke, the programme worked really well with Dale and the other children and ironically was similar to the technique we had devised long ago with the *Thomas* trains.

I certainly didn't want to compromise the wonderful work

Christine was doing with Dale at school and so when she arrived at the house I explained the situation regarding Henry and was greatly relieved by her advice. Knowing I was very 'tuned in' to Dale's autism, she said, 'As long as you use this technique constructively and responsibly, go for it.' She felt we had found a means to communicate with Dale that he was comfortable with and we could obviously aim to wean him off Henry's voice as he progressed over time. I assured her this would be our ultimate objective and that meanwhile we would be careful in how we used the voice.

Soon after this meeting, in the summer of 1995, Jamie and I attended a conference on autism at which Jim Taylor was one of the speakers. When we managed to corner him to ask what he thought of our unusual discovery, he told us, 'I'm not surprised. A third party can reduce the anxieties associated with one-to-one conversation.'

While Jim had never come across a talking dog before, he had been party to a situation at Struan House where a worried young boy was only able to tell Jim what was wrong by turning his back and picking up a telephone to speak to him. They were both in the same room, but this indirect means of communication allowed the boy to express himself without all the non-verbal pressure that is involved in a face-to-face conversation.

We understood exactly what Jim meant. Henry had become Dale's telephone; with his unthreatening face and eyes, he was not making the type of social demands on Dale that a person would. He had also become Dale's first real friend, teaching him how to be successful in a relationship without all the pressure that would come with a human friend.

When we got home, we saw how Jim was right. If we

used Henry's voice, Dale would look at the dog's face, with correct eye contact and proximity to Henry, whereas when we spoke as ourselves, he either avoided looking at us or got right in our faces as before.

In these early days of the voice, I became virtually hoarse from talking through Henry, progressing from fleeting moments of interaction to almost constant three-way conversations. These included doing homework with Dale, playing with him and reading bedtime stories. Henry would pay dutiful attention throughout, cocking his head from side to side, as if intrigued by the sound of 'his' voice. For my part, such was Henry's involvement that it felt as though he had indeed become my second child. Tantrums with Dale still happened, but not as often or for as long, because Henry could talk him through his upset and reassure him more quickly than ever Jamie and I had been able to do. When Dale was almost seven years old, he himself poignantly confirmed his appreciation of Henry to me: 'I love my soft, cuddly dog. He's beautiful. If I didn't have him, I would be crying and sad for a long time.'

Another really encouraging change around this time was in Dale's drawings. He had constantly drawn Thomas and the other trains in the past, but now they were given obvious different facial expressions – happy and sad. What surprised us even more was that even though he still struggled to give us eye contact, he would draw the trains looking directly at each other; in other drawings to follow, Dale was starting to introduce figures as well as trains, including perhaps himself and Henry, showing signs that his imagination was starting to improve.

As Dale's seventh birthday approached, we tried to get

him used to the idea that his age was going to change and reminded him of all the fun we had had on Henry's first birthday. This seemed to help a lot, as did the fact that the school was working on the problem, too – children's birthdays in the unit were used as a social learning time for all of them, as far as possible with a few mainstream children joining in as well. The teacher asked us to supply a birthday cake for Dale, and as he was also going to have a small family party at home, I let him choose a *Thomas the Tank Engine* cake for school and a Dougal one for home, after the *Magic Roundabout* character.

All in all, I think everyone's concerted efforts paid off because when Dale's birthday finally arrived, he happily trotted out to the school taxi, looking forward to his party. I gave the escort girl the bag with his cake in and then noticed that one of the other boys in the taxi, who had severe autism, was in a sulky mood.

Trying to cheer him up, I told him, 'Raymond, be happy – it's Dale's birthday today and he's got a cake for you all to share.'

Raymond was unimpressed. His firm and disappointed reply was, 'Oh, no, it will be a train,' and he looked even more unhappy as they all drove off.

It was ironic that even other children with autism were bored with Dale's obsession, and perhaps little wonder that he had no friends. We tried to help him with this by resurrecting our Boring Bertie stories, but it was still difficult to get him to understand an abstract concept like boring.

He also had trouble understanding various words he would hear other children use at school, such as 'hate'. He thought this was something you would say when things were not going your way and so would exclaim, 'I hate you,' if one of his trains fell off its track. And no matter how hard we tried to demonstrate 'love', particularly at night to try to settle him down, it was still too advanced a concept for him to grasp.

We knew Dale wouldn't understand that our gift to him for his seventh birthday was given with love, but we thought he would at least like it. Mindful of his obsession with transport, we got him a tyre swing for the garden, thinking this would give him the pleasure of having a car wheel as well as a swing. How wrong could we be? Dale was completely horrified and flew into a tantrum because 'Tyres belong on cars.' We had to cover the entire thing with a big sheet as he wanted nothing to do with it and would not even let his two young cousins, here for his birthday celebrations, play on it. Such was his wrath that he drew a picture of the swing and put a large teacher's cross through it, adding on an accompanying piece of paper the words 'No, Mum and Dad.'

We nevertheless managed to have a fun time as Granda George diffused the situation with a game of pin the tail on the dog – Henry being at a safe distance of course. Dale participated well, especially in waiting for his turn, and was sufficiently recovered from his tantrum to appreciate the small gift of another toy car later presented to him by Henry, who was proudly sporting a cluster of balloons on his collar, with the car attached.

Everyone sat as I cut up the Dougal cake and then Dale opened his other presents, one of which was a memorable dog-themed game named Fleas on Fred, which he really liked and learned to play right away with his cousins and me.

So, despite the swing disaster, all went well – until the moment when Dale, while helping Granny Madge clear up in the kitchen, suddenly let out a piercing scream. He was hopping around as though in real pain and I hurried to check his bare foot, only to find a small piece of curly lettuce stuck to the underside: he was clearly less than taken with the strange sensation it gave him. Although we knew it wasn't sore, he was really upset and would not be comforted, so my mum suggested, 'Pop a Mickey Mouse plaster on it and see if that calms him down.' I had used such plasters on him in the past if he cut or hurt himself, even if it was just a tiny scratch, and they had seemed to help. Fortunately, this time was no exception and a major tantrum was once more averted by Mickey.

This gave me an idea. Jamie and I had decided we would have to change the tyre on the swing for a normal seat, but I thought as a last resort I would try to enlist the help of Henry and Mickey. Although pretty much redundant since *Thomas* had come into Dale's life, the large Mickey Mouse doll was still sitting at the foot of his bed.

The next day, Dale came home from school as usual, little knowing what was in store. Henry suggested excitedly to him, 'Come on, Dale, let's go and play in the garden,' and we all went outside. Dale shrieked in dismay at the sight of the now uncovered swing with Mickey strapped to it. I quickly ran over and started frantically swinging the wretched mouse all over the place, much to the delight of Henry, who leaped around barking as he tried to grab hold of Mickey's leg. While this madness unfolded, Dale at least stopped screaming and looked on dubiously. Henry then took it upon himself to tell Dale of all the fun he was having: 'Whee! Go, Mickey. Push him to me, Mum.' My young boy finally found his sense of humour and began to enjoy the spectacle – so much so that Henry continued with great glee, 'Mum, take Mickey off. It's not his swing, it's Dale's.' Sure enough, Dale was by now so happy that I was able to leave him, Mickey and Henry playing together with the swing. When Dale jumped on to the tyre, Henry jumped too and shrieks of laughter echoed around the estate.

Later, when Jamie was home, Dale forced something on to his lap as he sat trying to read the paper. It was another picture of the tyre swing, this time with just a big teacher's tick beside it.

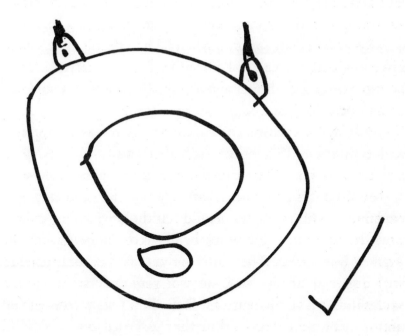

Despite the regular little breakthroughs via Henry and the intensive education Dale was receiving at school and at home, we knew he still needed as much integration and socialisation as possible, preferably among his peers locally. In August 1995, because Dale was already familiar with the church environment and enjoyed Sunday school, he joined the Anchor Boys at Jimmy and Dorothy's church. Fortunately, this group was led by the same lady who ran Sunday school, so Dale already knew her. We still suspected, however, that he might have a problem with the fact that she and her daughter would now be carrying out a different role; not only that, they would also be in a church hall that was being used for something other than Sunday school. Many people with autism have difficulty seeing those they know outside of a familiar setting and do not always learn from previous experience; they struggle with lateral thinking and the application of what they have learned from one situation to another. We had witnessed this trait ourselves with Dale one day when he had become extremely upset at seeing his teacher Paula at Hillend Nursery. As far as he was concerned, she belonged in the PSLU and he could not comprehend how she could be anywhere else.

As always, therefore, careful preparation was paramount and so Jimmy and Dorothy took Dale along to see the Anchor Boys in action before he joined the group properly. Knowing it would be difficult to get him to wear the uniform, they explained to him how you could tell the boys were Anchor Boys because they all wore bright-red jumpers with an Anchor Boy badge. The leader, who was a natural teacher with a special affinity for Dale, was very understanding and said it didn't actually matter if Dale didn't want to wear the uniform; it was more important that he settled in successfully. But because we wanted to reinforce to him that he was no different from the other boys, we thought it would be worth trying to get him to wear it. We told him, 'Dale, all the other children will be the same, so that's all right.' We then had a rehearsal with the jumper at home, where Henry informed Dale approvingly, 'Dale, with your red jumper on, you'll look like Jealous James.' This had the desired result. Dale pulled on the jumper and ran outside to his running area, where he pretended he was indeed Jealous James. Henry joined Dale in his run and told him how good he looked in his red jumper, reassuring him that when he wore it to go to Anchor Boys, Henry would go along in the car with him and be waiting to take him home again afterwards. 'Dale, you're becoming a big boy,' added Henry. 'Like me.'

And so the deal was struck. Off we all went to Anchor Boys, with our dog in tow. Henry was already known to the church minister and elders as he spent time there with Jimmy and Dorothy when they were looking after him for us, so he was afforded the privilege of being allowed into the church to wait for Dale. Thankfully, Dale responded to the leader's gentle approach and settled in really well, even if he was understandably quiet at times. In this happy, well-structured environment, he gradually blended in with the other boys and began to learn from them how to adapt socially.

This was a big step forward, but given the amount of input Dale had needed just to get to this stage, I was all too aware that he still had mountains to climb in terms of progress. He continued to have no awareness of other people's feelings and emotions, let alone empathy, which was one of the most difficult concepts for a person with autism to grasp. Jamie and I had resigned ourselves to the fact that it would take years of specialised input to achieve even the most basic level of understanding in this area.

*   *   *

One afternoon when Dale arrived back in the school taxi, he seemed in a really good mood and happy to be home. Buoyed by this, I took a chance, saying, 'Hello, Dale, how was school?'

The fact that I had used my own voice was my downfall. With great disapproval, my son shouted, 'Don't say "school".'

Immediately under pressure to put things right, I made my second mistake, one with which I was all too familiar. 'OK, Dale,' I let slip, 'we'll talk about it later.'

That did it. Dale reacted with a rage I had not seen in a long time. Knowing a violent tantrum was now inevitable, I tried to restrain and calm him, but with the strength of Goliath he broke away from me. He was crashing around holding his head, hands covering his ears, and before I could get to him he started banging his head into the wall, screaming, 'I hate you. Don't say "OK".' I desperately tried using Henry's voice to reassure him, but he was too far gone.

Henry by now was stood at the opposite end of the room, looking understandably anxious. I tried again. 'Dale, it's Henry. I'm scared – you're frightening me.'

Dale was having none of it and, to my complete horror, ran at his dog, with his school shoes still on, and gave him an almighty kick, screaming, 'I hate you.'

Poor Henry yelped and ran to the corner, where he lay down, bewildered.

At this moment, I lost it. 'Dale, that's it, finished,' I yelled. 'You are not going to make this dog's life a misery.'

Unused to seeing me at this level of anger, Dale sat down, moaning and crying as I checked Henry over and comforted him. Fortunately, he seemed fine, but I was not yet ready to be placated and shouted across at Dale, 'I'll take Henry back to Val's.'

Dale just rocked back and forth and echoed without understanding, 'Back to Val's.'

Shortly afterwards, Jamie arrived home from work.

'We need to talk in the kitchen,' I told him, as Dale whimpered in his chair, feeling very sorry for himself.

I explained to Jamie what had happened and how I was really concerned for Henry's welfare. 'Dale might think he can take his anger out on his dog now,' I said, 'physically, like he still does with me.'

'But it's not like he really hurt Henry,' said Jamie, still trying to absorb the news. 'It's probably just a one-off.'

'We can't risk it happening again,' I disagreed. 'Ever.'

Both of us were at a loss as to how to get this across to Dale; and if we couldn't, then for his own protection our beloved Henry would have to go.

Sometimes the best ideas are born out of despair. As I stood in the kitchen unable to face the thought of losing Henry, I happened to glance at the cupboard where I kept the medical box containing the Mickey Mouse plasters. This simple act inspired the makings of a plan, which I cautiously explained to Jamie. We worked up the idea together, but then as I started to realise the potential implications, I began to have doubts.

'We have to be sure about this, Jamie. Otherwise I'm not going to be able to go through with it.'

Jamie considered a moment, then replied, 'I'm sure. This is too important – we have to give it a try.'

Anxious but determined, we went through to the lounge, where Dale was sat in the armchair, calmer now, but still crying. Jamie went over to Henry in the corner and knelt down beside him to comfort him. Then, using Henry's voice, he said, 'Dad, please help me. I'm so sad. Dale hates me. He hurt me – my back is very sore.'

I slipped out into the hall and returned with a suitcase that Dale knew we used when we went away. I placed it on the sofa and started to fill it with Henry's things. In went his food bowls, his toys one at a time and his grooming tools. Dale sat and watched, teeth clenched, swaying back and forth, moaning. I picked up the phone and, while Jamie continued to collect items for the case, pretended to call Val, feeling terrible about what we were doing, but knowing we had to see it through.

'Hello, Val,' I lied. 'It's Nuala here. Something terrible has happened. Dale has kicked Henry and hurt him. He hates his dog.' I paused and gestured to Jamie, who disappeared into the kitchen, knowing what I wanted from him. 'Val, poor Henry is very sad,' I continued. 'His back is so sore.'

Jamie returned with a big adhesive dressing on which I'd drawn a felt-tipped Mickey Mouse face and he proceeded to stick this on Henry's back where he was kicked.

'We'll have to bring him back to live with you, Val,' I concluded into the phone.

Neither of us could possibly have been prepared for Dale's reaction. To this day, we remember vividly how he screamed in shock and ran over to Henry, frantically cuddling him, burying his head in his fur and crying hysterically, 'My dog, my dog, what have I done to my dog?'

Although shocked at seeing Dale in this state, we nervously carried out the rest of our plan. In a subdued voice,

Henry said, 'No, Dale, you hurt me and hate me. I want to go back to live with Val.'

Desperately distressed, Dale started kissing Henry on the head, telling him, 'Henry, I'm sorry, I'm sorry. Please don't leave me – you're my dog.' He collapsed again against the dog's fur, and his next words left us gaping in disbelief. 'I love you, Henry. I love my dog.'

We looked on, quietly stunned. Dale had never before expressed sentiments of love and it mattered not a jot to us that it was a golden retriever who received them first. We also realised that Dale did understand what he had done and so Henry told him forgivingly, 'I love you, Dale, and want to live with you.'

I sat consoling Dale, with Henry beside us, while Jamie unpacked the suitcase and returned Henry's things to where they belonged. I made sure Dale felt better, though he still seemed a little shocked as I pretended to phone Val back, telling her that Henry was going to stay with Dale, who had promised he would never hurt him again.

Over two hours had gone by since the onset of this nightmare and Jamie and I felt drained, mentally, physically and emotionally. We sat trying to reassure Dale for what seemed like ages, but he remained upset and we cuddled him up with Henry on the sofa, wrapping the cosy train duvet round them. 'Dale, Henry will always be your dog,' we told him, 'and he will never leave you.' We managed to get him to take a drink and a biscuit and Henry listened attentively as I read them a story of Dale's choice, to try to regain some sense of normality.

By the time we took Dale up to his room to settle him for the night, he was much calmer, although he insisted that

Henry stayed with him at all times. Even when Henry was lying beside him on top of the duvet, Dale still needed reassurance that his dog was not going away and was feeling all right. I had an idea and whispered to Jamie, who then said in Henry's deep voice, 'Dale, I'm feeling much better now. Please take my plaster off.'

Jamie gently removed the plaster, saying, 'Dale, I'll put this in the bin – we won't need it any more.'

Dale's face immediately flooded with relief and Jamie left me to say goodnight to him.

'Dale, give Henry his night-time kiss,' I told him. 'It's time to sleep.'

He turned and did so, saying, 'Night, night, Henry. Love you. See you in the morning.'

I snuggled Dale down and kissed him, saying, 'Goodnight, Dale,' as I cautiously turned to leave.

Then came his quiet, upset little voice, wanting more reassurance: 'Mummy, Dale loves his dog.'

I didn't want to make any more of a fuss and carried on, saying, 'Yes, darling, and Henry loves Dale.'

As I opened the bedroom door wider, Dale repeated softly, 'Mummy, Dale loves his dog.'

'Yes, that's good,' I replied, still trying to leave. Then I stopped dead in my tracks as his next words hit me.

'And Dale loves his mummy.'

Just five little words, yet I was numb, paralysed with shock. Then somehow my brain started to function again, although my heart was pounding – I desperately didn't want to get this wrong. I turned round and knelt down beside Dale's bed, where I gave him a cautious and gentle hug, telling him, 'Mummy loves you, too. And Daddy loves you. Goodnight, Dale.'

His sweet, small voice replied, 'And Dale loves Daddy.'

I kissed him on the head, quietly left the room and wept – copious, silent tears. Through this mist I noticed Jamie, who had been waiting on the landing to see whether Dale had settled. We just gazed at each other, disbelieving. Then he took me in his arms as I continued to weep.

Downstairs, we badly needed a cup of tea – not just any old cuppa, but more a remedy for shock, like after an accident. We spoke about what had happened over the previous four hours and acknowledged just how precious Henry had become to Dale and all of us. While we thought we had understood our son's condition to date, we had abruptly learned a lot more about both him and his autism that night; it was as though this traumatic episode had given us the final piece of the jigsaw we needed. Now we had been shown so dramatically just how important Henry had become to Dale, and that he did love us and understood the meaning of love, we felt the sky was the limit in terms of what we might now be able to unlock deep within him.

A few days later, with the stress of that night behind us, we headed off to Tesco, with Henry on the back seat of the car, strapped into his seat-belt harness. Once there, as I was scanning the shelves, Dale ran ahead to collect dog biscuits for Henry. In the maze of aisles, he disappeared out of sight and Jamie hurried after him, leaving me anxious as to whether he would get to him before something dastardly happened. Next thing I knew came a voice across the aisles as loud as the shop tannoy: 'Mummy!'

'I'm here, Dale,' I had to reply loudly, 'but you need to talk to my face.'

This prompted one or two strange looks from other shoppers, and not least a response from my son for the whole world to hear: 'Love you, Mummy!'

I ran round to the aisle where Jamie was staring at our wee lad in amazement, and knelt down, arms wide open in delight. 'Dale, come here,' I shouted back, 'I want a big hug. I love you, too.'

At the checkout, Dale helped me put the shopping on the conveyor belt, while Jamie packed the carrier bags. To my great surprise, Dale suddenly leaned forward and kissed the top of my left hand, which was resting on the bar of the trolley. The lady behind us in the queue couldn't help noticing and commented, 'I've never seen a child do that before – it's lovely. He must love you an awful lot.'

I smiled and carried on, thinking, 'My God, if only she knew the half of it!'

Sometime after the shopping trip, our friend Lindsey arrived for the weekend with her near-white golden retriever, Ollie. For an English-bred dog, he was remarkably similar to Henry in both looks and temperament, and definitely a real geezer. Dale took an immediate interest in this new dog, but none of us could have anticipated how bringing Ollie into the house would again illustrate Dale's blossoming understanding of his emotions.

As Dale was cuddling Ollie on the floor, being really affectionate with him, I couldn't resist observing, 'Dale, you love Ollie, don't you?'

'No, Mum,' came his emphatic reply. 'I *like* Ollie. I *love* Henry.'

13
Make or Break

There was no doubt that on that fateful night of the kick, Dale had through Henry taken two enormous steps. For him to have the ability to empathise, let alone love and be loved, was more than we could possibly have hoped for. With all the progress and breakthroughs we had witnessed, it seemed reasonable now to take Dale even further. I had learned from the early days of the tree that there was no harm in trying for more, because if necessary we could always rein things back in again. Better this than never to have tried at all.

Days were spent with Jamie and me talking via Henry virtually throughout. As time passed, I was gradually able to decrease the emphasis on the voice – for example, starting a conversation through Henry but then throwing in little snippets of my own voice. In this way, without even realising it, Dale would not only communicate with me directly, but also correctly – just as he would speak to Henry at the right distance and with appropriate eye contact, he began to do this with me, too, with the result that his confidence in talking to another person soared.

I could also use Henry's voice to show Dale that I was even more interested in what he was doing than Henry was; Henry would simply ask Dale to involve me. If Dale was engrossed in drawing, he always involved Henry and showed him the picture, so I took to suggesting through Henry, 'Dale, show Mum the drawing, see if she likes it.' Dale naturally complied, but whereas Henry would only sniff at the picture and wag his tail, I would go over the top in my enthusiasm, sometimes even rewarding Dale with a chocolate from his *Thomas* tin. The resulting masterpiece would always be put up on the wall.

Over time, Dale learned that he got more attention and response from me than he did from Henry. As he continued to do anything the dog asked of him, through this technique Jamie and I were both slowly able to get him to accept us into his world. We could see Dale gradually becoming the little boy we had always dreamed of and hoped we would soon be able to wean him off Henry's voice completely. But such was Dale's anxiety about non-verbal and direct communication that we hadn't really appreciated quite how bonded he had become to communicating through Henry. It was to take quite a while longer before Henry ceased to talk.

After such an intense summer, Jamie suggested that we have a weekend away, but wasn't sure where we should go. For a variety of reasons, I thought of Blackpool. There would be no flights involved, which was all to the good as we still could not be sure Dale would go on an aeroplane without immense preparation, which at this point we did not have time for. I also thought that, Blackpool being famous for its trams, we could continue helping Dale to learn by using his obsession with transport themes. So once we had found a nice boarding house in the Saturday paper and booked their traditional September weekend package, we were all set.

We told Dale that Henry was taking a weekend break of his own, and when the big day arrived, we stopped by at Val's to drop off Henry. We couldn't bear the thought of putting him in kennels, and after all he really did deserve a holiday. From then on, Val always came up trumps for us and Henry never spent a single night in kennels.

Six hours later, after a couple of pit stops to refuel ourselves and the car, we arrived at the B&B. Dale demanded we instantly get ourselves out. 'Look, Mum, trams!' he exclaimed excitedly, as he spotted one at the end of the street.

That first evening, we took Dale to the Pleasure Beach, where he went on all of the rides he was tall enough for, as long as Jamie accompanied him. Not surprisingly, his favourite was the miniature railway. The next morning, we all went down for breakfast, to be greeted by the landlady in her northern English accent, 'Morning, love.' She made a special effort for Dale, saying, 'Morning, duck, what would you like for breakfast?'

Dale replied crossly, banging on the table, 'I'm not a duck, I'm Dale.'

After breakfast, we ventured out along the promenade to the North Pier, where we knew from some brochures that there was a Venetian carousel which was accessed by a little train. At the end of the pier, there was a nice lounge where we could have lunch. As we made our way along the seafront in the autumn sunshine, being buffeted by strong winds, we noticed above us a whirring sound. Dale looked up and cried, 'Mum, Dad, look – it's Harold,' his inspiration being of course a certain helicopter from *Thomas the Tank Engine*.

A little further along, I noticed a board advertising pleasure flights in the helicopter we had been watching. These left from the North Pier. As we were heading there anyway, Jamie and I looked at each other, the same thought going through our minds.

Then Jamie shook his head. 'Nah,' he said. 'It'll be sixty pounds for me and Dale for just five minutes.'

'If he goes up in that helicopter with you,' I replied, 'I'll give them a thousand pounds.'

When we arrived at the North Pier, the helicopter could clearly be seen and heard, as it waited on the helipad ready for the next trip. Jamie knelt down beside Dale and asked him, 'Dale, would you like to go on Harold with me?'

To my eternal surprise, Dale instantly replied, 'Yes, Harold, Harold the Helicopter.'

Was *Thomas* once again going to help Dale achieve a major breakthrough?

Jamie headed off to buy the tickets for Dale and himself, and I explained to Dale, 'It'll be very noisy, but Dad will be there and you'll see all the trams in Blackpool from Harold in the sky.'

Jamie returned and let Dale see the tickets. Then the two of them were shown to the helipad. I was back behind the barrier, about twenty-five metres away. Because of the noise of the helicopters, I couldn't hear what was going on. I saw a party of four adults and Dale, the only child there, being fitted with bright-yellow life jackets. Only then did I fully realise the enormity of what was unfolding. A few minutes later, to my horror, I saw this little figure beside Jamie start to bounce up and down, just as he did sometimes when heading into a tantrum. I feared the worst, but I couldn't hear what was happening over the noise. Then as some returning passengers disembarked and passed between me and the helicopter, I lost sight of Jamie and Dale. When the way was clear again, my two boys were nowhere to be seen. I went over to the stairs, but there was still no sign.

Because history had dictated that if I feared the worst there was generally a good reason, it was not until the helicopter had actually taken off that I realised the only place they could be was on it. I couldn't control my tears of joy and excitement at the thought of my incredible boy up there in Harold. Though they were only away a few minutes, to me it seemed longer. Then, suddenly, the familiar whirring of the rotors signalled the end of the circuit of the Blackpool seafront and yet another amazing achievement for Dale.

After their life jackets had been returned, Dale was given a certificate to prove he had flown in a helicopter. He still has it to this day.

When they got back to me, I asked Jamie, 'Why was he jumping up and down? Was he scared?'

'He was beside himself,' said Jamie. 'He was going to fly in a real Harold!'

Over a celebratory drink in the hotel lounge that evening before dinner, Dale was still buzzing with excitement about his trip. 'Mum,' he said joyfully, 'Dale wants to tell Henry about Harold.'

'Henry's not here,' Jamie told him. 'You have to be in the same room to talk to him.'

Our son's retort took us both by surprise: 'All right, Dale will phone him.'

With that, Jamie pretended to dial a number on the payphone in the hall and answered in Henry's voice. 'Hello, this is Henry, who is it?'

'It's me, Dale. Dad and me were up in Harold,' came the ecstatic response.

'Do you mean Harold the Helicopter? That sounds very exciting. Was it good?'

'Yes, it was great,' replied Dale.

'Excellent, Dale,' said Henry, adding in case we were there all night, 'I must go now, it's my dinnertime. Good-bye, Dale.'

From then on, Dale would frequently phone Henry, which meant of course that he was continuing to communicate with us via Henry's voice, so we knew it would take a lot longer to wean him off it than we had originally thought. Still, as we now only used it when he phoned Henry, and Dale had previously shown real signs of accepting the weaning process, we felt we would get there eventually.

Despite all the wonderful things that were taking place, we knew that nothing could compare to Dale getting a brother or sister. It was painfully clear by now, however, that we would need specialist help. One evening in October 1995, Jamie and I had a consultation with an infertility consultant at the private Glasgow Nuffield Hospital. It was decided that we should try a procedure known as intra-uterine insemination (IUI). I would be stimulated by the drug Clomid to produce extra eggs, then artificially inseminated at the peak of a cycle. We went through this process the following month, but sadly it did not result in a pregnancy.

*　　*　　*

Dale's second year at St Anthony's went well and he made steady progress, particularly in relation to his drawing ability. In his pictures at school and at home he began to develop a sense of perspective, his railway tracks disappearing into the distance and the trains themselves making obvious eye contact. This was the period during which he started doing what we called his 'Xerox drawings'. They always had the same background and composition, two different trains facing forwards, with distinct facial expressions. Dale would reproduce five or more of these drawings at a time if you let him. More encouragingly, he also began to draw more pictures of people, starting with an easily identifiable likeness of Granny Madge, who was delighted to be one of his portrait subjects.

In the early summer of 1996, with life so settled, in spite of our fertility problems, we felt we should book a proper holiday and this time, because of the success with Harold the Helicopter, we decided to venture to Paris by plane. We knew by now that one small setback could undo a great deal of progress, so we put in plenty of preparation before the trip. We visited the airport with Dale, had lunch at a table from which he could watch the planes and then took him to the check-in area to get him familiar with the process. Coincidentally, he also had a visit from a pilot to St Anthony's and, as a result of all this groundwork, took the flight in his stride.

To get from Glasgow to Paris, we had to change in Birmingham. On the first leg, Dale ate his breakfast and was enjoying the flight when the man sitting beside me, a young pilot travelling down to get a connection, asked, 'Would your boy like to see the cockpit?'

I asked Dale and he replied that he would. I considered telling the pilot about Dale's autism, but, as things were going so well, decided not to on this occasion.

They disappeared off to the cockpit and returned about five minutes later, Dale with a big smile on his face. The pilot said it had been a while since he had shown anyone round like this and that Dale had made his day. 'He was so interested – he really enjoyed it,' he said. 'A lot of kids nowadays aren't bothered.'

On the second leg of the journey, when a stewardess offered us drinks from the trolley, Dale turned to Jamie from his window seat, saying, 'Tell the lady Dale will just have tea.' Even at 30,000 feet or so he was not going to pass up the chance of a cuppa.

We arrived in Disneyland on Dale's eighth birthday and booked up the special Disneyland Hotel party tea, the highlight of which was Dale being served his chocolate birthday cake by none other than Mickey Mouse. Jamie quipped, 'Minnie can't make it, Dale. She's still in the kitchen baking other cakes.' Then there was a poignant moment as Dale got up to give Mickey a big hug, as if he appreciated all that he had meant to him in the past.

Needless to say, Dale had a wonderful time at Disneyland and we were so glad we had chosen this as the place to spend our first proper, trouble-free family holiday.

One summer's day in 1996, shortly after our Paris trip, the three of us were down at Seamill with Henry, enjoying the fine weather. We were throwing Henry's plastic bone into the water, trying to get him to swim, but he wouldn't go any further than paddling depth. Most retrievers know perfectly well they are water dogs and will swim for hours if they get the chance, but not so our Henry. He was a complete wimp: if the bone went too far, he would wait for the tide, or one of us, to bring it back. Jamie and I even tried supporting him in the water, just out of his depth, to teach him, but all he would do was swim straight back to the shallow water where he was comfortable.

'Will you teach me to swim?' asked Dale, who had participated in all of this. 'Then I might help Henry.'

We made a brief start, which was consolidated in the next school year when Dale's class began swimming lessons, and by the end of the first term he could swim. Unfortunately, Henry never mastered this skill. We had many more fun days at the beach, however, often precisely because of our dog's unwillingness to get too wet, even though this invariably meant that we did.

Over the following year, Dale continued to make steady progress at school and enjoy looking after his dog at home. Again, life seemed settled, although changes were on the way.

Despite all the progress in his classes and at home, Dale still had no friends at school. During the summer holidays of 1997, when Dale was nine, I was faced with the usual problem of keeping him occupied for the seven weeks that he was off school. He was still socially quite immature and I felt that involving him in play schemes might exacerbate the problem. Even so, I still wanted to find something that would occupy him and help him develop the social skills that he lacked because of his autism. It was crucial that he acquired some confidence, otherwise he would continue to have problems fitting in with other children. And without this ability, of course, his all-important chances of integrating into the mainstream classes at St Anthony's would be compromised.

I saw an advert in the local paper for a two-week drama workshop run by the local council, where a show would be put on at the end of the fortnight for parents and friends. I had heard and read that many people thought drama was not a suitable activity for children with autism, so before I launched into the process of priming Dale, I phoned up and spoke to Margaret Lambert-McNeil, who would be running the workshop. She sounded lovely, with a gentle and understanding nature, and her main profession was working with young adults with learning disabilities, including autism. I explained all about Dale and she fully supported the idea of trying to socially integrate him more. She was very happy for him to become involved in the group, and we discussed various ways in which we could help him take part.

Before the workshop started, Jamie and I once again gradually worked with Dale to get him accustomed to the new experience. We also reinforced to him that because it was a summer fun-time class, everyone would have a treat break each day. So I then took him to a nearby shop where he spent about half an hour choosing ten treats, ten drinks and ten packets of crisps in readiness.

When we got home, I spent time with Dale – Henry at our feet and very much involved in the discussion – preparing ten little treat break bags, each with the appropriate day written on them. This meant Dale would understand that his fun-time class would have to end, and I also thought the treats would give him extra motivation to attend and cope.

On the first day of the workshop, Henry went along in the car with Dale to put him at ease. I offered to stay with him during the class, but Margaret rightly felt it would be better to leave him be, although she suggested I stay in the building for that first day. I spent the two hours reading in the foyer and Margaret knew where to find me if I was needed. When I picked Dale up, Margaret gave me the great news that the experience had been a success. Although Dale had hovered silently around the edge of the group throughout, he was not unhappy and really did enjoy the break time. Margaret had occasionally seen him showing a fleeting interest in what was going on and she felt, as I did, that Dale would slowly become part of the group, in his own unique way.

The other children in the group were not fazed by Dale's presence and at times, especially during the breaks, tried to include him. They all simply accepted him for who he was. The bags of treats diminished until, at the end of the two weeks, Dale stood on stage with the other kids for their public performance in Gourock's Gamble Halls, in front of an audience of over a hundred people. To get Dale to do this, we had promised him a prize if he did well, in the form of a new train from the *Thomas* range, which we wrapped up for Margaret to give him at the end of the show. It did wonders for his confidence and self-esteem to be 'chosen' by Margaret, as he thought, out of all the group. We would often tell Dale little white lies like this to motivate him in new situations and it always worked. Overall, Dale's involvement was so successful that for the next three years he would attend not only the summer drama workshop, but also one at Easter and a weekly evening classes, all run by Margaret.

Thanks to Margaret, he gained enormously in terms of self-esteem, confidence, imagination and socialisation with his peers. Even more memorable was the fact that these workshops also led to a huge breakthrough – they gave Dale his sense of humour. Before attending, he did not understand the concept of telling a joke, but he learned his first one in Margaret's class. He would tell his joke to everyone he encountered and loved the laughter it produced. 'Why did the orange stop running?' he'd ask. When he got the response, 'I don't know,' he'd start laughing himself as he delivered the punchline: 'Because it ran out of juice.'

In the weeks that followed, Dale would attempt to make up his own jokes – some funny, most not, because he still tended to miss the point due to the abstract nature of a joke. Over time, this process helped him to develop the good sense of humour he now possesses. It also did wonders for his self-confidence because when people responded to his jokes in a positive manner, he realised they were interested in him. It was also invaluable in developing his learning because he was much keener to embrace a topic if we could make it funny. If he was behaving inappropriately, for example, we would copy the behaviour in an exaggerated and animated way so he could see how funny it looked and understand how others saw him.

Many friends commented on how great it was to see Dale telling his jokes, all the more so after I taught him a lengthy and really funny story concerning a millipede, with the punchline 'I'm still putting on my boots.' Dale would tell this at any opportunity, clearly understanding why it was funny, and it was a joy to watch his sense of humour evolve.

Jamie always took his annual fortnight's holiday during the last two weeks of Dale's school holidays. We wanted to find somewhere that Dale would enjoy as much as Disneyland and London sprang to mind – there was lots to see and we could also work in a trip to Legoland while we were there. This had the added bonus of a steam train to entice him.

Because of Dale's involvement in drama classes, I thought he would like to see some West End shows. Once again we used his obsession with trains, deciding that his introduction to London theatre should be *Starlight Express* because the excitement of seeing a show about trains should overcome any worries on Dale's part about the crowds and noise. We ensured we were at the very front of the theatre so Dale could see the show but not how many people were in the audience, and we booked the aisle seats in case we needed to make a quick exit. Happily, this wasn't necessary and Dale loved the show, leaving the theatre proudly clutching his programme. He seemed to understand the concept of people being trains, and I think it gave him an insight into how he could play at being a train himself. We noticed on our return that when doing his *Chariots of Fire* run, he would incorporate the circling piston action of a train with his arms, as well as make the sound of its whistle.

On the next two nights of our London trip, we successfully took Dale to *Beauty and the Beast* and *Cats*. He especially liked *Cats* as we had been playing the tape of the show in the car to let him get to know the music. He'd been looking forward to seeing a railway cat named Skimbleshanks and was delighted at the spectacle of this feline and his friends forming a train on the stage out of mock rubbish and various props. He was intrigued by the use of rubbish in this way and loved the surprise of it. When the cat characters went through the audience demanding to be stroked, Dale was overjoyed, howling with laughter as he stroked the 'cat' beside him. At first, he had got a fright because it sneaked up on him in his aisle seat, but once he composed himself the female cat character intrigued him so much he responded to it as if it were real.

Not surprisingly, another aspect of London that Dale loved was travelling around on the Underground. The lure of the trains meant that he took the crowds in his stride, and he really seemed to like the hustle and bustle of London life.

Needless to say, Legoland was also a great highlight that reminded us of Dale's first building blocks and of how far he'd come in the interim.

When the holiday came to an end, Dale insisted on giving Henry a call from the airport to let him know we'd be home soon. He had seemed to have learned a lot about imagination thanks to this weekend as he had this conversation with Henry using his own hand as an imaginary phone.

On returning home, I discovered a really good nursing position was available. Dale was progressing so well, so I felt I could not miss the opportunity. The local health centre was looking for a community senior staff nurse to work with an assistant on night shifts for fifteen hours a week. It was rare for such a professionally challenging and rewarding position to come up, and the hours would fit in ideally with Dale. Also, if I was ever to succeed in having another child, the job would accommodate my needs nicely. I was therefore delighted to be offered the position, and for the first time since Dale was born felt I could function as the professional I had been all those years ago at St Luke's.

Another positive change was that Dale was due to move up from the Anchor Boys to the Boys' Brigade Junior Section. The boys from both groups got together once a year for their end-of-term display night, so Dale was aware of the junior section and familiar with its leaders. The only stumbling block was that he wasn't happy about changing from a red to a navy-blue jersey.

As we weren't aware of any train in this particular colour, we thought perhaps someone else could help with the problem, so one day when Dale came home from school, a smartly dressed Henry greeted him with the words 'I liked this navy jumper so much, Dale, I just had to try it on.' Dale laughed heartily as Henry continued, 'Do I look like a grown-up dog now, Dale? Can I join the junior section?'

Dale answered, giggling, 'No, Henry, dogs are not allowed in the junior section. You'll still have to wait at the door.'

Dale thrived in the junior section. Whereas some boys might have found its more structured and disciplined approach difficult to adapt to, this suited Dale's needs perfectly and he thoroughly enjoyed it.

* * *

In October 1997, Jamie and I attended a review of Dale's progress at St Anthony's. The staff graciously acknowledged how our efforts to help Dale were paying off handsomely, but we still had a major concern: Dale had no friends. To try to address this, we had actively manipulated him into a more socially acceptable obsession than *Thomas*, in the hope that he would then be able to mix with his peers. The craze of the day was the computer game *Sonic the Hedgehog* and we had bought Dale a Sega Megadrive and accompanying games for his ninth birthday in June. He learned the game quickly and it rapidly became a new obsession, but at least it was 'in' and something he could talk about in the playground.

Despite this and the fact that Dale was integrating well locally in his after-school activities, the worry remained that he had still failed to integrate into mainstream academic classes at St Anthony's. Of even greater concern at the review meeting was the doubt of the educational psychologist and staff that our son would ever integrate into his local school, which of course had been the goal all along. They said they were planning to keep Dale at St Anthony's for the whole of his primary education and then send him to Glenburn, a special-needs school in Greenock.

We reiterated our hopes that Dale would ultimately have a good quality of life and decent level of independence, stressing the need for a mainstream secondary education and that his route into this should be a period attending his local primary school. Sadly, Jamie and I were the only people present who felt this was achievable; we were told that Dale had not integrated at St Anthony's to a level where he would be able to cope fully in a mainstream setting. I pointed out that a major concern while he remained in the unit was that he was regressing, in that he was picking up autistic mannerisms and copying inappropriate behaviour from the other children.

Thankfully, the educational psychologist did agree to leave the options open, but if Dale's level of integration remained as it was, nothing we could say would alter the school's view.

I left this meeting in despair. It seemed that no matter what Dale had achieved, there was a major obstacle to a positive future for him. What was needed was something to help him with his academic work, to break down the barrier to integration. The biggest hurdle for Dale was definitely maths, in that the language involved was preventing him from understanding the questions, making the whole environment of the subject frightening and alien.

We were going to have to find a way to prove Dale could cope at his local primary school as soon as possible. Time was running out.

14
A Fitting Tribute

In October 1997, during the half-term break, Dale had a successful week at an art workshop for schoolchildren, which his drama teacher, Margaret, had told me about. He loved all the different activities, apparently fitting in well alongside the mainstream kids.

While I was waiting for him to finish one day, I noticed a poster about the Kumon maths system and saw that the Guild was running classes after school on Mondays and Thursdays. The more I read about the programme, the more I felt it was suitable for Dale. It was a 'drop-in' system geared towards children of all ages and abilities, many of whom participated because they were finding schoolwork difficult and had lost confidence. The programme tied in with the National Curriculum, but would be adjusted by the teachers to suit each individual pupil's needs and abilities, letting them progress at their own pace – they would work on their own within the class, so there would be no pressure to keep up with the other kids.

I was quite excited; this seemed tailor-made for Dale. I met with one of the teachers, Mr Gordon, who carried out an assessment on Dale to determine his starting level, and it was agreed that he would join the programme. Dale immediately adapted both to the teachers and the class – it was an ideal, non-threatening environment and he took the whole thing in his stride. He particularly liked the reward system and, thanks to the patience, support and understanding of Mr Gordon, was to attend these classes for the next three years.

With this new class and all the other activities Dale was involved in, his self-esteem and confidence soared. I dearly hoped we now had the weapons we needed to win the coming fight to get him into full-time mainstream education.

It had been three whole years since Henry had found his voice and we were at last slowly managing to wean Dale off it. He was getting more used to conversations, although these were still limited. We encouraged him to respond to Henry's non-verbal signals and facial expressions, just as you would with any dog. 'Dale, look at Henry's tail,' we would say, 'he's so pleased to see you.' In this way, Henry also finally helped Dale to understand the concept of hide-and-seek. When Dale hid, we would tell him, 'Stay quiet and Henry will sniff you out with his big nose.' Somehow the knowledge that Henry could smell him taught Dale that he needed to try to trick his dog by hiding in different places – without his usual cry of 'Here I am!' Such was Henry's ability to find Dale that one day Dale turned to me and announced, 'Mum, it's not fair that dogs have good noses.'

By increasingly dominating the conversation and including Henry in only a small way, Jamie and I were able to get to a point where Dale was happy with only fleeting moments of his dog's voice. Then eventually the day came when Henry was silent, just like any other golden retriever.

While Dale was now progressing and able to converse

with us, there was no denying the void in his life caused by the lack of a real friend. Apart, of course, from his very special canine friend, he had no one to share his life with, and no matter how much he learned, it all seemed so sad and purposeless if he was to remain on his own. Fortunately, our introduction of the *Sonic the Hedgehog* obsession started to reap benefits and Dale slowly became more socially acceptable in the school playground.

At around this time, a nice, quiet young boy named Ryan, also aged nine, started in Dale's group in the unit at St Anthony's. Aware of how difficult Ryan would find it to settle in, the staff assigned Dale to be his mentor. Ryan had problems with communication and fell within the autistic spectrum, although he was high functioning, with good language, albeit immature social use of it. Over time, in their own quiet way, Dale and Ryan were to become the best of friends.

We had thought it would take years for Dale to establish a friendship in his own area and so it was ironic that just after Ryan came on the scene, another chance occurrence boosted Dale's social life still further.

Sometimes we would try out a new brand of dog food for Henry and Val would arrange to get a big bag of it for us. We would all go along to collect the food and seize the opportunity to see any dogs she had at the time. On one such occasion, Dale told Val's mum, Sheena, all about *Sonic the Hedgehog*, which struck a chord with Sheena as her only grandson, Robert, also nine, was really keen on *Sonic* too. Knowing Dale had no friend to play with at home, Sheena said to him, 'Robert could play *Sonic* with you, Dale. Would you like that?'

The very mention of the word '*Sonic*' was enough to prompt the response, 'That would be good.'

Soon after, we tried a short visit with Robert at our house, and to our eternal relief, it was a total success. We told Robert that he was in charge, and although Dale was quiet, he accepted Robert's guidance and played along well. Soon afterwards, it was established that Sunday was Robert's day; he would come after lunch and stay beyond teatime. He was so patient and very understanding of Dale's at times bizarre behaviour and responses.

When Robert asked what was wrong with Dale, we came up with the explanation that he had language blindness and so was still learning how to communicate as well as Robert. We felt that the concept of autism was too complex to explain and might also be a bit off-putting for a nine-year-old. Robert was happy with our explanation and many a time would pick up on something Dale had said and put him right, which Dale was more inclined to accept than if we had tried in a similar way. Perhaps this was because Robert was his peer, and Dale was showing the natural desire of children to fit in with each other.

Not only was Robert one of Dale's first real friends, but there was another bond between the two of them, just as important as *Sonic*: Robert was a dog-owner, too. His own dog was a little shih-tzu called Mitzi – not a golden retriever, but at least he was surrounded by goldies whenever he visited Val's – so he understood Retriever World, as we jokingly called it. Robert didn't bring Mitzi to our house, but he and Dale always had Henry in the room with them as they played on the computer. For our part, we were overjoyed that Dale now had three good friends – Henry very much included, of course.

With Ryan at school and Robert at home as an ideal role model, these two new friendships really started to reap rewards in terms of Dale's communication and confidence. We made sure that we regularly took Robert out for an evening meal with us all as a thank you for his helpfulness and loyalty to his new chum. We went to many different restaurants and places, which both boys enjoyed greatly and which had the additional advantage of opening up another social world for Dale.

During this period, with Dale changing for the better in every way, we decided once again to address the problem of not conceiving. We saw another consultant, Dr Yates, at the Glasgow Nuffield Hospital and agreed to try an intensive programme of intra-uterine insemination (IUI) and ovulation induction. This meant having three cyclical attempts to stimulate my ovaries to produce healthy eggs via hormonal injections. Then hormone blood analysis and internal scans would monitor when two, or at most three, large follicles containing eggs were present, and at the peak of the cycle Jamie's sperm, specially treated at the lab to select the most viable, would be artificially paced in my womb to try and increase the chance of conception.

The whole procedure was similar to IVF and I had to take the same drugs as for that process and inject myself daily. Despite my determination and perseverance through all this and the many blood samples and internal ultrasound scans, three attempts ended in failure. I was despairing. I had put myself through emotional and physical hell and yet it now seemed that our infertility was another concrete wall – like Dale's autism, but one that we might never be able to break down.

As this was a stable time in Dale's life, the desire to have another baby began virtually to consume me. Apart from my own feelings of emptiness and loss, I just couldn't bear the thought of Dale being on his own. So even though the chances of success seemed to have slipped further from my grasp, I was determined to go all the way with the infertility treatment. Jamie was fully supportive and we were prepared to go to financial extremes if need be. I was not going to stop until failure itself was inevitable.

As Dale and Jamie got on with their daily lives, I became a recluse, living from one chance of conception to the next, taking every possible measure to help increase that chance. Just as I had before Dale was conceived, I took all the vitamins and minerals thought to aid the process and even stopped socialising, staying at home with Henry as my only companion.

Jamie would have the occasional night out with his friends, but knew that too much alcohol consumption might adversely affect his fertility. Knowing this and abiding by it, however, were not entirely the same thing and there were a few instances when Jamie would come rolling home with his mate John Turner, both well oiled in drink. They would want one last beer for the night and John would get Dale involved in their antics, which included virtuoso air-guitar performances to full-blast rock music. Although Dale didn't understand the concept of drunkenness, he was aware of the change in John's personality and found it highly amusing, doing anything John asked of him no matter how silly. John was so ebullient and animated that whenever we had friends round or went to their houses, he was the only one who could get Dale in full party mode, joining in the dancing or whatever games were going on at the time.

Another member of 'the team' also played an important role in Dale's life at this time. To give me some space, Jamie would take Dale down to visit George and his Ford Zodiac, made famous by our wedding. George would take Dale off for a run in the car and let him help fill it up with petrol, all of which Dale loved, just the two of them together.

George was a mechanic working for the health board. As another treat for Dale, he would show him the depot where he worked on the ambulances, demonstrating the ramp and all the tools involved. Dale was intrigued to see where the ambulances 'lived' and that it was George who fixed them. This might not seem like such a big gesture, but to Dale – and to us – it was. The ambulance depot was just round the corner from our home on Dresling Road and many a time Dale would suddenly exclaim, 'Look, Mum, George is driving the ambulance,' as he saw George setting off on yet another test run. Through his time with George, Dale was not only engaging with another adult, but also acting out his transport obsession in a real context, not just an imaginary world. Most important of all, this was the first time Dale had ever pointed out a family friend by name, rather than just inanimate objects as was his wont.

There is no denying how fortunate we were to have such good friends playing the roles that they did and how much more fortunate we are that they remain close friends to this day.

*　　*　　*

In June 1998, following the failure of the IUI treatments, I embarked on my first course of in-vitro fertilisation, or IVF. On 13 June, Dale celebrated his tenth birthday, but because I was in the middle of the gruelling cycle of injections and the commitment this treatment entailed, we did not have a party for Dale. He wasn't exactly hard done by, however, in that Robert came over for the day and they broke in Dale's new GameBoy together, attended as ever by Henry. This was followed by a slap-up meal, although I wondered at our wisdom in taking them to an expensive restaurant and letting them eat whatever they wished – the pair were developing a taste for the finer foods in life, like fillet steak and fresh scampi.

In stark contrast with that happy day was the reality of my mother's slowly failing health. She had fought breast cancer when she was forty-two and unfortunately hadn't got the type of help and support that is available today. Nonetheless, her fighting spirit, which had been so vital in her relationship with Dale, made her an inspiration to others at the time. Due to artherosclerosis, she had subsequently survived a risky operation to graft her carotid artery, but the weight loss and general health deterioration that followed were now cause for considerable concern. Although virtually housebound, she was at least stable at this time, which is why I had made the decision to go ahead with my IVF treatment.

I felt the pressure mounting as the big day for the egg-retrieval procedure approached, but once it was all done and I came round from the general anaesthetic, I was told to my enormous relief that I had produced ten good eggs for fertilisation. These would now be mixed with Jamie's sperm in a test tube, then monitored in a strictly controlled environment while the embryos, hopefully, developed. I was excited and uplifted because retrieving so many good-quality eggs was in itself a great result. Jamie and I then faced an agonising twenty-four-hour wait for a phone call from the unit informing us how many embryos had resulted.

After a sleepless night, I waved Jamie and Dale off to work and school, and then the phone rang. I picked up the nurse's tone of voice immediately she said my name, 'Nuala, I'm so sorry to have to tell you bad news.' She sounded genuinely upset as she continued, 'We don't understand what's happened. All the quality procedures were followed, but you have no embryos.' She tried to offer support and arranged for us to see the consultant to discuss what had gone wrong.

I put down the phone in shock, then wept as the reality of yet another failure started to bite. Everything I had gone through was for nothing. Albeit for different reasons, I experienced a similar sense of loss and grief as when I had found out about Dale's autism. That night, once Dale was settled in bed, Jamie took me in his arms and did his best to console me. I vowed to treat this setback like all the other obstacles that had been put in my way – I was not giving up.

Although Jamie was also hugely disappointed by what had happened, he was worried for my health and well-being if we continued, but I pleaded for one last chance.

'If the consultant thinks it's worthwhile,' I told him, 'we could always try ICSI.' This was intra-cytoplasmic sperm injection, similar to IVF, but more advanced. An embryologist would specifically inject each egg retrieved with a single 'good' sperm. I desperately hoped this would be an option for us, because although I had had no problem conceiving Dale, the doctors were unable to give me a definitive reason as to why I was now suffering from secondary infertility. They offered various theories, but basically it all came down to the same thing: ICSI was a last resort, and if we didn't meet the right criteria for this procedure, my chances of having another baby would be at an end.

While Mum's health remained a concern, the community day nurses, whom I knew through my job, couldn't have been more helpful and ensured that she had all the equipment and home support needed to make her comfortable. My mum was only sixty-seven, but she adapted bravely to the change in her lifestyle, somehow retaining her cheerfulness despite hardly ever being able to leave the house. She and George were happy with the care she was getting from my colleagues and felt strongly that they didn't want to put the family under any more stress than was necessary.

Reassured that Mum and Dad were settled and coping, Jamie and I set off to see the infertility consultant at the Nuffield to see why IVF had failed. He was very sympathetic, but could only conclude that although healthy in form and numbers, Jamie's sperm may not have had the 'strength' to penetrate the eggs. Then he said the words I was longing to hear, 'We could try a cycle using ICSI.'

He explained that, as with IVF, the process was by no means guaranteed and even carried an increased risk of failure. In fact, two-thirds of all ICSI procedures fail, because it is such a delicate process, whereby sperm may become damaged or those selected might not be the best ones genetically that Nature would have chosen.

With the consultant's advice, we decided to go ahead only after giving my body a rest from all the drugs and trauma to date. So it was that in September 1998, with Dale now in primary five at St Anthony's and Mum remaining stable, we started a cycle with ICSI. Jamie and I vowed to tell no one. It wasn't that we didn't feel anyone could support us, but rather that the stress and disappointment of failure was simply too much to bear. The grieving process was easier if people didn't know and constantly ask, 'How are you?'

As usual, I got on with all that was involved, except this time I felt quite unwell as my abdomen swelled considerably. I couldn't wait to have the eggs retrieved, I felt so bloated and uncomfortable. By now, I had also reached saturation point, and had menopausal symptoms caused by the drugs involved in the treatments to date.

The day before the retrieval, as I prepared for my trip to the hospital, the phone rang and I received terrible news. My mum was acutely ill in the Glasgow Western Infirmary; she was in renal failure and the prognosis was poor. Struggling to take this in, I phoned Jamie, who immediately came home and we went with my dad to see her. Dale came, too, and although he understood in a small way that Granny Madge was ill, he was pleased to be talking to her. In spite of her weakened state, she managed to talk back.

When I spoke to the nurses, I learned that as well as renal failure, it seemed Mum had a recurrence of breast cancer. I explained my situation regarding the pending egg retrieval and went home to tell the rest of the family of my mum's prognosis.

The next morning, on Monday, 5 October 1998, after yet another general anaesthetic, my swollen ovaries yielded twenty eggs. Thirteen were good enough to be injected with a single sperm each and then we again had to face the excruciating twenty-four-hour wait. Due to the high number of eggs yielded, I felt unwell and had slight signs of over-stimulation. Because of the state my body was in, there was currently no chance that any resulting embryos would take and so I was told they would have to be frozen. The staff let me go home later that afternoon. Despite the way I felt physically, I asked Jamie to take me to see Mum as I desperately needed to be with her.

Again she was cheerful, but very frail. I told her what I had been through, so that she would know there was a real chance that Dale would have a little brother or sister and that she would hopefully be a grandmother again. She was having to deal with so much and being so brave that I just wanted to give her some positive news to hold on to.

My poor mum's arms were covered in bruises where numerous blood samples had been taken, and because of her acute state, she had also had a barrage of other tests and biopsies. She hated all that and, I think, knew it was futile. It came as no surprise when she told me what the doctors had said about the cancer and she pleaded with me, 'Please, Nuala, tell them no more. I've had enough. I want to die in peace.'

Hard as it was, I promised Mum I would ensure that this request was honoured and would return in the morning with my sister Linda and Dad. Mum was very cold and I tucked her up in a blanket and kissed her goodbye.

'Don't worry any more, Mum,' I told her softly. 'I promise you'll get your own wee room tomorrow and all you need to make you comfortable.'

I watched as she fell into a contented sleep, then told the nurse to phone the family and me if there was any further deterioration, in which case we would come back to the hospital immediately.

When I got home, I felt really uneasy and the dread of the phone ringing was at times unbearable. I couldn't settle, but went through the motions of trying to watch television. Physically exhausted but mentally fully awake, I finally went to bed, only to toss and turn and watch the hands of the alarm clock drag round its face.

Eventually, I turned away from the clock, determined to get some sleep. Then my heart jumped as the phone rang. I knew straight away it was the hospital, but I was not prepared for what I was told.

'Mrs Gardner, I'm sorry, it's your mum. She needed some pain relief, and when the nurse went back later to check on her, she had passed away.'

In deep shock, I said that we would come to the hospital in the morning as we had planned, only now it would be to collect Mum's belongings. I felt cold and numb, shattered that I hadn't been there for her; but I think that after the pain-relieving injection she would have been comforted to know that her suffering was to end and must have relaxed enough to slip peacefully away. One thing I could still do for her, however, was ensure that there would not under any circumstances be a post mortem. I spoke to Linda and Dad, who agreed that she deserved to be left alone while we prepared a fitting funeral for her.

The next morning, after a sleepless night, I got away early to meet Dad and Linda to make all the necessary arrangements. Jamie stayed at home with Henry while Dale was at school, as I didn't know how long I would be. I said I'd phone him later to find out the ICSI results. My head began to throb both with the grief for my mum and my anguish over whether I would get any embryos. I felt like an empty vessel.

Because Mum came from a large Catholic family, we arranged a Mass at St Patrick's Church, which was just fifty metres from the funeral parlour where her body rested.

When I later tried to phone Jamie, badly needing to know the ICSI results, he wasn't in. After a busy morning, I invited Dad and Linda back for a cup of tea and a break from the stress of the day. My dad was deeply stricken by his loss, and I knew that he was going to need our support now more than ever.

There was still no sign of Jamie, but then I noticed that the mantle over the fireplace had been cleared of its usual clock and ornaments to make way for the first eight *Thomas* trains, all in order. I was initially confused – what on earth was Jamie thinking? – but then it clicked. This was his way of letting me know the outcome of the call from the clinic: each train represented an embryo. Dad and Linda didn't bat an eyelid, as Dale was always leaving trains around the house in the strangest of places, but I knew it was Jamie.

Shortly afterwards, Jamie arrived back with Henry. 'I didn't want to leave you a note,' he explained, 'but I thought you'd understand the significance of the trains.'

Only this news, and Jamie's way of breaking it, could
have made me smile at a time like this.

I was still consumed by thoughts of Mum, but at least
there was now a little hope amongst all the pain. The only
other pressing issue was how to tell Dale about the loss of
his wonderful granny, who had meant the world to him.
That night, we were sure Dale could sense something was
wrong and Jamie decided to speak to him. We agreed he
would have to explain at a level that Dale would understand.

Gathering Dale next to him, he began. 'Dale, Granny
Madge was very sore. The hospital medicines and Mickey
Mouse plasters did not work because Granny Madge was
just too sore.' Dale sat silent and solemn as Jamie continued, 'So she has to go away to a nice place in the sky
called heaven and we won't see her any more. That is why
we are all sad, because we loved Granny Madge very
much.'

Dale remained solemn, but snuggled into Jamie, who
planted a gentle kiss on his head. After a little while, still in
silence, Jamie left Dale to reflect, but checked in on him
periodically – he was playing quietly with his trains on the
floor.

The next day, I decided to take Dale into town with me
and involve him in choosing a wreath. I wanted the nicest
possible arrangement for my mum, so we went to my
favourite florist, which, although expensive, had a big
book of designs for Dale to choose from. We flicked
through a page at a time, with me not caring what Dale
chose or how much it cost – I just wanted him to be fully
involved, to help him understand what had happened.

Jamie and I had explained to him that Granny Madge would go up to heaven in a special heaven bed and that all her flowers would go with her to make her happy when she got there.

As I turned the pages of the big book, I came across a floral teddy bear; it seemed to intrigue Dale, so I asked, 'Dale, would you like to give the teddy flowers to Granny Madge to take to heaven for you?'

I was not expecting his response. 'No,' he said, 'I'll give Thomas.' I tried to explain there was no floral train, but he insisted, 'No, Thomas, Thomas flowers.'

Realising how much Thomas meant to Dale and that for him this would be the ultimate tribute to his granny, I asked the florist if there was any way she could do a train like Thomas. Not surprisingly, there wasn't.

I left the shop to phone Jamie, who agreed that if it would help Dale, then it was worth trying to find what he wanted, and we could always get a separate arrangement from ourselves. So I spent the entire afternoon visiting every florist in Greenock and phoning others, even as far away as Glasgow, but no one could help. I felt really disappointed for Dale because he had seemed so happy at the thought of Thomas flowers for his granny, but there didn't seem to be much more I could do.

As we made our way back to the car, passing the various shops adjacent to the row of bus stops, we came to a greengrocer's that sold fruit, vegetables and a few flowers. It was a nice shop, but I never usually used it and the flowers on display were nothing like what I was looking for. Nonetheless, I concluded that there was no harm in asking. In we went and I explained my predicament to the large, pleasant owner, who announced, 'I've done guitars and animals before, but never a train.'

In excited disbelief, I suggested, 'If I give you a picture, could you do something as near as possible?'

He said he'd do his best, although as he would have to spray some flowers, it would be very time-consuming and therefore costly.

'If you can do this,' I told him, 'I will be happy to pay whatever it takes.'

The day before Mum's funeral, the kind greengrocer came to the house with the fruit of his labours. True to his word, it was big, but very definitely a Thomas wreath and, at a cost of £120, hopefully for Dale worth every penny. I thanked my saviour profusely as he left and then turned back to the wreath. It might not have been what I had planned for Mum, but it was perfect for Dale.

When Dale came home from school, the huge floral train was sitting on the dining table. Dale ran straight to it and jumped up and down with joy. 'Thomas flowers,' he cried. 'Thomas for Granny Madge.'

We were so relieved to hear this, as Dale was never normally willing to be parted from Thomas and we had feared he might want to keep the wreath for himself. We explained that we should take Thomas to the place where Granny Madge was in her heaven bed and then she would go on up to heaven in the morning with all her flowers. Dale calmly accepted this and we prepared to leave.

Jamie carried the wreath to the car as I locked the front door. I turned with Henry and stopped, stunned. As I looked at Dale, I was overcome with silent tears. There he was following Jamie down the path, both of his arms circling just like the train characters in *Starlight Express*, contentedly chanting in a rhythmic train beat, 'Puff, puff . . . puff, puff. Thomas is taking Granny to heaven. We won't be seeing her any more. Puff, puff . . . puff, puff.' He continued until Jamie had safely installed the wreath in the car. Then we set off, Jamie and I quietly touched by what we had witnessed.

I had explained the situation in advance to the staff at the funeral parlour and when we arrived we took a photograph of Dale sitting with the wreath. Then I told him it was time to give the flowers to Granny Madge, who was in her heaven bed behind the big doors. Jamie took the wreath in and laid it on the floor beside her coffin. After a little nervous hesitation, Dale cautiously popped his head round the door, holding my hand and waving, 'Bye, bye, Granny Madge. Thomas will puff, puff with you up to heaven.'

15
The Miracle

The days following Mum's funeral were tough. The loss of such a wonderful mother and grandmother was unbearable. We particularly worried about how her passing might affect Dale, but looking back, it was as if he reverted to his contented, happy self almost immediately after the handover of the Thomas wreath. Although Dale had lost his Gran, he still had Henry, and without their strong bond at this time I think Dale would have been lost.

We took Dale up to Granny Madge's graveside to reassure him that Thomas had indeed taken her to heaven. The uniqueness of the Thomas wreath had obviously touched the gravediggers as they had propped it up with some bulky earth at the head of the grave. All the other beautiful tributes people had brought covered the remainder of Mum's resting place like a luxury floral duvet.

We told Dale that the graveyard was where the heaven beds were put and later, when it was dark, Granny Madge's 'spirit ghost' would float up to heaven with all the flowers. He understood in a very basic way about people becoming 'ghosts' as one of his favourite films, *Casper*, had dealt with death in this manner, though we had to explain that, unlike in the film, spirit ghosts stayed up in heaven for ever with all their flowers beside them. Dale seemed passive and accepting and Jamie and I wondered if he really did understand. But then, as I took his hand and we slowly walked back to the car, I heard his lovely, by now familiar chant: 'Bye, bye, Granny. Thomas will puff up with Granny to heaven.' With his free arm, he was again doing his train actions, which he kept up with the chant until we reached the car.

A couple of weeks afterwards, I went back to the grave to find that due to the harsh weather it had been totally cleared of flowers. Armed with this knowledge, Jamie and I took Dale back with Henry and explained that, led by Thomas, Granny Madge had now arrived in heaven. Dale just stood quietly, as did Jamie and me, each with our own private thoughts of her.

Dale was by now a well-grounded ten-year-old and was continuing to progress both at school and in his extra-curricular activities. Although the major concern remained about his inability to integrate with the mainstream kids at St Anthony's, one of the most positive things at this time was his now firmly established friendship with Robert. Our Sundays were totally taken up with his visits, and the two of them spent hours playing with the Sega Megadrive. To prevent the boring obsessive factor from taking over, however, Robert fortunately became adept at diverting Dale on to other activities, both inside the house and out in the garden, often playing football games, which Henry joined in with enthusiastically.

With this stability in our lives, although it was only a few weeks since the loss of Mum, I felt it was time to face the reality of my ICSI treatment. At the right time in my cycle, four embryos were thawed, which was in itself a big hurdle to cross because of the risk of the embryos perishing during the process. The hospital informed us, however, that we had two viable embryos and so, with great anticipation and anxiety, we drove up to Glasgow Royal Infirmary for the process of implantation. Once the embryos had been placed in my womb, all we could do apart from being generally sensible was wait fourteen days and see whether Nature now took its course. At the end of that period, I provided the usual sample to the hospital, which was tested as we waited in a side room. When the nurse returned, the news was gently broken to us that the embryos had failed.

This hit me really hard. Because I'd been pregnant before with Dale, I had honestly believed that if I had real embryos inside me, the process would work. I had so desperately wanted it to work, not just for us as a family, but for Mum, who I missed so much. I also wanted to give my grieving dad, George, something to look forward to. Despite knowing that ICSI treatment is a form of emotional and physical hell for so many couples, Jamie and I felt that our personal hell throughout this process was on a scale all of its own – one that we could barely cope with, let alone get anyone else to understand – so much so that we decided that if we had a successful pregnancy and birth, we would donate any remaining embryos to help other couples, and signed a consent form to this effect, although we did have to inform the consultant of Dale's condition.

We had taken the decision not to tell Dale of our quest for another child through infertility treatment. We felt that if it didn't work, he might be upset unnecessarily, and, more importantly, if it did work, he would need full preparation for such an enormous change in his life.

Meanwhile, I tried to console myself with the fact that there were four frozen embryos left.

Since 1990, Jamie had been employed at Motorola's design centre in East Kilbride, and his work over the past year or so had necessitated trips to Austin, Texas. In January 1999, he was due to return there for three weeks. Dale was getting used to his father's absences and Jamie assisted in this by always spending time with him before he left – for example, making a detailed chart with a drawing of an aeroplane and a number of squares below it to illustrate how long he would be away. This would let Dale cross off each day so he would understand when his dad was coming home. Each time Jamie returned, it would be like a mini Christmas as Dale was given toys or games that were not available in the UK. Jamie would also bring Robert the same things as a mark of appreciation for everything he had done for Dale. Needless to say, it was no time at all before Robert and Dale were filing requests for games with Jamie well in advance of his next trip.

To keep Dale busy during the weeks that Jamie was away, Granda Jimmy worked on making a large wooden Henry train from scratch. On Jamie's previous trip, Jimmy had made a Thomas train, but this time Dale wanted to help and they worked together in Jimmy's big joinery workshop in the attic of his house. Dale would be involved in any way he could and would update Jamie on the train's progress each night on the phone. Such was the quality of these trains that to this day Dale has them displayed in his room, together with a picture we managed to capture of Henry the dog lying beside Henry the train.

When the next four embryos were thawed, sadly, again only two were viable. The day that I was due to have these implanted was to fall during Jamie's forthcoming trip to Texas. We spoke to our friends Lorraine and Brian, and as Brian offered to drive me to the hospital in Glasgow on the day, we resolved that Jamie should go on his trip as planned.

Brian made me feel so relaxed and was very positive about the whole thing. We had several laughs along the way because various members of staff kept thinking he was my husband. One nurse in particular spotted him sitting on his own while I was in theatre having the embryos implanted and tried to drag him in to be with me. Thankfully, he took the day in his stride, even to the extent of using his relaxed and pleasant nature to calm down other anxious men waiting.

The usual two-week wait followed, then the sample and the wait for the final result, which even through familiarity became no less agonising. I stood in the hospital feeling sick, bracing myself for the inevitable . . . then the nurses from the Assisted Conception Service came in, one saying cheerfully, 'Nuala, sit down, we have good news. Congratulations, you're pregnant.'

I just couldn't absorb what the sister had said. My heart pounding out of my chest, I asked her to repeat those words I never thought I'd hear. She duly did, and after thanking her as if she alone were responsible, I wept with joy. The feeling of happiness was indescribable and I loved every minute that followed that simple conversation.

I was bursting to tell Jamie, but had to wait until that evening when he called from Texas. I proudly announced that while he was 4,000 away, I had got pregnant, with my friend's husband at the conception! This caused no little hilarity between Lorraine, Brian and ourselves over the next few weeks.

When I was about eight weeks pregnant, Jamie took me up to the Nuffield for a routine scan. There was nothing routine about it, however, because it clearly revealed that I was carrying twins. After all we'd been through, and still raw from losing Mum, we felt better than if we'd won the lottery – no amount of money could have bought us such happiness.

A couple of weeks later, I started to bleed, not just spotting, but obvious bleeding that was clearly abnormal. While the midwife in me told me that this sometimes happened, I felt the same sense of unease that I had had from the day Dale was born: deep within me, I suspected this impossibly precious pregnancy was doomed.

Since a thread of hope remained, however, I fought off my distress and spent a whole week trying to stay calm and doing all I could to prevent what seemed inevitable. I followed all the advice and took total bed rest, but nothing stopped the continuous bleeding. When Jamie took me back to the Nuffield for another scan, the nurses and my consultant showed great compassion as the ultrasound probe was placed next to the neck of my womb. I could hardly bring myself to look at the monitor as the consultant searched and searched, but in vain. There were no heartbeats. Only black masses of conceptual contents remained.

Utterly destroyed, I was then told that because of the bleeding and risk of infection arising from the retained products of my pregnancy, I would have to be admitted to hospital for a minor surgical procedure. To try to bring an end to my mental turmoil as soon as possible, the consultant arranged a prompt admission to the Glasgow Royal. Yet again I would have to undergo a general anaesthetic, only this time with no hope of a baby beyond it.

I will never forget being admitted to the ward for this procedure. Here I was in the same hospital where the embryos had been implanted, desperately wanting to keep them but having to endure the nightmare of having their remains removed. The nursing staff were very supportive, but somehow they also knew to leave me be.

Such was my grief that I never wept once throughout the time I was there; I was just numb. I wanted everything over and done with, and I think my silence spoke volumes about how I was feeling. I'd never experienced grief like this before and I couldn't help but think back to that young mother with the stillborn baby who had been in a similar state all those years ago. The only thing that kept me going was that Jamie was as determined as I was that we shouldn't give up. The very fact that I had become pregnant at all gave me the strength to carry on.

In April 1999, Jamie started a new job in Livingston, which was a 120-mile round trip. He had no option but to take this post because the office where he had worked in East Kilbride was moving all of its design activities to Texas. We had been offered the chance to go there, too, but had felt that because Dale's quality of life had now improved so much, such a move would have been devastating for him and may well have set him back years. It just wasn't worth the risk.

Around this time, I attended a parents' afternoon at Dale's unit in St Anthony's. I went along feeling encouraged by the fact that Dale was generally progressing well, at school, at home and in all of his out-of-school activities. When I spoke to his teacher, however, I learned to my horror that Dale's fate for secondary education now seemed to be sealed. Although the unit had tried to bridge the gap regarding his integration, it was felt he had not reached an acceptable level to cope with mainstream education.

When I asked the teacher what the plan was for his secondary education, she confirmed that Glenburn in Greenock would be recommended for him. She already knew my feelings on this and nothing had changed. Glenburn was a good special-education school, catering for children from five to sixteen years of age with a diverse range of physical and learning disabilities, but I passionately did not want my son educated in this environment, possibly never mixing with mainstream kids, who I knew could teach him so much. I remember telling the teacher that I didn't understand how Dale could integrate fully in his local area with all the mainstream activities he was involved in, yet wasn't able to do so at St Anthony's.

Dale only had two years of primary education remaining. I left the meeting knowing that unless we took strong action to get him into an appropriate educational setting, then 'special' secondary education was going to be inevitable. I went home in a panic and related all to Jamie.

We discussed many options, but the one thing that was clear to us both was that if Dale stayed at St Anthony's, he was never going to integrate to an acceptable level. We concluded that the success he was having with his out-of-school activities was due to the fact that these took place in his local area and he knew the children involved. Another factor was that the class size at St Anthony's was very large in comparison with our local school. It also concerned us that by remaining in the unit Dale was still picking up various autistic mannerisms and having to take part in social activities below his level. This in itself was counter-productive, and we felt that if he transferred to Glenburn, little would change. It was time for him to move on.

Feeling more determined than ever, we started to look into other options. We were also aware that Dale had started to show an insight into the fact that he was different from other local kids. One time as we walked Henry up the hill past Overton Primary, about five minutes from our house, Dale asked, 'Mum, what's that place there?'

'It's the school where all the kids in the houses near us go,' I explained.

'Why can't I go there?' came Dale's reply.

At this time, a really nice young boy named Fraser lived across the road from us and would sometimes visit to play with Dale. Thinking of his friend, Dale then asked, 'Is this Fraser's school?'

As I explained more about it, I could see Dale had a real desire to be like Fraser. 'Would you like to go to school with Fraser?' I asked him.

'Yes, that would be good. I like Fraser.'

I couldn't ignore the fact that I had uncovered this motivation in Dale and set about trying to fulfil his wishes. Jamie and I rapidly concluded there was no harm in trying Dale at Overton if the alternative was to leave things as they were. We prompted a meeting via the educational psychologist at St Anthony's. We put our argument to them, but everyone else present had serious reservations about our plans. With the summer holidays approaching, however, it was decided to leave the final decision until the next term.

In late May 1999, shortly before Dale's eleventh birthday and knowing we had done all we could for now about the school situation, we embarked on another cycle of ICSI treatment. After more gruelling injections and general anaesthetic number four, this time only eight eggs were sufficiently good to be injected. Twenty-four long hours later, the phone rang ominously and we were informed that there were just two viable embryos. Jamie and I felt this news was very much a wake-up call and had a frank discussion.

While we were both delighted that we at least had the two embryos, we obviously knew from our previous experiences that the odds were not good. To compound this, the fact that I had only produced eight eggs was a strong indication of the pounding my body had taken over the two years of almost constant injections and operations. Although it was an incredibly tough decision, we both agreed that if this attempt resulted in failure, enough was enough. Quite apart from the mental and physical punishment, we had to be realistic as we had spent over £12,000 on fertility treatment. The whole experience was unforgettably draining, but we tried to tell ourselves that at least we had Dale and in comparison with some couples, our troubles were insignificant.

On a wing and a prayer, we decided to try to repeat the

previous winning formula, in terms of becoming pregnant at least. So Jamie went off to work as usual and Brian drove me up to Glasgow Royal for the implantation process. Two weeks later, I supplied the sample, knowing we were at the last-chance saloon. I couldn't bear to go with Jamie to the hospital for the pregnancy test, so I watched him drive off that morning, convinced the result would be negative and preparing myself for the worst.

Jamie told me it was the longest twenty-mile journey he had ever taken. He had said he would only phone me if there was good news. He arrived at the unit and a nurse took away my sample to do the test while he waited in a side room.

A few minutes later, the sister came in and simply gave him a big hug. 'You'd better give Nuala the news,' she said, and handed him a phone.

As the phone rang, with shaking hands I lifted the receiver. 'Hello?' I said, almost sick with nerves.

There was a deep breath at the other end, and then came Jamie's voice. 'We've done it! We've actually cracked it.'

I could barely speak. I just couldn't take in that I was pregnant again.

The next day, both of us went up to the unit to see the consultant. Aware of my previous miscarriage, he advised me to take hormonal pessaries to thicken the wall of the womb and hopefully allow better implantation and embedding of the pregnancy. He had also uncovered some research that suggested that patients like me, with a history of bleeding in pregnancy, would benefit from taking 75 milligrams of enteric-coated aspirin daily and so he advised me to do this right up until a month before the birth was due. I would have to stop then because of the need to be able to clot well after giving birth.

At around eight weeks, we returned for my first scan. To our absolute euphoria, two normal pregnancy sacs were clearly visible on the monitor – I was again expecting twins. We felt we were the luckiest people in the world, although given what had happened before, our joy was naturally tinged with apprehension.

Hard though it was to stay quiet, we told no one our news except Lorraine and Brian, who were obviously already in the know and, true friends that they were, ready to support us throughout.

A happy by-product of Jamie's business travels was the amount of Air Miles he had clocked up, so we decided Dale should have a special trip away with his dad while I took things easy. Jamie had spotted a *Thomas the Tank Engine* weekend at the Bluebell Railway in Sussex and so booked up flights to London for the two of them, leaving me with Henry. My dad, George, came by, as he often did, to walk Henry around the estate. We had taken Dad very much under our wing since my mum's death, and I took over the role of my mum in doing his washing, helping him shop and so on. As Dad loved football, Jamie would take him out to his local to see the big games on Sky. For Dad's self-esteem, Jamie would also go down to Dad's with a couple of beers to watch some games in his house, as Dad liked being the host.

After they had gone, I was happy and content to be on my own and couldn't help thinking ahead to the future, daydreaming about my babies. We had always wanted to call our children Dale and Amy, but now another name would be needed. As I relaxed in a warm bath that night, my mind was buzzing with possibilities.

And then I started to bleed.

I screamed in a voice I did not recognise as my own and fumbled for the phone.

'It's happening again,' I cried to Lorraine, distraught, 'just like last time.'

She said she'd come straight round and then I called the hospital, who advised me to take no risks such as lifting anything heavy and to take time off work and go on bed rest.

I saw no point in calling Jamie and ruining his trip with Dale, so Lorraine stayed with me until it was time to pick them up. The first Jamie knew of anything wrong was when he was greeted at the airport by Lorraine instead of me and Henry. Out of Dale's earshot, he was appalled to hear her quiet explanation.

After a few days of total bed rest, with confidence low and anxiety levels high, the threat did not recede and Jamie took me to the hospital for a scan. My feelings of doom were overwhelming as the procedure began, but after a few moments of searching with the probe, the consultant found a glimmer of hope: one clear heartbeat. While this meant that one of my twins had tragically perished, I was literally clinging on to the other for all it was worth. I returned home to the confines of my bed and lay there for three long, anxious weeks, continuing with the aspirin and pessaries. Terrifyingly, the bleeding persisted, but not as heavily. Desperately hoping that the pregnancy still had a chance, I did all I could to nurture it. Throughout my period of bed rest, Henry was my constant companion, lying beside me for cuddles, which relaxed us both.

During this period, Dale took part in a show through his drama group. I obviously couldn't go, but Jamie told me that for the first time Dale was right in the middle of the other kids, singing and dancing. It was a 1960s-themed show where Dale played a car salesman and delivered such lines as 'What car would you like?' with considerable aplomb.

That summer, another opportunity to help Dale arose in the form of a project known as Artism 2000. The eminent artist Peter Howson, together with the Scottish Society for Autism, had secured funding to allow children with autism to attend Saturday art workshops in a real artist's studio. What made the project unique was that the Scottish Society had given a number of artists training in working with kids of all ages and levels of autism. Dale was fortunate to be included in the project, the culmination of which after five months would be an exhibition of the children's work at the Glasgow Museum of Modern Art. Our weekends were now full, with Saturdays involving trips to Glasgow for Dale's class and Sundays still being reserved for Robert. By this time, my bleeding was scanty and so, while I was still doing very little at home, I occasionally left Henry at home with Jimmy and Dorothy or my dad, and accompanied Jamie to Artism 2000, or Projectability, as it had now become known, where we sat in the waiting room chatting with other parents during the two hours that Dale was occupied there. Little outings like this kept me sane, and at least I was in Glasgow and therefore closer to the hospital in the event of an emergency.

Dale thrived in Projectability, and we were given a further break in that Jamie managed to get a job closer to home when Intel opened a new design centre in Glasgow. At last things appeared to be going our way.

I was delighted to receive my clinic card from the Southern General Hospital, where I had trained as a midwife and hoped to have my baby. As the bleeding remained minuscule, I had really started to believe that fate was on our side and we were at last to be blessed with our second child.

One morning in August, over three months pregnant, I awoke in a pool of blood. My cry of horror woke up Jamie, who immediately phoned the doctor, while blood continued to pour from me like water from a tap.

Not surprisingly, the doctor wanted me admitted to hospital and advised us to call for an ambulance, but rather than wait for it, I lay in the back of the car as Jamie raced me to the Southern General. The bleeding had by this time all but stopped, although the consultant and I both felt that the profuse haemorrhage meant the chances of my baby surviving were virtually nil. Jamie and I prepared each other for the worst as we awaited the inevitable scan.

The radiographer was very supportive and sympathetic. Resigned to the fact that it was all over, we couldn't bring ourselves to look at what we knew would be a black mass of clotted blood within my womb. Still unable to look, I grasped Jamie's hand tightly as the radiographer moved the probe around, searching, and finally stopped as she found something. Her next words rocked us to the core: 'Look at this amazing wee creature that's causing all the trouble.'

Jamie and I gazed at each other in disbelief and then at

the screen. There it was as clear as day, a cheeky wee foetus waving its arms and dancing away happily in its own little world.

'Someone's having a great time,' said the radiographer.

Jamie and I were both in tears. Not only was this a perfectly active foetus with a strong heartbeat, but there was no evidence of clots within its sac and placenta, nothing to put the pregnancy at further risk. It seemed that the astuteness of the infertility consultant in putting me on aspirin and hormonal pessaries had saved our precious baby. No one could be certain what had caused such a dramatic bleed, but it could have been due to the remnants of the other pregnancy sac.

The consultant, Dr Naismith, had some junior doctors with him and informed them of my history. It transpired that the haemorrhage had been so severe that I had lost half my blood volume and Dr Naismith advised that delivery should ultimately be by Caesarean section to minimise any further risks. That the baby had held on, he said, was nothing short of a miracle.

I was discharged with the advice to soldier on with the aspirin and hormonal treatment, as well as a supply of iron tablets. Inevitably, I had to remain on bed rest and take no risks. While remaining indoors for almost five months would be a tall order, I was prepared to do absolutely anything to keep my baby. We told Dale that I was simply having a little trouble with my stomach, which was something he could relate to as he had a scar on his abdomen due to a problem with his tummy when he was small.

Everyone pitched in and Jamie's mother, Dorothy, helped considerably with shopping and cooking for us all, as did Lorraine and Brian. The family also helped us to make sure Henry was looked after, taking him out for strolls around the estate. Jimmy kept Dale amused as usual and we felt blessed to have such supportive family and friends.

To get out of the house, Jamie and Dale would sometimes take Henry down to the beach at Lunderston Bay for a paddle. Henry never did get to grips with swimming, but they had fun watching him retreat from the waves and run back to the safety of dry land. That's not to say that they had to take Henry out for my sake – he seemed to understand that I was not myself, and whenever he did stay at home, he would lie on the couch beside me, providing me with lovely, peaceful companionship. He was, as ever, a gorgeous member of our family, faithfully giving us a lift during these times just by being himself.

During those summer months, we began to prepare Dale for changes in his schooling. Even though official decisions had not yet been finalised, it was perfectly clear to Jamie and me that we couldn't leave our son at St Anthony's purely as a gateway to Glenburn. That's not to say we didn't respect Glenburn as a school; we just felt it was the wrong environment for Dale.

For his part, all Dale wanted was to be like the other children he saw having fun on the estate. He still played with Fraser, and it was especially heartening that other boys would now also call at the door to ask if Dale was coming out to play. Jamie and I will always remember one night in particular when this started to reap benefits.

For years we had what we thought was an obsolete bike lying in our garage. Dale had shown no interest in it at all and so we'd never taught him how to ride it. On this night, however, he came and asked for it as Fraser and all the other kids were playing on their own bikes. Jamie duly fetched the bike and pumped up the tyres, reminding Dale of the small matter that he'd need to be shown how to ride it. To our eternal surprise, he calmly announced, 'It's OK, Dad, I know what to do.' And off he rode to meet the others.

He later told us that seeing Fraser and the rest on their bikes had made him simply want to be the same, so he got the hang of it to be with them. Ours was not to reason why – autistic children have a gift for just suddenly doing things and Dale had, after all, gone from a crawl to a steady walk in only two days.

Dale had a really full and successful summer simply being just one of the kids on the estate. While the boisterous games outside were not always suitable for Henry, when Dale and his friends played together in the house, the dog made sure he was with them and became a popular member of the gang. Dad would come and take him for short walks, then sometimes tether him on a long lead outside the front of our house so that he could see Dale and vice versa – we did need to tether him up so he couldn't wander off or butt into the kids' football games. If any children came over, he was always delighted to roll over and let them pat him, seeming to understand their tender age. One little girl was frightened of dogs, but because of Henry's amazing nature, she soon bonded with him, although she remained scared of other dogs. This was probably because Henry seemed to understand that small children didn't like dogs jumping at them, so he would always lie down as they approached, to let the children stroke him. In Dresling Road, Henry was a bit of a star.

Dale's art was progressing really well. As luck would have it, I discovered that the Glasgow School of Art ran week-long workshops for all children. So, after a discussion with the principal and meeting with the teacher, Dale was enrolled and successfully completed a week of painting and sculpting. The teacher was much taken by his natural ability and how well he fitted in and worked with the other children in the class.

This only strengthened our resolve to give Dale the opportunity to go to school with the children he'd been playing with all summer. Jamie and I wrote to Dale's educational psychologist setting out our case for him to attend Overton, which prompted a meeting at Overton itself. After much discussion and argument on our part, Jamie and I were delighted when it was agreed that Dale would have a trial period of one day a week at Overton, starting after the October holiday, with a review to follow in the New Year.

We had over the years become adept at writing strong letters to fight for Dale, as we'd discovered that to get anywhere you needed to state a good case in black and white. We would spend hours doing this when we could have been doing things with Dale; it was immensely frustrating, but it went with the territory.

Two weeks later, the head of the Support for Learning Service wrote to us requesting a meeting – we were very surprised, as we had never heard of anyone being summoned to such a meeting. When we met, he expressed a personal reservation that even if Dale might be able to cope at primary level, there was no knowing how he would fare at secondary school. After much deliberation, we pushed home the point that he should at least be given the chance to try, which would then give us all more knowledge for subsequent discussions.

After the October holidays, the momentous day arrived. Now showing a noticeable bump, I walked with Dale and Henry up to Overton Primary. We had carried out many practice walks prior to this and Dale was quite happy, especially as Fraser came with us on that first day. I was going to wait with him until school began, but he quite literally told me where to go: 'I'm just like all the other boys and girls,' he said emphatically. Thereafter, once a week Fraser would knock on our door and the pair of them would head off to Overton – and back again later – together. Henry and I might have felt redundant, but for the fact that we still collected and returned Dale at lunchtimes. This was firstly to give him some respite at home, avoiding the overwhelming situation of the school dining room, and secondly to give him more practice with the journey to and fro. After only a few weeks, however, he started going to the canteen and staying at school all day.

Friends and neighbours on the estate who had watched Dale grow up over the last six years shared our joy at his progress and seemed almost as thrilled as we were that he was finally going to his local school – even if it was only for one day a week. Many commented that they had never seen him so happy.

One afternoon, while we were at the Kumon maths class, Dale pointed at a poster and asked, 'Mum, what's that sign?'

'It's for another class called Weightwatchers,' I explained, 'for people who don't like to be fat and want to lose weight.' I should have known what was coming.

'Mum, why don't you go to that class?' Dale queried. 'You're getting very fat.'

The issue of my twenty-six-week bump could clearly no longer be ignored – it was time to tell Dale about our forthcoming arrival.

That evening, Jamie and I sat down with Dale and explained calmly and gently why I appeared to be putting on weight. When we concluded with, 'So you'll be getting a wee sister soon,' yet again, we were not prepared for our son's response. He was totally shocked and cried with real fear. We tried to soothe him and showed him a photograph of the scan, explaining that this was how we knew the baby would be a little girl. We thought it would help if he knew he would be getting a sister, rather than just a baby. We reassured him that we loved him and that we would love both him and his sister the same, telling him he could ask us anything he liked about the impending arrival.

It took a few moments for him to absorb all this and then he got right to the nub of the matter. 'Would she be allowed to touch my trains?'

We assured him she would not and that she would have her own toys to play with.

Later that night, I was putting away some clean clothes in the bedroom when Dale approached me. 'Mum, can I ask another question?'

Seeing his troubled look, I sat on the bed to give him my full attention. 'Of course, ask as many questions as you like.'

With an impressively direct look and worried tone of voice, once again he came straight to the point. 'Mum, if she pees herself, will I have to change my wee sister's knickers?'

Trying to keep a straight face, I reassured him accordingly.

Now that the threat to my pregnancy had at last receded, I was really enjoying it, just as I was the process of preparing Dale for his little sister's arrival. Thankfully, he approved our decision to call her Amy and we started referring to her by name right away, so we could all become accustomed to this new presence in our family.

To most people, the millennium was a big event, but with everything that was going on in our lives it paled into insignificance. We didn't ignore it altogether, spending New Year's Eve with Lorraine and Brian, toasting the big moment with Coca-Cola. I obviously wasn't drinking alcohol, but poor Jamie was also on the wagon in case he suddenly had to drive me to the hospital. I was now thirty-four weeks pregnant and Dale had arrived at thirty-five, so we took nothing for granted.

We didn't spend long at Lorraine and Brian's because there were fireworks going off, which we knew would alarm poor Henry, who was home alone with the TV on. While he had the patience of a saint, he was a total wimp on Bonfire Night, which caused him so much angst that he had to be sedated every time.

The new millennium brought two big changes to our life. After the holidays, Dale increased his time at Overton to two days a week because the initial transition period had gone so well, and the second change was in me physically – I was now hugely pregnant and ready to have Amy at any time. A few weeks later, my consultant confirmed I had signs of pre-eclampsia and a delivery date was set for 15 February.

While we had no concerns regarding Henry's reaction to a new member of the family, we thought we should at least involve him in the preparations. Many a time when I had sat with him, he would snuggle into my bump and I'm sure he understood I was 'with pup'; but in the hope that he would realise someone else was on their way, we set up Amy's pram on Sunday, 13 February and put it in the lounge for Henry to sniff.

We thought we had until the Tuesday before Amy arrived, but on the Sunday night it became apparent that she wasn't going to wait. At around 1.30 a.m., I woke Jamie with the news, 'Time to go – I'm in advanced labour.' He sprang into action and got Dale up while I called Lorraine to let her know we'd be dropping him off on the way to the hospital.

Sure enough, when we arrived at the Southern General at about 2.30 a.m., it was confirmed that I was indeed in advanced labour. I was promptly wheeled into the operating theatre, with Jamie alongside, now gowned up and looking like one of the staff. They were mostly familiar faces from all those years ago when I had trained at this hospital, and they celebrated with us at 4.11 a.m. on Valentine's Day as the newest love of our life was welcomed to the family – screaming and healthy.

16

Independence

'Of course what he most intensely dreams of is being taken out for walks, and the more you are able to indulge him, the more he will adore you and the more all the latent beauty of his nature will come out.'

Henry James

Knowing that Dale would need a lot of reassurance about Amy's arrival, we had a couple of nice surprises in store when he first visited the hospital to see his wee sister. A *South Park* video and new wristwatch were lying in Amy's cot for him. Lorraine had also had a wonderful idea: she used her computer to make a personal card from Amy to Dale, introducing herself and noting how he owned a dog, which he really liked.

In spite of all this preparation, however, Dale still seemed wary of his little sister, so we made sure we included him as much as possible and showed him that although things had indeed changed, we cared for them both equally. We knew of course that his bonding process with Amy would be different from ours, but hoped that with our help it would progress through time. When Jamie visited me with my dad, they both fussed over Amy, taking turns at holding her, while I spent the entire visit making a huge fuss of Dale. I loved seeing my dad's pleasure in holding his new granddaughter; after the trauma of losing my mum, he now had a thriving grandson in Dale and was looking forward to watching Amy grow up.

Aware of the impact Amy would have on Dale, his class teacher at Overton, Mrs Simpson, did something very special to help. She got all the children in the class to hand-make cards for Dale celebrating the arrival of Amy. Even the cards from the boys were lovely, but those from two of the girls stood out. They were so sweet and thoughtful I've kept them to this day. One had a drawing of a teddy bear holding balloons and was inscribed, 'To Amy, hope you have a great life.' On the other, the young girl had written, 'A special baby girl. Welcome to the world to the lovely baby Amy.'

After five days in hospital being spoiled rotten by staff and reminiscing with colleagues I hadn't seen in years, it was time to go home. Amy was now successfully breast-feeding, although I was very anaemic, having lost a lot of blood during the delivery. Life was perfect and I relished every minute of being a new mum again.

Driving home with Jamie, I couldn't wait to see every-one, but as he pulled into the estate, I burst into tears at the sight of the welcome awaiting me. Lorraine and Brian had spent a fortune on big, tied bundles of pink balloons, both outside and inside the house, and the lounge was looking like a florist's shop. Because Lorraine and Brian were such close friends – and Brian had played such an important part in Amy's 'conception' – Jamie and I decided to give Amy the middle name of Lindsay, after their surname. It was the least we could do as a gesture of how much we appreciated all they had both done for us. Henry was at the forefront of the welcome party, tail flying back and forth, with a giant helium balloon tied to his collar. I knew that I wouldn't get Amy inside the house without greeting Henry first, and sure enough he gave me his 'five-minute, five-year' welcome, ecstatic to see me again.

Once Henry had had a good sniff at Amy and satisfied himself that she was a fitting member of his pack, he accepted her graciously. We had no visitors that day, as everyone we knew gave us the space to get Amy settled in her new world. Then, on the Sunday morning, Val phoned to check if it was all right for her and Sheena to come up and visit. I told her we'd love to see them and they arrived bearing gifts of gorgeous baby clothes.

They were completely taken with Amy, and even though I was obviously biased, she was indeed a beautiful baby, with piercing dark-brown eyes and a full mop of wavy brown hair. Her skin looked and felt like silk, which was mostly, I think, an advantage of being breastfed. Unlike Dale as a baby, Amy was accomplished in making her presence felt, especially at feeding time.

True to form, Amy demanded a feed during the visit and Sheena handed her over to me. Jamie sat across from us all while Amy contentedly fed and I joined in the conversation. Then, while the other three carried on chatting animatedly, I took Amy off my breast to wind her and watched in horror as she collapsed on me, turning blue. Somehow my shock as a mother was overridden by my gut instinct as a midwife, and as she had just fed, I knew to hold her bolt upright and stimulate her with pats on the back.

'Breathe,' I pleaded desperately. 'Breathe!'

Sheena, Val and Jamie sat stunned as I tried to stimulate

Amy's floppy body. I knew there was a risk of her stomach contents entering her lungs, so I had to maintain her upright position and support her airway with my front hand clasping her jaw. One terrifying minute seemed like an hour, before her colour slowly improved and she gave a whimper in response to my efforts. Then she let out a loud cry and my pounding heart began to calm a little.

Jamie sat in total silence, deeply shocked, unable to comprehend what was happening. Then a knock on the door announced a visit from the community midwife, which allowed Sheena and Val to leave. I explained to the midwife what had just happened, and while she acknowledged the shock we had had, she felt that because Amy had apparently recovered there was no need for further action. She left saying we should obviously phone the local hospital if it happened again and that she would come back and see us in the morning.

Keeping Amy upright in my arms, her tiny head resting on my shoulder, I still felt very scared and was uneasy about the midwife's advice.

I told Jamie, 'I nearly had to fully resuscitate her there. If it happens again, I might not be able to.'

Jamie was in no mood for 'if's and 'but's. 'Call Eleanor,' he urged. 'She'll know what we should be doing. We can't just sit here and wait on it happening again.'

My friend Eleanor was at the time working in the neonatal unit at the hospital we'd only left two days beforehand, the Southern General. With great anxiety, I phoned around and managed to catch her at home. I didn't know where to begin.

'Eleanor,' I said, in the end, 'I know this is a crazy

question, but can you remind me how to resuscitate a newborn baby?'

As soon as she heard why I was asking, she told me, 'Don't feed Amy again. I'll call you back in ten minutes.'

Eleanor phoned back to advise that because Amy was only seven days old, she still came under the care of the Southern General. She'd spoken with a paediatrician colleague there who had said Amy should be brought to the neonatal unit right away. While I got Amy ready, Jamie collected my dad, so he could watch Dale and Henry at our house.

With Amy bolt upright in her car seat, we retraced our journey of Friday morning, but with much more speed and anxiety. The whole of the way, Amy remained motionless, silent and pale, with only her breathing on my hand offering any reassurance. We were greeted at the hospital by the paediatric doctor Eleanor had spoken to, who had already arranged for Amy to be admitted to the observation unit in an incubator.

Our daughter was very quickly settled and full monitoring established. She had an oxygen saturation probe attached to her foot, which also monitored her heartbeat, setting off an alarm if the rate dropped below 100 beats per minute – the norm for babies varying between around 100 and 120. In Amy's case, because she was cyanosed – having turned blue – when she collapsed, this might have been indicative of a heart problem. Later that night, she was put on a heart monitor because her heartbeat kept dropping below eighty, which was a significant concern in itself.

Our wee daughter was also hooked up to an apnoea monitor, known as an MR10. This involved a button-like probe being attached to her chest by a long, thin plastic line that was linked to the small monitor, which would sound an alarm if her breathing stopped for more than ten seconds. Even though technically I knew what this equipment was all about, my head was in a total spin and I was grateful for the fact that the midwife treated me primarily as a mother rather than a professional equal, explaining everything that was going on.

Amy was also screened for any source of infection, to rule this out as a possible factor in her collapse. The midwives kindly set up a side room at the back of the unit for me to stay with her throughout, and this also allowed them to monitor her while I was feeding her.

The holiday Jamie had taken to be with us all at home was spent in a way we could never have envisaged, but at least he was there to look after Dale and get him off to school, and could also spend lots of time with me. Dale managed to visit, too; although we could see he was a bit stressed, he generally coped well with the scary environment within the neonatal unit. I was touched when Jamie told me that Dale, as well as hanging on to Henry for comfort, had started cuddling up to him on the sofa at night – something he had stopped doing long ago – because he was so worried about his wee sister.

I felt very secure knowing Eleanor was looking after Amy, and when, after a successful feed, she told me to go and have a rest, I felt able to do as she asked. After seemingly endless tossing and turning, I even managed a few hours' sleep. I was awakened at around 7 a.m. by Eleanor pushing Amy into the room in a standard hospital cot, with only her MR10 and oxygen monitor attached. It seemed that we were out of the woods.

A midwife supervised for the day while Amy fed. However, just when I was confident enough to be thinking about going home, my little girl went blue and almost lifeless again. The midwife sprang into action and with the same management as before, together with some oxygen, Amy recovered. I'm not sure the same could be said for me, as by this time my nerves were in shreds. With every feed my heart was thumping in my chest. I knew I couldn't have coped without the midwives.

Later that evening, the paediatrician spoke to Jamie and me and concluded that Amy had classical symptoms of gastric reflux – the opening to her stomach was relaxing too much and allowing milk to reflux back up the food pipe and into the windpipe, which was why her breathing was stopping during feeds. While this was truly terrifying when it happened, the treatment itself was very simple. Before Amy was fed, she needed to be given some infant Gaviscon, an antacid mixture which neutralised the milk and thickened it within the stomach, to prevent reflux. As long as she was held upright after a feed and slept in a raised position, the problem would eventually be resolved.

To my eternal relief, two days later we were given the all-clear to take Amy home, together with her new treatment and the MR10 apnoeic monitor. This last was really more for our benefit than Amy's; the paediatrician knew what we had gone through to have her and thought the monitor would help reassure us. It would probably also be the only way we would get any sleep, as it was night-time when Amy was most at risk. Before leaving the hospital we were given full instructions on how to resuscitate Amy if she suffered another collapse, and while this was obviously a frightening thought, Jamie and I did now feel more confident that we would be able to manage.

My wonderful friend Eleanor has always been there for me. Through the hideous lows since Dale's birth and the highs as he improved, she has been my rock – just as she was through this horrendous experience. I am eternally grateful for Eleanor's unfailing friendship and support.

Back at home, our nightly routines differed in that we always attached the MR10 monitor before putting Amy down for a sleep. While this seemed strange at first, the paediatrician was absolutely right – the reassuring click from the monitor as it picked up Amy's chest movements allowed us to get some sleep ourselves. On one or two occasions, however, we were awoken in the middle of the night to loud screeches as the monitor went off like a smoke alarm. We would pounce out of bed only to find that the connection to Amy had merely dislodged. But for all this, it got us through a very frightening time in our lives. No matter what we had previously experienced with Dale's autism, the death of my mum, fertility failure and devastating miscarriages, the thought of actually losing Amy was the most unbearable of all.

We settled into our new routine, and friends and neighbours on the estate came to visit, kindly bearing gorgeous gifts. They were much taken by our daughter's beauty, and so happy for us. One neighbour Isobel, who lived across from us had even hand-knitted beautiful matinée coats for her, which meant so much to me as it was something that my mum would normally do.

Whenever people arrived to see Amy, Henry always

assumed that they were there to visit him, so he always ensured he had a 'present' for them, such as a rattle or a furry toy belonging to Amy. When Amy slept, Henry would adopt his position beside her pram or bouncy chair as if on guard, protecting the newest member of his pack. If Amy cried, however, Henry would get upset and go into the garden – he was sensitive when it came to the piercing noise of a baby's cry and it seemed to distress him almost as much as fireworks.

I remember one time when I was changing Amy's nappy on the floor and Henry was sat nearby, watching with interest as I wiped her clean. When I reached over for a fresh nappy, Amy's tiny feet in my hand and her bottom in the air, Henry decided my efforts were below par and began a clean-up job of his own. I couldn't help laughing as I gently discouraged his enthusiastic licking – although judging from the amount of water he then proceeded to drink from his bowl, I think he had learned his lesson!

Although Dale was still doing well, he found it very difficult to voice concerns to anyone and would bottle things up for months or even, it transpired, years. While he had in his way helped us to realise it was time to leave the unit at St Anthony's, one incident in particular convinced us of this.

St Anthony's was a Catholic school, and while we had told them from the start to teach Dale the basic morals of religion and of the school, we emphasised that we did not want him exposed to long, confusing Masses. This was not contentious because there was a very mixed group of children at the school and non-Catholics were allowed to opt out of Mass.

One night, however, as Jamie and I were getting Dale's things ready for school the next day, Dale announced angrily, 'I don't want to go to Mass tomorrow.'

'That's fine,' I told him, 'you don't go, anyway.'

'My teacher told me to stand in line and get ready for Mass,' came Dale's furious response. 'I told her back many times I wasn't going, but she wouldn't listen.' Then, as I tried to find out more, he blurted out in a rage, 'I'm not like Kyle in *South Park* – I'm not a Jew.' What he meant was that he knew that we were not a religious family and so knew that he shouldn't attend Mass. 'It's not fair,' he went on angrily. 'John and Harry don't go – they draw in class instead. So I went,' he finally concluded, 'but with my arms crossed instead.' We couldn't help but be impressed by this gesture of defiance and assertion.

It turned out that Dale had been going to Mass for the whole of the five years he had attended St Anthony's. While Jamie and I laughed at this revelation, more importantly Dale had been reminded the hard way of the true power of communication. With him at my side, I wrote a note to the teacher, appreciating that there had perhaps been a mis-understanding but asking that he be excused from Mass. Ironically, the incident did at least highlight to us that Dale was apparently ready to move on to Overton full-time. He had demonstrated a sense of independence by challenging his teacher.

We attended a meeting at Overton in late March 2000 at which Dale's teachers from St Anthony's expressed con-cerns that he would be unable to cope if he left the unit for a permanent move to Overton. We explained that Dale appeared very happy at Overton and, more importantly, had voiced this himself; he was thoroughly enjoying becoming part of his class and school.

Anticipating that we would meet with a degree of opposition, prior to the meeting we had sought the help of the Scottish Society for Autism, and one of its field workers attended the meeting on our behalf. She supported us in our arguments, emphasising that Dale was motivated to be at Overton and how important this would be in terms of maintaining his self-esteem.

The final decision was that Dale would go to Overton three days a week until Easter, with a view to moving to five days if all went well. True to form, with all his extra-curricular activities and the support of Overton, Dale continued to thrive and Jamie and I were over the moon when he moved to five days a week in June 2000.

Shortly afterwards, Dale confirmed not only that we had made the right decision, but also the extent of his awareness of being different: 'Mum,' he said, 'there's a boy I see in Overton's playground who needs my place at St Anthony's.'

For the rest of the term, there was a reassuring knock on the door from Fraser every morning and the two of them headed off to school together. Finally, after so many years, Dale was like any other boy on the estate. Jamie and I revelled in the normality of it all, though we will forever be grateful for what St. Anthony's did for Dale.

While Dale continued to thrive at Overton, I relished my time with Amy. She was a different baby from Dale in every way in terms of her reactions and how she behaved with her toys, but I still wanted to enhance her development and found a way that would in fact benefit both of us. A community nursing colleague was running baby massage classes, so I took Amy along. She seemed to love the whole process and we both enjoyed socialising with other babies and mums.

With all going so well, my only concern was Dale's lack of interest in his sister. Jamie and I had tried to involve him in so many ways and persistently reassured him that we loved them both equally, but he had great difficulty appreciating Amy's needs and how young she was. Often when we would try to guide him, he would shout, 'She has to learn the same as me.' He had no understanding of just how long his own learning process had been or how very tiny his sister was.

I thought it would be a lengthy and difficult process to bridge this gap, but yet again a certain toy train came to the rescue. With Henry and Robert's help, as well as the benefits of Dale's new life at Overton, we had at last managed to wean him off *Thomas*. Nonetheless, the bond with *Thomas* would always be there and I suggested to Jamie that we try using it to help Dale bond with Amy. The range of *Thomas* toys now available was endless and so we bought a miniature tabletop activity centre of Sodor, the island, with movable beads, trains and Harold the Helicopter.

I told Dale that we had a new toy to teach babies how much fun *Thomas* was and how *Thomas* could help them grow up. Then I gestured towards the toy and slyly asked, 'Dale, as you know *Thomas* best, could you show Amy how to play with this?'

As soon as the activity centre was revealed in all its glory, Dale sat with Amy and started to show and tell her all about it. So began a true bonding process. In time, he would read *Thomas* and dog stories to his wee sister and play with her and her toys, the love between them easy to see.

Now that Dale understood Amy a bit better, we thought he was ready to take another big step. Even before bringing Amy home from the hospital, we had reassured Dale that Henry was his dog alone. This had worked very well, and he was never jealous of any attention Henry paid Amy as he knew Henry was his dog. We now felt there was a way we could reinforce this to him.

As Dale's friend Robert was used to retrievers and had a dog of his own, we introduced a system whereby with Robert in charge he and Dale would walk Henry around the estate every Sunday before they had dinner together. The next step from there was that I took Dale out and prepared him to walk Henry on his own, ensuring he would always take the same circular route, have an emergency phone number in his pocket and follow strict safety rules. I also timed the walk so we would know when Dale and his dog were due back.

One afternoon, Dale had still not appeared some fifteen minutes after he should have been home; fortunately, he had stuck to the set route and I found him talking to the other kids on the estate. They were all fussing over Henry, who needless to say was not complaining. Dale feared he was in trouble, but I reassured him because I now at least knew that he understood the rules. From there, we were able to develop other, more varied walks.

Dale moved on to take responsibility for all aspects of

Henry's care, even to the extent of accompanying him to the vet's, and took all of these duties in his stride. It may have taken all seven of Henry's years to achieve this, but it was still a big breakthrough – all the more so because it meant we could now teach Dale to take care of himself in the same way that he looked after his dog.

With Henry's influence, I even taught Dale the basics of cooking. As a retriever's stomach is never full, I showed Dale how to make toast for himself and Henry, cook sausages – always an extra for his dog – and fry up the compulsory juicy steak for his canine friend's birthday. Dale clearly enjoyed this independence and never more so than when I taught him how to safely make a cup of tea. I showed him how to use the electric kettle and bought him a tiny single-cup teapot, which he used to practise pouring hot drinks. With careful guidance and strict rules, he was finally able to help himself to his favourite beverage whenever he felt like it. One day, I rather unkindly pretended I was unwell, suggesting a cup of tea might make me feel better. The result of Dale's labours was the most tasteless, cold, disgusting liquid I had ever drunk, but it was also the first cup of tea he had made me, so I told him it was lovely and that I felt much better, which in a way of course I did.

Jamie and I could hardly believe our luck. At long last our twelve-year-old son could greet us in bed in the morning with tea and toast. In time, if ever we had visitors and needed more than two cups of tea, Dale would fret about getting the 'order' wrong and write it down like any good waiter. He quickly became an expert, and visitors were very impressed with the quality of his service and drinks. The icing on the cake was that this much-practised task had the added benefit of improving Dale's social skills and increasing his sense of independence.

In August 2000, Dale returned to Overton for his final year at primary, which was to bring great steps forward. Out of school, however, there was a setback in that after all Dale's success with the church Boys' Brigade, the group was to be disbanded for want of a leader. Robert had been attending a local Scouts group since he was a young boy and suggested that Dale went with him there instead. Dale was put into Robert's group and the pair of them attended every Monday night. Dale did so well that even when Robert left the group, he continued on his own and was eventually promoted to group leader.

At school, one big event for Dale's class was a trip away to give a performance at a millennium festival. The teachers worked hard with Dale and his previous drama experience helped, to the extent that he felt confident to go on the trip and take part in the performance – no mean thing, given that an overnight stay in Inverness was involved. I was given this extraordinary news by one of Dale's teachers, Mrs Cannon, and remember virtually skipping down the road with glee afterwards. Mrs Cannon assured me that while she would keep a close eye on him, he would mostly be treated just like any other boy in the class. This was music to my ears because it had not been necessary to date to tell the other children of Dale's autism and I was delighted that the situation would remain that way.

By now, Dale seemed to be having this kind of positive effect generally on the people working with him, such was his motivation to be the same as everyone else. It was a time

I will never forget because he was taking the kind of steps that so many parents took for granted in their own children.

So, with a weekend bag packed by Dale himself, Amy in her pram and Henry by our side, we waved the school bus off. Some parents were crying, as it was the first time they had been parted from their children like this. So was I, but mine were tears of pride.

When Dale returned, we could only get one short sentence out of him as to the success of the performance: 'It was good.' There was no stopping him, however, as he told us of all the fun, antics and downright misbehaviour of some of the kids at night-time, which had kept him hugely entertained. He had obviously learned a lot of positive things, too, that weekend and we didn't worry about him picking up bad habits from the other kids. Because the process of teaching him right from wrong was so literal, we could pretty much guarantee his behaviour would be impeccable and that he would always respect his teachers and others in similar roles.

With the success of this trip and Dale's extra-curricular activities, he was now up for anything. On the many camps he began to attend with the Scouts, he took up a number of outdoor pursuits and his increased confidence and fearless nature particularly enabled him to master activities such as rock-climbing and abseiling. It seemed the sky was, literally, the limit.

17
Tough Decisions

Although the transformation in Dale was enormously pleasing and positive, his autism still had a major impact on the quality of his life. He was so anxious to learn, fit in and succeed that this became an obsession in itself – not entirely a bad thing, but it did create problems. He couldn't cope with not being able to do something and would get really upset if a particular task or situation was beyond his reach or control. Having successfully established himself at Overton, the biggest pressure of all in his mind was keeping up with homework and integrating with his peers without blowing his cover. Another major issue for Dale, albeit unknown to him at the time, was that he was still unaware that he had something called autism.

Neither we nor the school placed too much emphasis on academic success, but when it came to homework Dale always insisted it was finished, no matter how confusing or difficult he found it. His unfailing determination to be like everyone else left us no choice but to muck in and try to help him achieve this goal to his own level of acceptance.

This meant I would sit and help him, Amy suckling at my breast, Henry at our feet, night after night for two or three hours, until Dale felt he had satisfactorily completed his homework. Even with all the help from the Kumon course, mathematics remained a serious obstacle for him and I worried generally that the academic pressure of mainstream might be his downfall.

Dale's poor understanding of English within the various subjects was his greatest barrier to learning. Sometimes simply one strange word would alienate the context of an otherwise familiar sentence and totally faze him. For example, in a standard question like 'What are the perceived strengths and weaknesses of sheltered housing for the elderly?' the word 'perceived' would throw him and he would just guess at the answer. The school did everything possible to help him, but as the language used in all subjects was advanced, it caused him much anxiety. His 'word bank' book, however, in which he recorded any new words he came across, helped a little.

Despite this major hurdle, the physical games and activities he took part in at Scouts enabled him to excel at PE, especially basketball – Dale had grown tall and was older than his classmates, both of which helped. Dale also enjoyed subjects that were of social value, such as modern studies and religious education, where the class discussed issues like euthanasia and capital punishment. While most kids found this boring, we encouraged Dale here and had many a riveting talk as his capacity for self-expression grew and he became more aware of the society in which we lived. Not least, discussions on modern medical ethics, including topics like IVF, enabled him to understand the miracle that was Amy. Despite, or perhaps because of his difficulties with academia generally, no parents could have been more proud than Jamie and me when Dale ended up winning the Religious Education Prize in year four.

As Dale struggled to cope with the English barriers,

however, through each day and laborious night of home-work, his awareness of being different from the other kids steadily escalated, as did his frustration. 'Why can't I do this?' he would exclaim angrily. 'I'm fed up of having problems. Why have the problems not been left at St Anthony's?'

As the weeks went by, it got harder to reassure him, until one night, after three exhausting hours of homework, he screamed in fury, 'Why me? Why did I get born with problems?' He raged on and then suddenly turned to me, demanding, 'Do these problems have a name?' A day we never thought would come was now a reality.

With increased progress came increased insight and there was no denying that it was time cautiously to tell Dale the truth. As it was now very late in the evening, however, I promised him we would have a good family meeting the next day after school and tell him all he needed to know. He accepted this, as he was used to regular family meetings to discuss issues that may have occurred due to his autism. The only dilemma was how we would explain this delicate situation to him and make the word 'autism' as positive as it could be.

Jamie and I discussed what our approach should be and I hit on the idea of using a public role model to give Dale an example of what could be achieved in spite of having a disability. Through my work as a community nurse, I had contact with a patient, Margaret McAlleny, who had won a Paralympic gold medal for swimming. Such was her success in sport that she was a highly respected public figure locally. Because I knew Margaret well, Dale had met her on many occasions and I would always point out to him her outstanding achievements when they appeared in the press. Jamie and I agreed that his familiarity with her situation, in that she used a wheelchair but was an amazing swimmer, would help him to understand that his achievements were similar to Margaret's, albeit in a different way.

So, with cups of tea, Amy sleeping and Henry lying beside Dale, we started our meeting. We began by reminding Dale of Margaret's situation, which prompted the response, 'Yes, but what about my problems? I don't have a wheelchair.'

We reiterated an already familiar rule – everyone is different – and explained that Margaret's problem was known as a physical disability, which was why she needed a wheelchair. 'But your problems,' I said, 'are with not being able to talk and communicate like everyone else.'

We told him that when he was born, it was possible that his brain had been damaged a little, which caused problems in understanding people and knowing how to talk to them and socialise with them in the right way. Or it might have been that he had similar difficulties as Uncle Tommy, due to a link in the family.

We said the word to describe this type of problem was 'autism' and that it could range from being a very small problem to a very big one.

Dale cried, quite calmly, as this unfolded and then asked, 'What size is my autism?'

I took a subtle deep breath and told him, 'Unfortunately, yours is big and that is why you had to go to St Anthony's.'

We then reiterated everything that he, and Margaret, had achieved despite having got off to such a bad start, and that not all people with his problem did as well as he had. As his tears began to subside, we explained that he had managed to fight his autism so well because of the fantastic help he'd had from his school teachers, out-of-school classes, ourselves, Henry and, more importantly, all the hard work Dale himself had put in.

Jamie told him, 'If you didn't have such a strong desire to be like everyone else, you'd never be where you are now.'

Although quiet, Dale did understand and even felt quite good because he now knew what he was up against. Naturally, there were many times afterwards when there would be frustrated and angry outbursts, but we all agreed that telling him when we did had been the right thing to do. There was no doubt that it helped him to cope knowing his problems at least had a name and that some people understood what that meant.

A few nights later, a subdued Dale approached me. 'Mum, can I ask a question?'

'You know you can always do that, Dale,' I reassured him.

He sat down next to me and wondered out loud, 'This autism thing . . . Is Amy all right? Does she have it?'

Telling him that that was a good question to ask, I replied that we were all happy that Amy was all right and doing well.

Although Dale and Robert still enjoyed playing with Henry, they had now exhausted the potential of the Sega Megadrive and PlayStation, and so we started buying things for the computer that they could use instead. While they thought they were playing games, which of course was true, the benefit was that they were also learning.

Delighted at getting a free rein to access the Internet, Robert soon had Dale up to speed and surfing better than me. As I sat beside him, Dale would use the Web to help with homework, printing off any information he needed to complete the given task. This also served to open up his social world as his familiarity with computer games and jargon enabled him to blend in with his peers – an invaluable factor in the process of transition to secondary school.

While all the work at home and at school was undoubtedly paying off, no amount of such input could avoid the very real possibility of Dale's vulnerability in the playground resulting in bullying. Although he seemed contented enough, we noticed subtle changes in his behaviour and demeanour. Then he started to voice concerns, saying that he didn't like playtime and a boy he knew was 'taking charge' of him – he had to do what this boy said, even to the extent of giving him his dinner money. It transpired during yet another of our family meetings that Dale and another vulnerable boy were constantly being picked on by this boy, who dominated their school lives. The way Dale put it was, 'I'm fed up being a servant to the king.'

Knowing his confidence and self-esteem were being eroded, we told Dale that he had done the best thing possible thing in telling us and had been very clever to do so. We could now do something about it, which this boy would not expect, since all bullies relied on kids not telling. We reassured Dale that he had nothing to worry about and promised that the problem would be sorted.

I then had a meeting with the head teacher, who immediately took appropriate steps. A special social group had been running at Overton for children needing learning support and this was playing an invaluable role in helping prepare Dale for secondary education. The speech therapist in charge absorbed the bully boy into the group, along with a few other difficult kids, and then professionally covered the topic of bullying within it. Together with our support at home, this initiative gave Dale the confidence to deal with any further incidents on his own and, more importantly, let him know that his voice would always be heard.

The boy concerned immediately left Dale alone and became very wary and nervous around him, as he now understood that Dale would make his teachers aware of any problems he had, not least bullying.

The problem in the playground thereafter shifted from boys to girls. Although not unduly concerned, Dale told us that a few of the girls were mocking him and swearing at him. He was annoyed by this because he had been taught not to use such bad language. Jamie and I deliberated on how on earth to resolve the problem without Dale becoming known as a tell-tale over every little playground occurrence – things that other children would be able to deal with themselves.

Dale had told us, 'I shout back at them, but I can't be rude,' so we decided that, particularly with secondary school looming, our son needed to become streetwise. The tools I gave Dale to manage this problem were, to put it mildly, unorthodox. With Jamie's consent to my proposed 'alternative lesson', I initiated some role-play in Dale's bedroom. We sat in front of his mirror so we could see each other's faces and I carefully reiterated that bad language was indeed rude and unacceptable, but for teenagers at secondary school, like in Dale's *South Park* videos, swearing was a part of playground life and it would be OK for Dale to use it in the right circumstances. I emphasised that this should only be as a last resort and that really no one should ever use bad language, especially to anyone in authority and certainly not to their teachers.

Once this rule was firmly ingrained in Dale, we got down to brass tacks. I explained that the girls were only doing it because they knew he wouldn't respond. 'So you need to learn how to answer them back,' I told him.

Using the mirror and a determined, angry face, I demonstrated exactly what I meant. 'Fuck off,' I exclaimed. 'Get off my back.' And so it went on, with Dale copying me, then practising on his own.

'Fuck off,' he shouted. 'Get out of my face. Leave me alone.'

I knew for sure he understood what we were doing when he turned to me with an excited laugh and said, 'Mum, you're good at this – you're scaring me and I know it's only pretend.'

The other part of our lesson was teaching Dale the concept of a white lie. I gave him several examples of how we'd used this in the past to help him, so he could see that the white lie was a useful weapon to have in his armoury. If a situation in the playground arose in which Dale wasn't to blame, he was allowed to use the white lie to protect himself. If the girls 'told on him' for swearing, for example, he could tell the teachers it wasn't him. Thankfully, with these new playground tools, it wasn't long before the bullying stopped.

The alternative lesson also reaped benefits in an unexpected way. Dale's ability to deal with bullying incidents was so successful that he became like a minder on occasions for Fraser and another friend Tom and actually stood up to the school bully. He took great delight in telling us how this boy was now scared of him.

With the hurdles in Dale's transition process almost all cleared, our main focus became the fact that, now fourteen months of age, Amy was due to receive her MMR vaccine, to protect against mumps, measles and rubella. This vaccine was shrouded in great controversy at the time as there was a school of thought that it could cause autism. When I heard through the National Autistic Society that Dr Andrew Wakefield would be giving a lecture on this very subject at a conference in Glasgow in March 2001, I jumped at the chance to attend.

During the lecture, Dr Wakefield described in detail his theory of a correlation between MMR and autism. Dale had had the MMR vaccine at thirteen months, but Dr Wakefield's theory didn't ring true for me because we now knew Dale's autism had been present from birth. However, when Dr Wakefield went on to discuss an associated physical condition – autistic entero-colitis, as he called it – I was stunned. Dale had been plagued by every symptom since receiving his MMR vaccine in 1989. The type of vaccine he'd had was replaced after 1992 by the MMR-11, and I couldn't help but wonder whether the vaccine had contributed to or compounded Dale's physical problems. I certainly couldn't ignore the implications for Amy.

During the interval, I was lucky to get a chance to speak to Dr Wakefield personally and explain about Dale and my dilemma regarding Amy. Dr Wakefield advised it would be prudent to get Dale's problems checked out, as they could represent a significant obstacle in his progress. As our conversation continued, I also came to the conclusion that repeating the MMR for Amy was not an option. We could, however, consider giving the vaccines individually, since the only other alternative was not to give them at all.

Lorraine and Brian came to pick me up from the conference, bringing Amy with them as they had looked after her for the day. Everyone, including Dr Wakefield, fussed over her, commenting on how lovely and sociable she was. No one could possibly have guessed quite how proud of her I was, or how relieved that she was developing normally with appropriate language for her age.

For several nights after the conference, Jamie and I deliberated over what I'd learned. We arranged for Dale to see Dr Mike Thomson at the Portland Hospital in London, since he was familiar with the situation that Dr Wakefield had described. Dr Thomson prescribed some very simple medication and the problem soon resolved itself.

As far as Amy was concerned, we took the informed decision to give her single vaccines at six-monthly intervals. By a chance in a million, there was a measles outbreak locally and this really brought it home to us that we could never live with ourselves if anything happened to Amy because she had not had the vaccinations.

Another aspect we had to consider was the 'double-hit' element of the MMR controversy. There had been a few cases reported where normal school-age children had regressed into autism after receiving a booster of the MMR vaccine. Although many people believed the term booster was a milder form of the vaccine given at fourteen months, it was in fact exactly the same dose. Dale had never had a booster and we were certain that this should also be avoided for Amy – it was just too scary a step to take.

Statistically, one shot of each element of the MMR should be sufficient to cover Amy, so this was what we did.

We faced another difficult decision at about this time regarding Dale's education. There was a particular secondary school that the children from Overton would naturally transfer to, but because of Dale's special vulnerabilities, we had to accept that this school would not be suitable for him. Our research into the options available locally eventually convinced us to send Dale to Gourock High School, which had an excellent reputation. It had a unit for deaf children which fully accessed the main school, and because of this we knew the school would be a disability-friendly environment. It was a tough decision, however, as it meant that Dale wouldn't be going to secondary with his friends Tom and Fraser.

Because of the success of the Overton experience, we were fully aware of the importance of living in the same area as Dale's school and so there was no denying that we would have to move back to Gourock. Fortunately, we found a new-build house on a small estate with a park nearby, which would be good for Amy growing up, as well as ideal for Dale and Henry's walks.

The provision for Dale at Gourock was excellent, with a full support network including a classroom assistant. As usual, preparation was paramount and Dale made several visits to the school to meet the teachers, in addition to attending the normal induction days. While Jamie and I felt really good about all that was happening, we could see the head teacher had similar concerns as the Overton staff had initially had as to how Dale would cope, but thankfully she had an open mind.

Precisely because of the challenges ahead, we still took every opportunity to boost Dale's confidence and give him more experience of mixing in a mainstream setting. Because of his blossoming talent for art, we enrolled him in another Saturday class at the Glasgow School of Art, this time among kids of the same age and with no support geared to his needs – for the first time, there was no safety net. I remember a time when Dale skipped down Sauchiehall Street beside us, telling us with great excitement how the teacher had held up to the whole class his monochrome picture of a tiger as a perfect example of the day's work. We often wonder how he would have managed in Gourock High School without this boost to his self-esteem.

At Dale's end-of-term prize ceremony, we were over the moon to see him get the top prize for handwriting, and we still have his end-of-term report card, which described him as a happy and hardworking member of his year. The head teacher, Eleanor McMaster, commented that 'With support and encouragement and Dale's own commitment to work, he should cope with the challenges of secondary school.'

Just before he left Overton Primary, we gained a more unexpected insight into how well Dale had been accepted at school. A girl in his class asked if she could be his girlfriend. Dale politely declined, but thanked her for her kindness. On the final day of school, Dale came home in fine high spirits and with great pride showed me his school shirt, which all his classmates and even the teachers had signed.

Dale was worried that because of the move to Gourock, he would no longer be able to see Ryan, with whom he had developed a close friendship at St Anthony's. We assured Dale that if Ryan wanted to, they could keep in touch by visiting each other's homes at weekends. A successful phone call to Ryan's parents followed and indeed the two lads continue to see one another to this day.

The summer ended quickly, and once we were installed in the new house in Gourock, the need to prepare Dale for his journey to school was now top of the agenda. All the same principles as before, when we practised the walk to Overton, had to be covered again because this was a new area and experience for Dale. More importantly, he now had to cross a busy main road and be on time for the school bus. Ironically, this was the same road where Dale had caused so much havoc ten years earlier when he lay in the middle of the street head-banging because he had dropped Mickey. Ashton Road was even busier now, and this part had no pedestrian crossing. So, with Henry on his lead and Amy in her pram, many days were spent with Dale going through every stage from leaving the house to showing him where to walk and teaching him all the rules of the road and personal safety. Finally, I identified a 'marker' lamp-post at which he would cross the main road to the stop where the school bus would pick him up.

To increase Dale's sense of independence we had bought him a *Wallace and Gromit* alarm clock; he was into these characters at the time because he particularly loved Gromit, the dog. With the help of the clock, he practised getting up on time and preparing his own breakfast in readiness for when he started school. Dale would also feed Henry before going to school, and Henry would sit by his side while Dale ate his own breakfast, which would consist of toast for himself and an extra slice for Henry.

This new routine was amazing for me because if Amy was still asleep, I would enjoy the luxury of a lie-in. For my own reassurance, we introduced into the routine the rule that once school started Dale would always tell me when he was going – and with any luck I'd get a kiss goodbye, too. Dale learned the whole process by the book and I would get such a surge of happiness when he shouted as he left, 'Bye, Mum, I'm off now. Have a good day. I love you.'

On Dale's first day at Gourock High, Jamie and Henry walked down towards the bus stop with him. True to form, however, Dale wanted to be like the rest of the pupils and so told Jamie not to come down to the main road as he didn't want to stick out by having his dad with him. From that day on, Dale was totally independent in going to and from school and fitted in seamlessly.

One day when I went to pick Dale up from school to go to the dentist, like many other parents I waited at the gate for the school bell to ring. Once it did, amongst the distant onslaught of hundreds of emerging school kids, I spotted Dale, sauntering along with a couple of other boys, in full conversation and camaraderie with them. As they approached, I could see one of the boys was quite small and young-looking, yet seemed to be the leader of the group.

Dale waved them goodbye, then told me, 'Those are my friends. The wee guy, Scott, is really eleven and he's in the same year as me.'

Being thirteen and tall, Dale towered over his new

chums, but their emotional maturity matched perfectly and I was delighted to see they had accepted Dale as one of them.

Because Dale was a lot older than the other boys in his year, his desire to fit in was stronger than ever. He didn't want his school friends to know about his autism and especially not that he went to a special unit for more than five years. It didn't matter that the other kids wouldn't have a clue what autism was; he was not about to advertise his vulnerability and weaknesses, and just craved to be treated the same as the rest of them. I knew, however, that Scott and the other kids would sooner or later want to know why Dale was older than his classmates and so our old friend the white lie was resurrected.

When Dale was a baby, he had a stomach operation for a common condition called pyloric stenosis, which had left him with a very noticeable surgical scar on his abdomen. Jamie and I told him that if any kids asked why he was only in the first year, he should say that when he was younger he was sick a lot and needed an operation. Because of this, he had missed a lot of school and so had to repeat a year. The tactic worked a treat as the kids accepted the story without demur when seeing the evidence of the scar. Indeed, it would be five years before any of his friends learned the real truth. So Scott and another boy, Matthew, unknowingly guided their friend Dale through the teenage social life at Gourock High.

The speech therapist was still providing specialised resources that the mainstream teachers would incorporate into his schoolwork as needed, and Dale and another boy in his class got support as required throughout their school

lives. This, together with the fact that staff were so prepared to take on board our own concerns, undoubtedly
contributed to his success. A good example of the way we
worked with them was in relation to French lessons. It
seemed pointless to us that someone who had problems
fully understanding English should at this stage be trying to
learn another language. Our feelings were borne out by the
fact that Dale was clearly really struggling with French, and
there were other children who did not take French, so Dale
would not be seen as different if he pulled out.

Fortunately, Margie Carracher and her staff from the
learning support department agreed with us, and Dale's
French periods were put to better use. He received extra
tuition from the learning support staff and was also able to
get his homework done during this time, which allowed him
to relax later at home. Unknown to us then, the ongoing
support of this teaching initiative would prove to be a lifeline
later in Dale's life: tumultuous changes lay ahead.

It was April 2002 and Dale was due to visit his uncle Peter
and aunt Carol, who lived in England and had recently
moved to the Stratford-upon-Avon area. He had enjoyed
some wonderful trips with them, including a trip to Florida;
but the most memorable of all was still to come. Dale had
previously travelled down to visit his uncle Peter and aunt
Carol by air with Jamie's parents, Jimmy and Dorothy, but
this time Peter and Carol were off work for the Easter
holiday and came up with a different plan. They sent Dale a
ticket for a flight to Birmingham, where they would pick
him up, spend the week with him and then bring him home
when they drove up to Scotland for Easter.

This was a giant step for Dale – he had never before travelled on his own like this, and we had great doubts initially about whether he would be able to travel on his own, at just thirteen, in a plane full of strangers. We did the usual type of preparation, although because of his previous travels with Peter and Carol, little was needed. He was registered with the airline as an unaccompanied minor and would be given support accordingly. When we checked him in at Glasgow Airport, we nevertheless explained the procedure to him fully, just to make sure. He took to the whole thing in the same way as jumping on his bike and was entirely unfazed by this historic moment. To this day, he flies happily down to visit Peter and Carol on his own.

When Dale's first year at Gourock High was coming to an end, we looked back and felt it had been more successful than either Jamie or I had dared hope. Not only was he fitting in and working well at school, but he had made friends and was doing all the things kids of his general age group normally did together.

As usual with us, however, life was not straightforward. After the schools closed for the summer, we started to get calls from the police telling us they'd found Granda George wandering around areas where he'd lived many years before. I had been doing my utmost to support him, but his mental state was quickly deteriorating. Yet again my colleagues in the community service provided invaluable assistance, and sadly against Dad's wishes we had to establish a system of carers to enable him to continue living in his own home. They couldn't be with him twenty-four hours a day, however, and his trips back to his past became more frequent, resulting in several calls a week from the police to announce they had once again found him.

As if all this wasn't worrying enough, my dad accidentally set fire to his house. He was now clearly becoming a danger to himself, so my sister Linda and I started to look into nursing-home provision for him. Because of the tremendous demand for good nursing-home places, this was not an easy process and I ended up spending more time with Dad than I did with Amy.

One night, around ten o'clock, while trying to catch up on my household chores, the phone rang and Dad's alarmed night-time carer informed me, 'George is not in his house.'

I immediately alerted the police and started to drive around the places I thought he might be. About an hour later, the police rang my mobile to say they'd found him. The poor soul was in an almost collapsed state about three miles from his house, having struggled up steep hills to the gate of the cemetery where Mum was buried.

This poignant event at least had the effect of catapulting Dad up the waiting list and before long he had a place at the Merino Court Nursing Home. This was very appropriate as he had grown up in the area and it was just across from Dresling Road, where we had lived. Even better was the fact that I knew many of the staff well and was in no doubt that they would take excellent care of my dad. This home was to become a special environment in itself, and not just for Dad.

18
Harry

With Dad settled into Merino Court, Dale doing well at Gourock High and summer ahead, I could at last get back to my everyday routine with Amy. Such was the impact of my father's deterioration, I was aware that my daughter had been a little left out and I was looking forward to spending more time with her. I had been taking her to a mother and toddler group locally since she was only a year old and she mixed well with the other kids despite being the youngest. I had also become friendly with another mum, Pauline Graham, whose daughter, Nina, had been born in the same month as Amy. We'd met in the local park and would now visit each other every week to let the girls play together.

It was really good to be able to take time out to talk to another mum who was very much on a similar wavelength as me and shared the same sort of views as to how the girls should play and learn together. Amy and Nina soon formed a close bond. I remember just after they had celebrated their second birthdays, Pauline commented on how good Amy's vocabulary was. She seemed a little concerned that Nina's was 'nowhere near as much as Amy's'. I told her of my experience with Dale and assured her she had nothing to worry about with Nina.

It was great for Amy to play with Nina, and I had also

already put her name down for a place at a local private nursery, to get her used to mixing with as many kids as possible and prepare her for school when the time came. I was now particularly looking forward to her starting nursery because I'd noticed that she had become somewhat withdrawn, playing quietly on her own and watching more videos than usual. I'd been so involved with my dad's problems and trying to juggle all that was going on, in addition to my night-shift job, that I did wonder whether she was suffering from not having the same level of attention from me that she'd been used to.

One morning, Amy was happily playing in her bedroom and I stole a few moments of pleasure by watching her from the doorway, without her knowing I was there. She was lying quietly on the floor, gazing at the little figures dangling from the brightly coloured wooden carousel that was spinning in front of her face. I smiled with joy as I watched my precious wee girl lying there so content. Then I shifted my position slightly and saw the look in her eyes. I felt a cold, terrifying chill pass through me. She seemed literally in a trance, completely transfixed – not, as I had thought, by the toy's dangling figures, but by its spinning motion alone. She was totally silent, with no facial expression, as the carousel spun round and round. My heart plummeted and I had to fight a wave of nausea as I slowly absorbed what I was witnessing.

I had seen this type of 'play' before. Before Dale's autism erupted. He would lie in a similar way, quietly transfixed by the process of pushing one toy car just a few inches with his little finger, endlessly back and forth. Now here I stood, a dozen or so years later, rooted to the spot by my daughter's echoes of her brother's behaviour.

I forced myself to move, going cautiously to Amy, lifting her up and hugging her to me gently. Voice trembling, I asked, 'Amy, do you like the carousel? Can Mummy play, too?'

She looked right through me, then laughed heartily in my face as if she had no idea who I was, but found my anxiety and intrusion hilarious.

I desperately tried to gain her attention. 'Amy, it's Mummy. Say hello to Mummy.' She ignored my efforts and continued to laugh as I pleaded, 'Talk to me, Amy. Please talk to Mummy.'

I felt both relief and despair as she finally blurted out in response, 'Winnie the Pooh.'

Now completely confused, I tried to play with her, but she resisted my intrusion and went back to the carousel. I sat glued to the floor, just watching her. This was nothing like the little girl I had spent all my time with until just a few weeks ago – she was a stranger to me, and, apparently, I to her.

I tried playing more boisterously, just as we used to with Dale, enlisting the help of Amy's sit-on toy dog that we had bought her for Christmas, which looked like a golden retriever pup on wheels. We had encouraged her to call the toy Harry, after our dog Henry's father and also because the name blended in so well with our beloved Henry. I had attached a strong red lead to Harry's red leather collar and Amy would sit astride him as I pulled her around the estate, much to her delight and the amusement of passers-by.

I tried so hard that day, saying, 'Come on, Amy, sing your doggy song.'

All I got back was, 'Winnie, Winnie the Pooh.' She was normally such a bright, happy child, and everyone marvelled at her intelligence, vocabulary and all the songs and rhymes she knew. Because of Henry and Harry, I had taught her a party piece and she would sing to all and sundry the three verses of 'How Much Is That Doggy in the Window?' I tried singing this to her now, waiting for her to do the 'Woof, woof' at the end of each line, but nothing happened right up until the end, when she did at least do the last two. My heart heavy, I took a long, deep breath and tried to remain calm until Jamie came home.

When I told him of my concerns, he said he had also thought Amy had become withdrawn, but like me had put it down to all the problems with my dad. From that day on, in light of everything we had learned with Dale, all sensory interruptions in the house were switched off and all my attentions were switched on to Amy. Jamie was fully supportive and equally determined to do all he could to help her. Whilst deep inside I was petrified to be taking such measures again, I really hoped that she just needed to have my full attention and would soon return to the vibrant little girl she was.

Day by day, as I had with Dale, I spent every waking hour with Amy, trying to encourage language, play and engage with her. I involved her in everything I did, from making breakfast to doing the household chores, taking things at her pace. Just loading the washing-machine could take half an hour as I tried to coax one new word out of her. One reassuring thing was that at least Amy's comprehension was much better than Dale's and most of the time she was easy to engage with, whereas Dale of course had always been such a challenge – until Henry had a word with him, that is.

From around May to August 2002, despite all my increasingly desperate efforts, my worst nightmare unfolded as I watched Amy slowly slipping away from me. Her frustrations grew, as did my anguish when I had to witness her tantrums – fists beating her head at full force – or watch as she stood flapping her hands and screaming in distress. There was no denying the reality of what I was once again facing. No matter how hard I tried to prevent it, the horror of autism was engulfing my wonderful little girl.

Most of Amy's language had now gone, having been replaced by futile echolalia. Like Dale's poetry, she endlessly repeated the jumbled and meaningless vocabulary she had left: 'Winnie the Pooh, Harry, Eyore.' At other times, all we would hear being chanted all day was, 'Oh, poor Winnie's stuck in the hole,' peppered with intermittent screams of frustration.

One day, I could no longer contain my grief and collapsed on to the sofa, distraught. Unknown to me, Dale saw me crying and suddenly he was beside me giving me a big hug. Never in a million years could I have anticipated his next words: 'Mum, it's OK. You're worried about Amy – you think she's got what I've got. Well, you got me back and you can do it again.'

With good preparation, Amy started at Madeira, a private nursery with a great reputation that ran drama and dancing classes, which would be good for her physical and social development. On the first day when I picked her up, all seemed to be well. Two weeks later, however, when I arrived to collect her, one of the staff asked to have a chat with me.

'I just wondered if you had any concerns about Amy,' she said.

'Well,' I began, 'I think she needs some more socialisation. She seems to have become a bit withdrawn.'

She confirmed this, but went further, saying that the staff were concerned that she was not mixing with the other children and her play and lack of language were poor for her age. As I cautiously opened up the conversation and agreed to a speech therapy referral, this pleasant young girl suddenly said, 'Don't worry, we've had children here before with autism.'

Shocked though I was to hear these words, I couldn't help also being impressed by how the girl had not in any way tried to fudge the situation. I maintained my composure and left with Amy.

I strapped Amy into her car seat and put on her music tape loudly, to drown the noise as I wept with the agony of my worst fears being realised. I felt the same pain as I had all those years ago when I lay on the kitchen floor at Ashton Road, facing death. What had I done to deserve this? My precious wee miracle was afflicted with the same condition as Dale. There was no justice.

I gradually composed myself. Let's face it, I knew how unfair life could be and I decided I wasn't going to be a victim. I wouldn't care what 'they' thought of me; I would fight tooth and nail to help Amy and get her everything she needed and deserved. Autism and 'the system' were not going to destroy all we had achieved. I was determined that, no matter what, we would do as Dale said and get Amy back.

That night at home, we had a delicate family meeting about the situation, including Dale, as he was now fourteen and able to understand. It was humbling to hear him say, 'Don't worry, Mum, I can help a lot – I know what it's about.'

We discussed the fact that the speech therapist coming to assess Amy was Grace, the same therapist who had done so much with Dale at Highlanders.

Dale gave me another big hug. 'Mum, it's going to be all right,' he assured me. 'Grace helped me a lot and she will do the same for Amy.'

It was ironic that during this horrendous time of our daughter's autism coming into our lives, Dale was my rock. Jamie did help, but he had his own grief to deal with. We told only Lorraine and Brian, Eleanor, Barbara and close family about Amy; such was our devastation that we were unable to talk to people without becoming upset.

Dale alone witnessed the full extent of my anguish and at times smothered me with love and reassurance. Such was his empathy for me that he would engulf me with hugs, many times a day. It could be a little overwhelming, but I never put him off, as his love for me and worry for his little sister were so touching.

I was drained at the thought of having to go through the whole nightmare again, not least because I knew from talking to other parents I'd recently met that nothing much had changed since my time with Dale and parents still had to fight for their children.

I felt completely alone and overwhelmed with grief and

despair. I was unable to sleep, and went to my doctor to get sleeping tablets, but even with combining them with alcohol, I would be lucky to get three hours' sleep a night. It got so bad that I slept in the spare room as I was disturbing everyone in the house.

One morning, a really cold, miserable, dark November day, I was unable to face the empty house, so I drove to the beach with Henry and tried to gather my thoughts. Mostly I just wanted to be alone and not risk meeting anyone. I let Henry off the lead while I sat on a large rock watching him wander around, trying to absorb the nightmare of what lay ahead and where on earth I would find the strength to do it all again. I looked over at Henry, who was as solitary as I was, but nonetheless brimming with happiness. I wondered how I would have ever got through this day if I hadn't had him with me. The solitude, with the empty beach and only Henry as company, gave me a chance to gather myself and to think, 'How could I let Dale, and even Henry down?' This thought alone gave me the strength to fight on.

A couple of weeks later, Grace arrived, bringing with her another speech therapist who would work with Amy while Grace observed and spoke to me. They could both see she had obvious autistic behaviour, especially when Grace tried to engage with her, holding a toy cup in her hand. 'Amy, what's this?' she asked. 'Winnie the Pooh,' came the reply.

I told Grace that although I could see there was much to build on with Amy, there was no ignoring the obvious problem that the little language she had held on to was predominantly echolalic, in that she would mainly just repeat what was said to her, without any real understanding or intention to communicate. This and the other deficits Grace and I discussed meant that a diagnosis of autism appeared inevitable, though this would only be possible after a full assessment and long waiting lists. I was shocked, however, by Grace's assessment now that, at the age of 2 years 8 months, Amy had the language level of an 18-month-old child.

I spent the next morning frantically phoning around to try to find somewhere that could give a diagnosis sooner. I called the National Autistic Society in Bromley, but they had a long waiting list and didn't accept private patients. I phoned Yorkhill, pleading my case, and while the nurse was very helpful, she told me they also had a long waiting list and would only see Amy to give a second opinion, if I didn't agree with an earlier local diagnosis. Once again distraught, I called Grace, saying I couldn't bear to wait. She was very understanding and fortunately was able to get an appointment there for Amy in a few weeks' time, in December. I couldn't thank her enough because I honestly thought I was on the brink of a nervous breakdown.

In the meantime, as with Dale, part of the process was that Amy would require the help of an educational psychologist. This was to be Mary Smith, the same person who had assessed Dale when we were so desperately trying to get a diagnosis years earlier. Given our suspicions that Mary had previously held a fairly low opinion of the way we handled Dale, we were hugely anxious that she was now coming to visit us at home to assess Amy. But Jamie and I concluded that as the main point was to get Amy a prompt diagnosis and the specific help she needed, we would give Mary another chance and not be obstructive.

On 11 November 2002, Mary Smith arrived at our house, bringing with her a speech therapist who had worked with Dale at the PSLU at Highlanders. Although I was determined to fight for Amy, when it came to meeting Mary again I knew I was emotionally very weak and so Jamie took time off work to support me through the encounter.

The speech therapist worked with Amy at the dining table, assessing her as they went along, while Mary spoke to us with exactly the same demeanour as she had twelve years earlier when we met her about Dale. I sat beside her on the sofa with Jamie rooted to a dining chair. Trying to control my anxiety, I told Mary about what we had witnessed with Amy and that we knew it was autism. I will never forget how she casually smiled at me and said that Amy was not like Dale, because 'He was severe.' This from the person who had repeatedly denied he had autism before we finally got him diagnosed.

I asked Mary when Amy would get a place in the PSLU because I knew that with early intervention and specific therapy there, as well as my continued efforts with her at home, she would thrive. To my horror, she told us, 'A place is likely to be available from August,' adding, just as we had heard all those years ago, 'Nursery provision is scarce.'

Jamie sat silent and shocked by the events unfolding and I could see the speech therapist was also uncomfortable – although I sensed she was in agreement because of the reassuring looks she gave me. As a last resort, I asked Mary if a record of needs could be opened for Amy as this would strengthen her case, only to be told, 'It would be better to wait until the professionals have got to know Amy.' This was already Amy's third assessment by professionals and I would have thought her needs could by now easily be identified as autism.

Voice trembling, I asked Mary if I could at least have Terri back to help me work with Amy pending further assessment. She conceded she would make the referral. Before she left, I asked her if she agreed that Amy had autism and she replied, 'Let's wait and see what the people up at Skylark say.'

With Amy in my arms, I showed Mary to the door and summoned all my willpower to bid her a dignified goodbye. I thanked the speech therapist for the way she had worked with Amy, commenting on the irony that Amy had responded well and would clearly improve much more quickly if only she could have ongoing help of a similar nature. Then I walked back into the room, set Amy down and yelled at Jamie, 'Why didn't you say something? You sat there totally silent!'

Struggling to respond he said, 'I can't believe what just happened. I can't take it in.' I hadn't realised he'd been in a state of shock the whole visit and had found it hard to participate.

Once Amy was safely up in her bedroom playing, I could no longer control my anger and despair. I sank into a huddle on the floor, sobbing, unable to comprehend that this was happening to us again and feeling totally at sea, with my husband 'lost'. But Jamie found me and clutched me to him, also crying. We held on to each other a few moments before I pulled back and looked him straight in the eye. 'That's it. We are not going to take this again.'

Over our usual remedy of a cup of tea, we decided once more to seek help and advice from Jim Taylor and Janet

Stirling, as they both knew us well. Jamie and I also wrote to the education department asking for a different educational psychologist to be assigned to Amy, and thankfully this led to the same person who was now dealing with Dale being allocated.

Unable to accept what Mary Smith had said about nursery provision, I phoned a local school, Moorfoot, which I knew had an excellent mainstream nursery. I was greatly encouraged when the head teacher, Sylvia Gillen, invited me to come and see her. She really understood my plight and said she would do her best to get a place for Amy in the nursery. True to her word, she was then able to offer a place from February for five mornings a week. I decided in addition to keep Amy's two afternoon slots at Madeira, to give her as much opportunity to socialise as possible.

Terri began to visit for one afternoon every fortnight and again became a lifeline, full of compassion. In the meantime, to fill the twelve-week gap before Amy started at Moorfoot, I channelled my grief into working intensively with Amy, using her obsession with Winnie the Pooh, just as I had with Dale and Mickey. This time, I wasn't totally alone, as the amazing Henry was once again part of the process, albeit in a slightly different way.

With Dale away at school all day, Henry was in Amy's face as much as mine, so in a sense she had 'company' to relate to. Either he would break into her play or she would want to play with him, and, as with Dale, she would help care for the dog and learn through this, especially his feeding sessions. Amy had always enjoyed a really healthy and varied diet, but as her autism emerged she developed obsessions with food, sometimes refusing to eat at all. Hungry Henry stepped up to the plate – or bowl at least – and taught her what the process was all about, just as he had her big brother.

Amy's imaginative play was poor, so I obtained out-of-date oxygen masks, a mini, mock intravenous fusion bag with a line attached to look like a drip, a child-size doctor's coat and various other medical accoutrements, all in a proper doctor's case which was being thrown out from where I worked. I threw in my old stethoscope, and with all these props we spent many a time playing animal hospital, with Winnie and his furry friends as patients. The best and most fun patient of all was Henry. He would lie and let Amy do anything she wanted to him, with a toy auriscope in his ear and mock syringes to give him his medicine. Through time, she would play appropriately with him on her own as he slept throughout his various medical treatments and examinations.

Such was Henry's success as a teacher that Amy herself developed a special way of connecting with him, even if she did insist on calling him Harry. No matter how hard I tried to get her to use his correct name, it was futile; she had quite clearly adopted 'Harry' as her dog, while Henry was Dale's. But we capitalised on this initiative as we had with Henry's voice – if it motivated Amy to play and get involved with the dog, we were happy to go along with it. And it did reap benefits by encouraging her to communicate; if she saw dog toys when we were out shopping, she would say, 'Nuala, buy this for Harry,' or, 'Amy want to give Harry a biscuit.' She always referred to herself by her name, just as Dale used to, and it would take months of patient correction and practice for her to master the use of pronouns. Funnily enough, she had also started to call both Jamie and me by name. This was because in an attempt to stop her butting in like Butting-in Betty, I told her once that she had to wait and say 'excuse me', and then the person's name, so they knew she was talking to them. Such was her literal interpretation of this rule that we knew it was too difficult for Amy to understand and so we allowed her to continue using our names – in a sense, she was right to do so, as this was what she had been told. However, to try and redress the balance, we would slip in a 'Mum' or 'Dad' when conversation allowed, to remind her of our roles.

Despite its incredible success with Dale, we didn't want to use Henry's voice with Amy quite simply because she was 'too good'. As she was easy to engage with and already showing great potential, we felt any attempt to use the voice would have hindered and confused her.

While we now had the help of 'Harry' and the Madeira nursery as well as my own input, there was still no substitute for Amy having someone of a similar age to play and interact with. Nina had become a wonderful friend, giving Amy a lot of guidance and even mothering her. It was as though she had picked up that Amy needed help and didn't understand things easily, and it was touching the way she took care of her and kept her on the right track. Amy would also quite often play with Lorraine's grandson, Reece, who was eighteen months her junior, but they still got on well together. Reece's mum, Lisa, was aware of how I was trying to break into Amy's world and help her socialise with other children, and one day she hit on a great idea.

Amy had developed a fear of bath time, so I would only

bathe her when totally necessary. Lisa suggested that every Monday evening I should drop Amy off at her house for a play session with Reece, followed by the two of them taking a bath together, in the hope that the whole experience would be fun for Amy. So for ten weeks while awaiting our place at Moorfoot, I would drive the sixteen-mile round trip this entailed and Amy would be waiting for me in her pyjamas, hair all done up in ribbons and bobbles. With all the fun of having company in the bath and lots of face-to-face contact, Amy slowly came alive again. Lisa was a natural teacher and Amy clearly adored her and the time she spent with Reece. As soon as I got Amy home, she would pull her hair asunder, but Lisa never gave up and every week when I picked Amy up she would look like a model child from a magazine, who, more importantly, radiated happiness. Lisa's scheme was ultimately completely successful and I was able to get Amy back into the bath again at home. Just as Henry had all those years ago with Dale, another friend had stepped in and helped us overcome a familiar hurdle.

With all the intensive input in the build-up to starting at Moorfoot, it was a huge relief to see the spark coming back to Amy. Her language and comprehension had improved and, crucially, much of the echolalia had now gone, which was reward in itself. A week before Amy's third birthday, the speech therapist came to reassess her in readiness for starting at Moorfoot and the PSLU. We sat at the dining table with Amy directly in the speech therapist's eye line, and Amy seemed to be responding well as they went through various different tests. Finally, the therapist turned to me, saying, 'You've been working hard, haven't you?' I didn't fully understand what she meant and watched cautiously as she checked the assessment tool to see what developmental stage Amy had reached. To my complete astonishment, she now had a language and comprehension level of thirty-two months – she had gained fourteen months' progress in three months.

I was both mentally and physically exhausted, but there was no denying this intensive and early intervention had worked. Not only could Amy now take full advantage of the education on offer at mainstream nursery and eventually Moorfoot school itself, but to my eternal relief, she was no longer a candidate for the PSLU, which would allow another child to have the chance of such a vital place.

On 22 January 2003, we made a second visit to the Skylark Child Development Centre in Greenock, the first one in December having been viewed by them as a preliminary assessment, just to see whether Amy was on the autistic spectrum. The outcome was that Amy did fulfil the criteria for autistic-spectrum disorder, but thankfully it looked as though she was at the higher-functioning end of the spectrum. We were given the opportunity to return in a year's time, to see exactly where Amy fitted on the spectrum, but in fact decided against this, for two reasons: firstly, we wanted to avoid the stress of unnecessary encounters with professionals, our sense of trust still damaged after our experience with Dale; and secondly, we felt we had enough to go on with what we'd been told about Amy not to want to block a vital appointment for another family desperately awaiting a diagnosis.

All this had not come without a cost to my health, though. In February 2003, I had a terrible headache and tightness in my chest like a vice. I had had many similar episodes before, but this was the worst ever. After seeing my GP, I was admitted to hospital for cardiac monitoring. The consultant, hearing of the situation at home, prescribed Valium for my blood pressure – following which I had the best two hours' sleep I'd had for a long time. I had to be careful from then on not to overdo it, but I didn't regret pushing myself because I was to find out from Amy herself how worthwhile it would be to see her return to almost the little girl I had.

When Amy started at Moorfoot Nursery, I kept in close contact with the teachers and staff and was delighted to find that she blossomed with their excellent input. As a result, her social skills improved tremendously, so much so that she was able to fully participate in both nurseries' nativity plays at Christmas. I think this was possible because of what she had done throughout her time at Madeira.

I also enrolled Amy in a drama class run by Carole Fry every Saturday morning at the Arts Guild. We particularly enjoyed seeing Amy at the usual end-of-term show in March, in front of a full house at the Arts Guild Theatre. After a scene featuring Amy in the chorus had finished, knowing her Granny Dorothy was in the audience, she ran back on to the stage and shouted, 'Hello, Granny!' She did this so naturally that the audience laughed with delight, thinking it had been rehearsed to look like an ad-lib. Her various other antics stole the show, especially at the end when the senior class were doing their grand finale. The plan was that during this the junior class would run into the theatre and stand below the stage to join in with the final number. Amy was having none of this, however, and ran up the stairs on to the stage to take part with the seniors. Following this, I managed to get her involved, as I had with

Dale, with many activities such as art, junior Brownies and gymnastics, all of which helped her social skills further.

Our daily life continued and I carried on with my community post, helping families care for their terminally ill relatives at home. A new part of our everyday routine was visiting my dad at Merino Court. I often took Amy with me and the staff there were so understanding that Henry was allowed to visit too. In a sense, he became a 'Therapet' to the home's residents and would lie in the communal lounge as if he were a permanent fixture. Many a subdued resident who showed no interest in interacting with people would acknowledge and respond to Henry. Everyone looked forward to his visits – as in fact did he, perhaps because the nurses gave him treats.

The staff embraced Amy as much as they did Henry, which allowed me to spend quality time with Dad. They thought nothing of letting Amy 'assist' the residents' hair-dresser or activity therapist for hours, and in a way these visits for her became like the Wellpark had been for Dale. One day in particular, Amy had disappeared off with the hairdresser as I sat with Dad in the lounge and Henry at his feet. Over an hour went by and I periodically checked that the hairdresser was happy with her young assistant. She never demurred, but when she finally came back to me, hand in hand with Amy, she gave a big smile, saying, 'She's a lovely little girl, but can you take her batteries out now?' This was a perfect example of how Amy was now 'over-sociable', getting involved with and literally interrogating anyone who was willing to listen.

Amy got to know a few of the residents personally and one of her favourites, for obvious reasons, was a lady called

Winnie. Winnie would ask Amy to draw her a picture, as would other residents and even staff members sometimes, and she was always happy to oblige. Due to the nature of this type of environment, however, it was inevitable that days came where there would suddenly be a new resident in a chair where Amy had known the old one and so she slowly grew to understand the concept of old age and dying. We told her that the person who used to be in the chair had gone to heaven like Granny Madge and that it was a nice place that looked like Teletubby Land, only without the Tubbies. She confirmed her grasp of the situation one day with the pronouncement, 'When it's Granda George's turn to go to heaven, there'll be a new man in his bed when we go back.'

When we were facing the most challenging aspects of Dale's behaviour all those years ago, I'm sure we'd have jumped at the chance of dealing with a child at the opposite end of the autistic- spectrum disorder, but Amy's superior ability with language didn't necessarily make our lives any easier. Because she was able to manipulate a situation or obsession and interrogate us about it, as she had with the hairdresser and many other hapless victims, this made handling Amy even harder. With Dale, once he was 'pro-grammed', he adhered to family and school rules, which made dealing with him a lot easier in the long run. As far as Amy was concerned, however, you would have to jump out of a cake to motivate her to do something and then let her eat it – or at least have a consistent reward system in place to reinforce the message. We have therefore learned that it doesn't really matter what level of autism you are dealing with; it is how an individual's particular autistic traits impact on their life that is important.

19
A Whole New World

In August 2003, when Dale was fifteen and Amy three and a half, Amy's ultimate obsession entered our lives – one that we would all have to learn about from scratch, and which would enable me to conquer a lifetime fear.

We had again decided on a family holiday at a nice hotel in Blackpool. One day, while walking along the beach, Amy saw the famous Blackpool donkeys arrive – a dozen of them, names inscribed on their collars. She immediately wanted to go on one and when the lady in charge asked, 'Would you like a ride on Harry?' no further prompting was needed. Off they went, with Amy sitting completely naturally and Jamie observing, 'She looks like someone in a posse from *The Magnificent Seven*.' When they returned, Amy was beaming from ear to ear and the owner of the donkeys remarked that it was a long time since she had seen a child this happy on one of them.

No sooner had Amy dismounted than she insisted on another donkey, called Harvey this time. Four donkeys later, we finally managed to persuade her to leave and headed off to the Pleasure Beach Carnival. Here, we progressed from donkeys to horses, of the carousel variety, and from that day our lives were transformed; whether we liked it or not, it was welcome to the world of all things equine.

Although I loved the idea of horses, I knew absolutely nothing about them and in fact had a real fear of their size and power. Even so, with the same excitement as when I was on my mission to find Henry for Dale, I set about using the obsession with horses for Amy. I resigned myself to having to overcome my fear, and when we returned from Blackpool, I called the local stables, which were less than a mile from our house. I discovered pony walks were available, as well as tuition in stable management. I explained Amy's condition to a young girl who was the yard manager and was delighted when she said that getting involved with horses would be very good for Amy; they would help her in any way they could.

I booked Amy in for a pony walk every Sunday and then once a fortnight she would have a lesson in stable management, where she would get one-to-one tuition from a stable hand on how to care for a horse. This type of interaction would be a very constructive way to use her obsession and open up a whole new social world for her. Amy and I became Sunday regulars at Ardgowan Riding Centre and made many friends there, one of whom was Rosemary Gisbey, whose nine-year-old daughter, Iona, owned a lovely horse named Rocky. I actually felt quite comfortable around him as he seemed to share the nature of a golden retriever, albeit with hooves. On many occasions Amy would be allowed to help Iona with Rocky's care and even got to ride him sometimes. Such was the success of this friendship that the day came when Iona and Amy entered Rocky in a 'tack and turn-out' competition.

It was a hot day, with as many as thirty in the group, children and adults alike, going through their paces. Amy looked both cute and immaculate in full riding dress as she sat astride Rocky, with Iona leading them round the ring. The judges knew nothing of Amy's autism and she competed in the same way as everyone else. It was a wonderful experience for Amy, and although she and Iona weren't among the prize-winners, they were clear winners in Rosemary's and my eyes, with not a single fault between them. There is no doubt that the day will come when another four-legged animal will be a part of our family, this time definitely belonging to Amy.

In December 2003, we moved house yet again, to our present home in Gourock, overlooking the River Clyde. At long last we had managed to recreate the view we had so loved in Ashton Road, but this time in an ideal environment for us all – especially Henry, who had his own floor-to-ceiling window from which to survey his domain. The old house was too far from the town centre, which had left Dale isolated from his friends, and had left Jamie and me as his taxi drivers, so we thought the move would help him establish his independence.

Dale's friends were now virtually permanent fixtures in his life, either hanging out at our house or all off somewhere together for weekends and holidays. The boys had taken it upon themselves to form a band, in which Dale played guitar, so many a time we'd come home to find our lounge being used for rehearsals by a gang of budding rock stars. To help with their inspiration, they started going to big rock concerts and this in itself highlighted another major step in Dale's life: it was time to get him a mobile phone. As well as allowing our fifteen-year-old to fit in with his peers, it would be important in terms of personal safety, as despite his increasing independence, he was potentially still quite vulnerable. This was, however, going to mean a lot of help from us to teach him how to use the phone; I'd only just got to grips with how my own mobile worked! Plus, although keen to learn the many aspects of using a mobile phone, Dale's ordinary teenage nature meant he had pretty much reached saturation point in terms of Jamie and me being his teachers for such things.

Dale was very fond of our friend Kenny, who just happened to work in the mobile-phone industry, so we were grateful when he offered to source the most suitable package and phone for Dale and, more importantly, show him how to use it. Kenny selected a top model with a built-in camera and all the trimmings and off Dale went to Kenny's house for a crash course in mobile-phone technology. Thereafter he was just like his friends, sending texts and taking pictures, with Henry of course duly installed as a screensaver. We were indebted to Kenny, who, like so many others over the years, had stepped in to help in their own way and made a world of difference to the quality of life that Dale and Amy are able to enjoy today.

Even though Dale was growing up and becoming ever more independent, all of his friends, including Robert, Ryan and the boys from the band, loved Henry and understood that he was a huge fixture in Dale's life. On those occasions when the band took a break from practising in our lounge to go to the local shop, they always took Henry with them. Many a time, even if Dale had him on the lead when they left, it would be one of the others walking Henry on his lead when they returned. Whenever they crowded round the computer, Henry would be there among them. Dale's friend Scott showed how he understood about Henry's bond with Dale when he gave him with a beautiful golden retriever ornament for his birthday, which he still has in his room.

A great advantage of the house move was that Dale was now within walking distance of all of his friends and was on a bus route for when he wanted to go to Greenock Shopping Centre. He could also walk to Gourock Railway Station and would now travel up by train to see Ryan, who lived twelve miles away, which was a bonus to Jamie and me since it saved us running him there in the car. As ever, it was crucial to prepare Dale with a practice 'solo' run, with me stalking him from a safe distance.

Another benefit of the house move was that we were now within a ten-minute walk of Moorfoot Primary, which we hoped Amy would attend as a natural follow-on from the nursery there.

Despite all the positives of the new house, we also had to face the emerging concern of Henry's deteriorating mobility. There were thirty graduated stairs up to the house from the road and we noticed that Henry was having increasing trouble with them. Now at the grand age of eleven, he was also struggling to stand up sometimes, especially in the mornings, and I would often have to assist him by gently helping to ease up his rear end as he tried to stand. I knew that he had arthritis, but Dale and I nevertheless had him checked out by his vet, Nigel Martin, who prescribed a glucosamine medication called Seraquin to help. Fortunately, we had fully insured Henry for such medical treatment as soon as he had come into our lives.

Nigel explained that Henry's arthritis would inevitably advance and it was a matter of managing it carefully. As Dale was still responsible for Henry's care, he would be his main walker and give him his medication. Being less active, Henry was starting to feel the cold more, so we bought him a really good dog coat, and as he was now unable to get upstairs to Dale's room, I made him a supportive bed so he could sleep in our room on the ground floor instead.

Henry's new bed consisted of a king-size high-tog duvet, which I folded and quartered and covered with a soft fleece material; he looked as snug as a bug as he slept on it. The day I went to buy the material for the cover was memorable in that I had 'the interrogator' with me. We were in the busy local fabric shop and Amy was delighted that the blue fleece material we found had a paw-print pattern on it. As the assistant cut the fabric to length, true to form Amy butted in: 'Excuse me, lady, do you have any horse material?'

'I'm sorry, we don't sell horse material,' the assistant replied with a smile.

'Could you order me some in, please?' was Amy's snappy response, prompting spontaneous laughter from everyone in the shop.

Just like her older brother, no matter where she was, Amy was an expert at bringing her obsession into the situation.

Around this time, Uncle Peter and Aunt Carol took Dale on another trip, their destination on this occasion being New York City. Jamie took Dale to Glasgow Airport to meet up with them, and Dale waved a cheerful goodbye as they set off on this latest adventure. He had enjoyed visiting

London so much that we knew he would be comfortable in New York and, in any event, now seemed happy to go anywhere with Peter and Carol – to this day, they all still get on wonderfully well.

When Dale returned, he was his usual laid-back self, stating simply that he'd really enjoyed the trip. We asked if he'd done anything particularly special and were both quietly taken aback by his reply: 'I went up in a helicopter at night-time to see the Manhattan skyline all lit up.'

He casually sauntered back to his room as Jamie and I reflected on how far he had come since the days of the lost little boy in Roxburgh Street who had created from Duplo bricks the very place he had just described. Locked as he was then in his autistic world, we could never have dreamed he would have another extraordinary connection with that same skyline all these years later.

Shortly after the New York trip, I noticed an advert for a junior car mechanics' class at the local James Watt College. This would be after school, for kids aged from fourteen to sixteen. Now that Dale was working towards standard grades, I thought this would be an ideal opportunity to get him used to the college environment and might open up an option for future employment. It would certainly stand him in good stead for when the day came to have a car of his own. I remember feeling ridiculously happy as Dale was fitted out with steel-capped boots and a boiler suit – he looked so grown-up. The outfit certainly did the trick as he went on to fit in seamlessly with the other boys in the class.

Another memorable event at this time was that it was Amy's turn at nursery to get chickenpox. She was totally covered in spots and, most unusually for her, very lethargic.

The inevitable itching was bad enough, but she became hysterical as the spots erupted all over her face and body. 'Rub them out, rub them away. Get them off my body!' she cried.

I did everything I could to help, eventually trying to divert her with children's TV. Luckily, a favourite character of hers in the *Tweenies* also had chickenpox and this settled her a little. Then her antihistamine medicine kicked in and she fell asleep.

Amy had been so distressed that I hit on the idea of enlisting Henry's help to reassure her. I got some tomato purée and dotted big red spots all over his face and ears. He indulged this latest nonsense with his usual equanimity and, I have to say, really looked the part.

When Amy woke up, I pretended not to notice Henry's affliction, but as soon as she saw him she burst out laughing and said, 'Mum, look – Henry's got chickenpox.'

I gave Henry his 'medicine', in the form of a small spoonful of syrup, making a big fuss about how Amy had passed on her bug to him. Realising she was not alone, her spirits lifted considerably and she coped well thereafter, not least because her spots went away before Henry's.

After Amy had recovered, another big event was approaching for Dale. Ever since his autism had been recognised, Peter and Carol had supported the Scottish Society for Autism and Peter also took part in various events for the charity. On 17 April 2005, Peter was due to do a sponsored abseil off the Forth Rail Bridge, only this time he wasn't doing it alone – he had persuaded Dale to join him. Dale had already done some abseiling in the Scouts, albeit on a slightly smaller scale, and so I told him, 'You do the jump and I will get you the sponsors.'

The day of the jump was a big event, with many other charities also represented and a tannoy system giving a running commentary as each person did their abseil. It was a clear, sunny day and the huge crowd had a great view of the gigantic column of the bridge where the jump was taking place. It took us a while to get through the crowd to the others because people kept stopping to pat Henry, which of course he loved, believing the whole event had been laid on specifically for him.

When I saw the height of the abseil and how slow and cautious people were in going over the edge, I was really worried for Dale. I overheard some people who had just done their jump saying how terrified they had been and started to wonder if this was a good idea for him after all.

'Are you OK with this?' I asked him. 'You don't need to go through with it if you don't want to.'

'I'm a bit nervous, Mum, but I'm with Pete – it'll be all right.'

So off they went to start the mountainous climb up the stairs of the column – it would take them about fifteen minutes to reach the top. While we waited, we took Amy on to the beach, where, with her usual knack of creating something horse-related out of anything she could find, she made a unicorn from seaweed and shells.

While we were admiring Amy's unicorn on the beach, we heard over the tannoy that the next participants in the jump would be Dale and Pete. Jimmy had his camcorder at the ready as we all stood rooted to the spot, but almost before the tannoy had finished announcing, 'Dale Gardner now for the Scottish Society for Autism,' Dale had popped himself over the edge and zipped down to the bottom like a pro. Uncle Pete followed, somewhat more slowly, a few minutes later.

When Dale got back to us, I gave him a big hug and kiss on the cheek and told him we were all so proud of him. Then I laughed, saying, 'Sorry, Dale, please don't hit me.'

He gave me a look. 'Very funny, Mum.'

By now he was able to appreciate how difficult his autism had been in the past and would join in with good humour when we joked about some of the things he used to do – like try to destroy the house and everyone in it because I'd told him I was proud of him.

Dale's abseil had raised £730, which was a decent contribution to the charity, but by far his biggest achievement that day was what he had done for people with autism by participating himself.

After a busy summer doing up the house, we delivered Amy to Moorfoot Nursery. With the help of the staff and educational psychologist, we had repeated the same preparation and formula as for Dale and she settled in successfully. Entering mainstream full-time was a big step, so Amy was to receive special educational needs (SEN) support, but mainly on the periphery as all concerned wanted to promote as much independence for her as possible. Her nursery teacher was aware of what had been achieved with Dale and was very willing to work with me to ensure Amy reached her full potential and would be able to cope when the time came to start at Moorfoot Primary.

The only real blot on our horizon was Henry's arthritis.

He had to go on to a stronger medication as his mobility deteriorated further. The treatment was called Metacalm, and while it did give Henry a new lease of life, we had to stop it sometimes because it caused gastric irritation, making him very nauseous and sick. This created a vicious circle of its own and I started to worry. Now eleven and a half, he could only tolerate small walks and it took two of us to lift him in and out of the car. He still had a good quality of life, however, and we would do all we could to maintain this; we just adapted to his disability accordingly.

Meanwhile, Dale was preparing to sit his exams. Throughout his time at Gourock High there had inevitably been a few occasions when problems had arisen for him, but with his teachers' incredible support and liaison with us, on the whole he had flourished. A major influence in his success was no doubt Margie Carracher and the staff in the learning support department. It was Dale's idea to sit his exams and do the best he could; Jamie and I never once pushed for him to achieve academically, wanting only for him to cope within the school environment and succeed socially.

One teacher, Marie Stewart, had previously worked at Glenburn School, for children with special needs, and had a lot of experience with autism. She was determined that despite his condition Dale should reach the peak of his potential and she was a great support to him in his studies. She was also his mentor and scriber when it came to sitting his exams, as he needed someone to write his examination answers for him. Although the results weren't important, I told Dale he should just do his best for his teachers. They deserved it.

One by one, day by day, Dale sat his seven exams. We let him be and didn't make a fuss. When he came home with his English paper, there was a question about trains, which needless to say he had chosen to answer. We were concerned about how Dale would handle the ambiguous way questions were often asked and whether the English exam would be difficult. We didn't know if he would get any pass results at all, and did wonder whether the lack of an English qualification in particular would affect his chances of gaining decent employment in the future. But for now it was over – he had done his best and we would enjoy the summer. Henry, too, benefited from the better weather and all was well as we began to prepare Amy for starting school in mid-August.

One morning in early August, the postman awoke us bearing the big brown envelope that contained Dale's standard-grade results. I took it to Jamie, who was still in bed, and we discussed how no matter what, even if Dale had no passes, he had nevertheless tried his utmost and we would reward him with a slap-up meal in an exclusive restaurant. I then went up to Dale's bedroom and left him to open the envelope on his own. A few minutes later, he came down to our bedroom with his usual laid-back demeanour and a big smile on his face.

'Mum, I think I've done quite well. Do you want to see?'

Jamie and I sat in bed and stared at the certificate. It took us a while to understand and absorb the list of grades in front of us. There it was in black and white: Dale had passed seven exams and gained a C in English.

Sensing what might be coming, Dale looked at me and

said, 'Mum, I don't want a fuss – you know I don't like that.'

So I sat where I was in bed and took a few moments of careful thought about how I would respond. I concluded that while Dale's autism may not want a fuss, I wanted to show Dale how happy I was for him. So, like many times in the past, I took a risk. I leaped out of bed and jumped up and down like a lunatic, screaming with joy and waving the results paper around as if it were a winning lottery ticket. Jamie and Dale were laughing. Then Dale rapidly worked out that I was coming for him next and ran away. I managed to catch him and smothered him with kisses and hugs, still jumping around and squealing with elation. I think he was pleased I was so happy for him and, judging by the fact that he was still laughing, at least enjoyed the crazy way I had shown him.

That evening, we took Dale out to an excellent Thai restaurant in Glasgow, leaving Amy at home with our Barnardo's sitter, Suzanne, whom she loved and would have a great time with. As a special token of how pleased we were for Dale, we gave him a surprise gift. Over the years, he had built up an impressive standard-gauge Hornby train collection and I had encouraged him to enjoy this with other enthusiasts by joining the local railway club in Greenock. Most of the members were older men, a couple of whom had young kids and Dale took responsibility for them when he was at the club. So this made for a very healthy and constructive use of his enduring interest in trains, yet again with all the social benefits that came with it.

The gift we presented to Dale in the restaurant, therefore, was a Henry train by Hornby, which he had been saving up for for some time. The following week, Dale gave the kids and adults at the club a great thrill by running not only his Thomas and James trains, but the new Henry model as well. He still goes to the railway club every Tuesday evening and helps set up and demonstrate the trains at big shows. He recently told me that when he goes to these shows, he can easily spot kids and adults with autism as they walk around the halls looking at the train displays.

With such great exam results, the teachers and school were delighted for Dale and he decided to carry on and do a fifth year. He had also started to give some thought to what he would like to do for a future career. He had recently done some work experience with his friend Scott at a local children's nursery and had received a very positive report from the staff there, who had been unaware of his autism. Also, he had started working towards a Duke of Edinburgh Award and, as part of this scheme, had become a volunteer at the local Beavers, or junior Scouts group. He had discovered here, too, that he had a good understanding of children and, after much deliberation, concluded that this was an area where he could use his drawing and guitar skills. He wanted to use the insight he'd gained from his own condition to help other children. More importantly, children were fond of him, warming to his patient, gentle and caring personality.

Amy also had a successful summer, attending mainstream art and drama workshops, as well as a large play scheme at the local sports centre. Because of our experience with Dale, the educational psychologist implemented a transition plan to assist with Amy's big move, straight into mainstream at Moorfoot Primary. This included a book of pictures being put together to familiarise her with the school, classrooms, PE hall, teachers and even the canteen food. Quite simply, it was the same as Paula's book for Dale, but without dear old Henry.

For the first time in our lives, Jamie and I learned what all the hype was about regarding a child's first day at school – and we loved every minute of it. Amy did, too, as she was so well prepared. There were no tears from her or us, and after taking a photograph of her in her class, we left her to enjoy the rest of this momentous day. The joy and sense of achievement we felt was on a par with the day that she was born.

With the excellent support of Moorfoot itself, together with the outreach service from the local school language base, speech therapy staff and a teacher specialising in special educational needs in Amy's class, she settled well into her peer group and thrived.

About six weeks later, in mid-September, while driving past Val's house with Amy in the car, I spotted her working in her front garden with her mum and stopped for a chat. Amy interrupted and began interrogating them about horses, so as a distraction Val turned to me with the bright idea: 'Why don't you let her see our new puppies?' One of the bitches had recently had eight pups, all of which already had homes to go to. I suggested we leave it for now so that we could all come back with Dale.

So, with Jamie confident that all the pups had been sold, we went back that weekend, taking Henry with us. We went out to the big shed in the back garden that housed the pups and had a dog run for the older dogs. While we all fussed over the pups, Jamie walked Henry around in the garden. On seeing this, Val and Sheena had a gentle word with Dale about Henry, explaining that his arthritis was very advanced and that at twelve years of age he was now quite an old dog. Then, while Amy continued to play with the pups, Val mentioned that one of the males was now available because the people who had said they would take him had changed their minds about getting a dog.

After a pleasant visit, we headed into town to get a DVD and pizza, which we often did on a Saturday evening. Staying with Dale in the car, I sent Jamie and Amy off with instructions as to what to get in both shops, and then turned to Dale. I had noticed something was upsetting him and wanted the chance to speak to him on his own. When I pressed him about what was wrong, he began to cry.

'I feel awful,' he told me. 'I can't bear the thought of not having Henry in my life.'

No matter how many times we had tried to explain to Dale that Henry might not have that much longer to live, it had taken his chat with Sheena and Val to make him fully understand that there was only so much the vet could do.

We talked a little further and I very quickly reached a decision. 'Do you think you should take the wee pup that Val has left?' I asked Dale.

We'd already agreed on how no other dog could ever replace Henry, but Dale reflected a moment and said, 'I think it would help. I couldn't go from having Henry to nothing.'

With some relief and Dale's permission, I phoned Val from my mobile. 'Hold that pup,' I told her, 'we'd like to take him.' I then called Jamie, who was by now in the pizza shop, and gave him the news.

There was a long pause, followed by a typical Jamie observation: 'This has been the dearest pizza I've ever bought.'

The only remaining decision was what to call the new arrival and we naturally felt this should be Dale's choice. Things never being straightforward in our household, Dale informed us, 'I know it's strange, but I always want to have a Henry in my life, so I'd like to call the pup Wee Henry.'

We had our reservations about this, but had to acknowledge Dale's needs and concluded that we could emphasise the word 'Wee' with the pup and shout 'Sir Henry' for the older dog. I came up with this as Mum had always been used to having mongrel dogs and because of our retriever's pedigree would often refer to him as 'Sir'. Henry was in any event already used to various other names, such as Harry, courtesy of Amy, and also Tigger when we visited Dad, who thought he was his old pet. We knew it wasn't the most sensible choice, but we'd given up doing things the normal way years ago. And of course we understood that when the horrendous but inevitable day came, Wee Henry would simply become Henry.

Unlike the day when we had collected Sir Henry all those years ago, this time Dale was very much picking up his own pup – not a replacement, but a second dog to love.

When we arrived back outside our house, the new bundle snuggled into Dale, we could see Henry through the window, lying on his bed in front of the fire. We let the pup in, to see how they got on. Sir Henry looked up in shock as Wee Henry trotted over to his bed and peed on it.

After the pup realised that Henry was not up for playing just now, he cuddled up to him and went to sleep, as though Henry was his mum. Sometimes he would go a step too far and try to suckle Henry, who, although tolerant, would show his displeasure by barking loudly at the young upstart.

Very quickly the two bonded well and would often play together like pups, with Wee giving Sir a new lease of life. Occasionally they needed to be separated like a couple of misbehaving children.

As both dogs were Dale's and registered and insured in his name, he took full responsibility for them. Once Wee Henry was old enough, Dale started taking him to dog-training classes, run by Val and a friend every Wednesday night. He still attends now, in an attempt, as Dale puts it, 'to find Wee Henry's brain'.

20
Granda George

As we'd learned throughout Dale's life, it was always prudent to plan well ahead. Once Dale had received his exam results, he decided that after completing his fifth year at school, he wanted to go on to a third-level college and so I started to investigate what type of help and provision he would be entitled to once he got there. The other item on my agenda was to find the college and course that would be most suitable for him. While we knew that officially there should not be any disability discrimination, we were also aware that given Dale's chosen career path of working with children, his autism could be a potential problem.

When I phoned around various colleges and explained Dale's situation, many were supportive, but some were shocked that someone with autism was even considering this kind of course. Thankfully, Dale understood that regardless of his personal and academic achievements, he would have to work harder to prove himself than someone without autism. This shouldn't have been the case, but it was a sad fact of life that we couldn't ignore.

What we wanted to avoid more than anything was Dale being in a 'revolving-door situation' at college, finding that there was no suitable employment available at the end of a course and having no choice but to go back into college to start another one. I spent an intensive day on the phone and then ironically made the call I perhaps should have started with. The helpline people for the National Autistic Society (NAS) in London told me about their employment service, Prospects, that among other aims provided support for students at college and university. More importantly, once in the chosen workplace, support would be offered not only to the new employee, but also the employer. They had presences in London, Manchester, Leeds and Glasgow, so I contacted their Glasgow office and spoke to them about Dale.

Dale embraced all that Prospects had to offer and, with the dedicated help of the staff and Anna Williamson in particular, gained a place on a national certificate course in childcare that was due to start at the James Watt College in August 2006. The learning support staff at the college worked well with Prospects to ensure that Dale's transition to college would go smoothly.

Meanwhile, though, Dale was working so hard to succeed at his schoolwork that there was no denying he was placing undue pressure on himself and suffering as a consequence. Following a meeting with the immensely caring and supportive Margie Carracher, Dale and I concluded that the best option for him now would be to leave school. He would be sorely missed by his teachers and would himself be upset to leave them and his school friends, but Margie's delicate handling of the situation helped Dale to cope with this momentous decision.

There were four weeks to go before Dale's leaving date and he wanted to fill them productively. By the end of his fourth year, his art portfolio had comprised several good pieces, one of which, a drawing of a sultan, had been pointed out to us by Dale's art teacher at a parents' evening as an exceptional portrait. We had been very pleasantly surprised by the standard of this drawing, as we'd never seen Dale's talent at this level before. When we thought back to our five-year-old boy who could barely hold a pencil, instead using a toddler's palmer grip to create meaningless scribbles, the quality of this piece really touched us. We told Dale we'd like a copy of the sultan to hang up with pride in the house, but he had his own ideas, suggesting, 'If you like that one so much, why don't I do something even better to hang in the house?' When we asked him what he had in mind, he replied, 'I'd like to do a portrait of Henry.'

Margie approached the art teacher, who agreed to allow Dale to work on this drawing rather than coursework during his remaining art classes at the school. This would help him to relax as he prepared for the reality of leaving a school and teachers who meant so much to him.

Dale set to work on what was to become a very special and significant drawing. He took his favourite photograph of Henry into school to use as a reference for the portrait and, although he hadn't drawn his dog in years, soon got into the swing of things. After many hours of painstaking effort, the final result was superb and was a much more powerful and meaningful piece for us to hang than the sultan. Henry's wise and noble character and beauty were plain to see, but there was something more – Dale had captured the essence of his dog through the eyes. The love he had for Henry was somehow transferred on to the paper and Henry's very soul shone through.

Dale was naturally upset the day he left school, especially at the thought of never working again with his wonderful teachers, who had contributed so much to his academic success, maturity and self-esteem. I suspect they gained as much satisfaction from seeing Dale prosper as watching another child get straight As. They were never arrogant, always listened to our views and we will be for ever grateful for all they achieved

In December, on one of my regular visits to my dad at Merino Court, I asked Jamie to come along with Amy. Jamie hadn't seen my dad for a couple of weeks and I wanted his opinion on my suspicions that my father's health was now a serious cause for concern. Jamie was shocked to see how much Dad had deteriorated. Amy also seemed to have picked up that her granda might soon be going to join some of her other favourite residents and Granny Madge in heaven. She went round to her 'dream room', a special room for the home's residents, with subdued lighting and soothing music to create a relaxed and tranquil atmosphere. Amy had previously drawn a horse for Granda George to see when he was in the room, but now she took it down from the wall – it was as if she realised that very soon he would not be there to see it. When we left, I asked the nurses to call me at any time if Dad's condition deteriorated; I hadn't been with my mum when she passed away and did not want my dad to have to die alone also. I would go up there first thing next morning and spend all the time that was necessary to be with him.

With this in mind, and concerned that Dale might not see his grandfather again, I took him back that evening to visit. Although Dad did not wake up, Dale sat on his bed and held his hand, speaking some kind words to him in the hope that he could hear – I had told him to talk to his granda normally and let him know that he was with him. As we were about to leave, Dale bent over the bed and kissed my dad gently on the forehead, saying with a mature and composed voice, 'Goodnight, Granda. I'll see you tomorrow. Have a good rest.' It was a gesture of love and compassion, telling and showing his grandfather everything that needed to be said and done. Such was the dignity and respect Dale showed his dying grandfather, it all but broke my heart and I needed every ounce of my emotional strength to stay composed.

I went home to get things organised so that I could be with Dad for the time he had left, with my sister Linda by my side. I put on washing and brought the usual chores up to date, then left things ready for Jamie and the kids for when the inevitable happened. Content that all was in order and with my dad very much on my mind, I eventually fell asleep, setting the alarm for an early rise so I could get to his bedside as soon as possible.

At five o'clock, however, the phone jolted me awake and my heart sank. It was the nurse from Merino Court informing me that my dad had died a few minutes earlier. I was distraught, not least because I hadn't been there at the end for either of my parents. Dale overheard my distress and understood what had happened, staying home to comfort me that day. As it was already 21 December, it would be difficult to hold Dad's funeral before Christmas, and because we also wanted to give family from Ireland the chance to attend, the date was set for the following Wednesday, 28 December.

We broke the news to Amy that Granda George had gone

to heaven to join Granny Madge and the others who had passed on from Merino Court. She took it well, although she said she felt sad that she would not see him again when she went back to visit her friends at Merino Court.

Just as we had in the past, we forced ourselves to go through the motions of Christmas, this time for a very sad and different reason.

Dale was very pleased with the set of *Dr Who* DVDs we gave him, in a package resembling the famous Tardis. Jamie and I had bought Dale a gift on behalf of his grandfather, together with an appropriately worded card. This was a themed alarm clock with a moving 3-D steam train and accompanying noises, which Dale was touched to receive. Amy had a card from Granda George, too, together with a Barbie Pegasus horse.

Amy's special present from Santa, however, had been in development for several months. On her many visits to her friend Nina's house, she had been very taken with Nina's enormous doll's house – or rather, the tiny replica rocking horse that resided in the child's bedroom in the house. Because of her autism, she would show no symbolic or imaginative play with the doll's house, as other girls would, but was nonetheless determined that this was what she wanted for Christmas.

In an attempt to kick-start Amy's imagination, we decided to involve her in the process of choosing and designing the house. We opened up an Internet website showing various styles of house and let Amy surf a little, ultimately guiding her towards a particular style and size of house. Basically, she 'chose' the one we thought most suitable! It had fewer, better-sized rooms than we'd seen in other houses and was in kit form, needing to be painted, built and furnished from scratch. By involving Amy fully in the process, it became obvious to us that she was recreating a replica of our own house, choosing the same colours for the rooms as we had. We seized on this and decided to run with it.

As we knew Amy's imagination would be limited in terms of how she would play with the house and dolls, we set out to replicate our own as best we could. For weeks on end, Jimmy was busy building and painting the house up in his attic, while we gathered together fittings and furniture that as closely as possible resembled our own, even down to the floor coverings. We also found lookalike dolls to match our family and Amy's friends, putting the name of each character on the sole of the doll's foot. Jimmy wired up the house with low-voltage lighting, which made it look different and more enticing to play with and had the added advantage that Amy could use it at night-time if she wanted. Amy took great delight in choosing the tiny rocking horse for her pink room, to replicate one she'd got from Santa two years previously, which she had proudly named Hero. No detail was spared: the house was given a number – number 9 – there was a kennel outside inscribed with the name Henry, as well as a wooden garden shed where characters who didn't live at number 9, like the Nina doll, would remain 'hidden' until they came to visit Amy.

True to form, on Christmas Day, Amy loved her house and spent many a happy time, with our help, engrossed in it. The only problem was that I now had double the housework – while Amy was out at school, after I'd tidied my own house I would do likewise with hers. One day, however, I decided not to touch it, so I could show Jamie just how Amy had left it. In the lounge, she had rearranged the furniture so that all of the seats, including dining chairs, were occupied by the entire Gardner family and all of the shed dolls were watching the television. The screen, which was normally blank, had a sticker on it with a picture of a horse, depicting the nature of the programme the dolls were so captivated by. Even the Henrys were there, sitting in front of the fire. Many a friend and other children have marvelled at Amy's doll's house and she still plays with it to this day – sometimes appropriately, sometimes rather differently, with Granda Jimmy having a ride on Hero in her bedroom, or Dale and the Henrys in our bed instead of their own.

With Christmas behind us, it was time for Dad's funeral. Amy did a drawing of a horse on a card to go with his flowers, and Dale wrote his own private message on a card to go in the hearse along with the coffin and flowers. There was a very good turnout and family from Dublin managed to make it across. Looking a fine young man in his suit, Dale coped with the day like any other adult, so much so that he was able to take one of the cords supporting the coffin and help lower his grandfather into his grave. Even though they didn't know my dad personally, Dale's friends Scott, Matthew and David all attended, out of respect for Dale because they knew he and his grandfather had been close. It was touching to see that some of the staff from Merino Court were present.

Ironically, given that Dale was now seventeen, his friends still didn't know about his autism. It was very poignant that day, seeing Dale helping to bury the man who had been one of the first to make a connection with him, breaking into that lost boy's world. At the funeral tea, family and friends who hadn't seen Dale for years were stunned by his transformation into the mature, well-mannered and adjusted young man before them, with his three close friends by his side.

In January 2006, all the work with Prospect and the college paid off and Dale successfully went through an informal induction period. He spent time sitting as an observer in an established childcare class, doing the same work as the students but on an informal basis. More importantly, the support staff and tutors were able to get to know him as a person and identify his learning needs for when he started his course officially in August.

By now, Dale's insight into his condition was such that he realised that doing voluntary work would bring benefits to other people with disabilities. As we had received help for Amy in the form of a Barnardo's sitter and befriender service, Dale thought it would be good to give something back to this charity. He attended an intensive six-week training course with Barnardo's to enable him to join them as a volunteer helper, working with children with a diverse range of ages and disabilities. To this day, Dale is a valued member of the team, which runs drama workshops and holiday play schemes, and his understanding of his own condition is surely helpful to them.

In the first few weeks of 2006, the Metacalm that Henry had been on long term for his arthritis began to upset his stomach more often, which distressed him greatly. We had no option but to take him off it until his stomach settled, to the detriment of his mobility. He was now twelve years old, which was a fair age even for a healthy golden retriever. Many drugs used in mainstream medicine are similar to those for animals and I was aware of the implications of the increasing frequency of these episodes with Henry. When I discussed my concerns with our vet, Nigel Martin, he told me we should prepare ourselves for the worst, saying that there may well come a moment when Henry would deteriorate rapidly. I really appreciated Nigel's honesty as he knew what Henry meant to Dale, having witnessed my son change from a withdrawn wee boy to the young man he had now become.

After an episode of sickness in early February, thankfully Henry's health seemed to settle down, albeit on a lower dose of the medication. We were glad of this for two reasons – firstly, because it was unbearable to see our wonderful dog in distress, and secondly, it was time to celebrate Amy's sixth birthday, on 14 February.

Willing as ever to use the obsession, we fulfilled Amy's birthday request for a 3-foot-high toy horse that looked like a small Shetland pony, which she named Butterscotch. Following the same principles as for the doll's house and to reinforce all she had learned at Ardgowan Riding Centre, we gave her not only the horse, but a replica stable to match, with all the necessary equipment and muck-out kit. Once again, Jimmy was set to work and we cannot thank him enough for bringing our designs to fruition with his wonderful joinery skills.

On one visit to check on progress when the stable was still under construction in Jimmy's bedroom, Amy told him, 'Granda, I love it so much. Can I sleep in it tonight?'

The stable now towers beside Amy's bed and looks decidedly unusual, but is totally appropriate for her, reinforcing how to care for a real horse, as well as helping to stimulate appropriate imagination, and not least letting her share with her friends her unique toy.

While Amy's birthday was memorable due to the stable, another event at this time stood out even more. Just as you would with any child, Jamie and I had always greeted Dale and Amy with a 'Hello', regardless of their lack of response. We had learned from the early days when Dale first called Jamie 'Dad' that our persistence might pay off eventually. We also wanted to treat them with respect, because their silence did not necessarily mean a lack of comprehension and it was always possible that they would ultimately learn through repetition.

Every morning as Amy and I walked up to school, three of the other mums, who knew of Amy's condition, would always make a real effort and greet her with a cheerful, 'Good morning, Amy.' For about six months, they never faltered as I tried to get her to look at them and respond, always using exactly the same expression in the hope that she would copy me. Day after day, she ignored them. Then, suddenly, one morning when they approached and gave their usual greeting, she stopped as they passed, turned after them with a beaming smile and shouted, 'Good morning, girls!' These lovely ladies were, I think, even more delighted than I was as they realised what they had finally achieved. From that day on, Amy has continued to greet them, as well as anyone else she encounters along the way.

In the middle of March, Henry had a severe sickness episode with the Metacalm and this time took longer to recover. In the midst of it all, Jamie and I had been concerned that the sudden deterioration the vet had described might now be upon us and that Henry would not be with us much longer. It's strange how your mind plans ahead for such an eventuality while simultaneously hoping against hope that it will not happen. Henry managed to pull through, although not without making me think about how we might like to remember him in the future. We had Dale's brilliant portrait of Henry, but I wanted something more, a final family picture of us all together, Wee Henry included.

At the end of March, we went to Simpson's, a photographer's in Greenock, who we always used for our family pictures, and this time Mr Simpson worked a minor miracle. He somehow managed to conjure up a lovely still shot of us all, despite Sir Henry's ailments, Amy manipulating the proceedings as usual with her latest horse and Wee Henry generally causing chaos.

Easter soon came and on Good Friday I decided to take Sir Henry out for a very gentle walk, not going too far from the house. At that time, there were two little girls a couple of doors down who often came over to play with Amy. One of them, seven-year-old Nicola, was terrified of dogs and had a real phobia. Just like the little girl in Dresling Road, though, she saw Henry was different and soon grew to know and trust him.

That day, as I was returning to our house with Henry off the lead to let him make his way inside, Nicola was leaving her house with her father. On seeing Henry, she ran towards him, shouting his name. Her dad, knowing she was scared of dogs, was shocked and asked her what she was doing. She replied, 'It's OK, Dad – it's Henry. He's special and I'm not scared of him.' Her dad was stunned.

In the evening, Jamie's friend Mark visited with his wife, Helen, for a social evening. Both Henrys were on good form, as you'd expect from a goldie when there is food around. Using all of their natural ability for emotional blackmail by drooling and gazing at us with their big brown eyes, they cadged as many titbits as possible and eventually, full to the brim, cuddled in together on their specially made bed in front of the fire. It was a lovely evening, with great company, the dogs well behaved and old Henry in relatively reasonable health. With the summer coming, Jamie and I thought we were in for a period of stability with him and felt all was well as we sat with our friends and watched the two dogs as they slept.

At bedtime, as that feel-good night ended, Wee Henry went up the stairs as always to sleep with Dale on top of his bed, the bond between them now firmly established. Sir Henry took up his accustomed position on his bed at the foot of ours. Sometimes the Metacalm would cause vomiting during the night, but I still wanted Henry with us, as at least then I would know if it was safe to give him his tablet in the morning. Apart from that, I just wanted to be there for him – he meant the world to me as well as Dale. He had done so much for us all and in a way it gave me satisfaction to be able to nurse and take good care of him. Many a night I would sit on the floor patting and stroking him or giving a little massage on his head as he drifted into a deep sleep. It was my peaceful, private time with this amazing dog who had helped return my special children back to me. The least I could do now was show him how much I loved him.

21
Letting Go

The following morning, we were awoken by the sound of Henry vomiting. I attended to him and massaged his stiff joints as usual, before helping him to stand so he could go out to the garden for his toilet needs. Thinking his sickness this time might be because he had simply overindulged the previous evening, I gently chided him for being his usual greedy self and broke the news to him that he should rest his stomach for now. Just in case, I withheld his Metacalm.

Despite this, Henry continued to vomit throughout the morning, although he did settle a little in the afternoon. As it was a lovely day, I suggested to Dale that he could try a gentle walk with his dog to see if some fresh air would help. We had previously worked out a system for walking Henry whereby Dale and I would carefully lift him into the car, then I would drive to the top of the hill, where both of us would lift Henry out and Dale would walk him back down the hill. In this way, our ailing dog could have some gentle exercise and conserve his energy for the difficult climb up the steep slope of our front garden. Dale had his mobile phone with him in case of emergency – for Henry more than himself – and I was reassured to see them both arrive back safely. Dale was so patient with Henry as they slowly climbed the slope together, understanding that his dog now had the frailty of a grand old man.

In the afternoon, Jamie and I took Amy to Braehead to shop. Amy had a wonderful new experience in the form of bouncing six metres in the air on a bungee trampoline. She loved it and we loved watching her. Then we moved on to some retail therapy, although with Henry playing heavily on my mind, I couldn't help phoning Dale to see how things were. Fortunately, Henry was fast asleep and there'd been no further vomiting.

Amy had emptied her money bank – which needless to say was in the form of a stable – with a view to blowing her savings in one go. There was a special shop in Braehead where children could choose and make their own cuddly toy from start to finish with the help of a shop assistant. Amy of course wanted a horse. For her, the experience was great fun; for me, it was another opportunity for her to interact socially with a stranger and constructively use the obsession. There was also a great incentive for her to return because the shop sold all manner of themed clothes for the toys the children could buy, and I knew Amy would love to come back and choose some of these once she had earned a bit more money. This she could do via our 'sticker reward system'; because she needed so much motivation, instead of giving her pocket money we would reward her various achievements with stickers, each of which would be converted to a pound at the end of the month.

True to form, the shop assistant was thoroughly interrogated by my daughter and also highly impressed with her equine knowledge, as well as the way she totally threw herself into the whole process of making her cuddly toy.

Back at home, Henry took a little drink of water and, to the relief of us all, managed to keep it down. By now, I felt guilty for accusing him of greed, because it seemed as though this was in fact his usual Metacalm sickness. We all settled down to bed and I sat fussing him on the floor for a while, as had become my routine. Although my gut feeling about him was not great, we all felt that he would cope better with the warmer months ahead.

In the early hours of the next morning, Easter Sunday, with Amy having joined Jamie and me in bed and now comatose between us, we were again abruptly awakened by the sound of poor Henry vomiting. This time, though, it was the worst he had ever been and he was in deep distress – as indeed were we. I immediately thought he must have some kind of intestinal spasm or obstruction and needed urgent veterinary aid. Even if he was still reacting against the Metacalm, I at least wanted him to have an anti-sickness injection as we couldn't bear to see him in this state. Jamie and I tried to get him up, but he couldn't stand and just collapsed in front of us, terribly weak, but alert and fully conscious. He lay there, panting excessively with the stress of it all.

Because it was a bank holiday, I phoned the pets' A&E in Glasgow and spoke to a nurse there, who advised that we bring him to the hospital right away. It was twenty-five miles away, but our only option. I woke Dale so he that could come with me, while Jamie stayed home with Amy.

I'm not sure how we managed what followed, but I think my nursing experience and common sense in a crisis kicked in. Due to his collapsed, floppy state, Henry seemed twice his usual size and weight as we tried to get him down the thirty garden steps to the car. Just as I would when moving a human patient, I rolled him on to a duvet cover and with Jamie at the back and Dale and me at the front, we were able to carry our dog in this makeshift hammock. Amy slept soundly throughout and Wee Henry, who had been barking because of the upheaval, now watched us quietly, peeking between the bars of the wrought-iron gate as we manoeuvred Sir Henry down the steps. There was the same 'worried-retriever look' on Wee Henry's face that I had seen with Sir Henry a long time ago, when Dale's violent tantrum had caused him to find his voice.

In moments of great stress, sometimes black humour acts as a release and I couldn't help muttering to Jamie how suspicious it would look if anyone saw us now, in the middle of the night, loading what for all the world could be a human body into the back of the car. I then proceeded to drive as fast as I could to the hospital, Dale on the back seat cradling Henry's head on his lap and remaining remarkably calm. He talked to his dog reassuringly throughout the journey. 'It's OK, Henry. You'll be all right, son, as soon as we get you some help.' Henry, bless him, fell asleep in Dale's arms.

We arrived at the hospital at 3 a.m., the vet and a nurse carrying Henry into the emergency room in the hammock. Although Henry was in a semi-collapsed state, I was cautiously relieved when the vet recorded his observations: 'Colour good, pulse good, chest quite harsh panting, bladder half full. Admit for IV fluids and routine bloods, etc.'

As I had anticipated, Henry was also given anti-sickness and gastric drugs to allow him to settle. Now that he was at last comfortable, Dale and I felt better. We stayed for a little while, but there was nothing further we could do and so we decided to leave him to sleep. Both of us planted a kiss on the top of his head, and I tried to explain the impossible to the vet and nurse. There simply were no words to convey what Henry meant to us and saying things like, 'He is a very special dog,' felt so lame. I'm sure the staff heard this sort of thing all the time, but in our case the phrase possibly rang a little bit truer than most. We left with the knowledge that the staff would do all that Henry required and would phone us immediately should there be any further deterioration. I couldn't shrug off the dreadful feeling that this was exactly like the situation with both of my parents, but I tried to convince myself that Henry had a good chance of responding to the drugs and IV fluids.

Later that morning, the vet phoned to say Henry was brighter. Although he was still panting, he'd had no more sickness and was attempting to stand. We arranged to visit that afternoon and the whole family went along at around 3 p.m., including Wee Henry for the ride. He stayed in the car while we all huddled into the confined space where sick dogs and cats lay in individual kennels, each with their respective drips and medical charts.

Amy, stood there with her horse tucked under her arm, was in her glory – it was just like *Animal Hospital*. She was intrigued by all the animals surrounding her, especially Henry with his drip and clipboard chart. As he lay there panting, she said, 'Where is Henry's oxygen mask? His lungs need help to work.' Due to having her own unique doctor's bag, she had obviously grasped the concept of her imaginative play and was now applying what she had learned to a real situation.

Henry was wide awake and, as soon as he saw Dale, tried valiantly to get to his feet, but he couldn't and flopped back down. Dale gave him a special cuddle while Jamie and I spoke to the vet. Henry's panting was still a concern and it was decided to X-ray his chest. I felt that in this alien environment, the stress alone could be a factor in his panting, but the only way we could be sure was by an X-ray. It was a huge wrench to leave our dog, but we knew he was in good hands.

Later that evening, the vet phoned to tell me that the X-ray had revealed that Henry had pneumonia. He was receiving all the appropriate antibiotics and treatment, and I was pleased to hear he had managed earlier in the afternoon to walk outside and eat two spoonfuls of food – a sign of great hope for our Henry. We felt a little more settled as we got ready for bed, allowing ourselves to believe that he might turn the corner.

Then, at 11 p.m., the phone rang again. My heart plummeted, just as it had with my dad. The vet who had been on duty the previous night told me that Henry's breathing had deteriorated and she was very concerned for him. Trying to absorb this news, I said I would phone her back.

In great distress, I called Val. Normally, I would be the medical advisor to friends and family, but I was completely out of my depth emotionally now and needed someone to help me rationalise. Val was immensely supportive and gradually brought me to recognise what I was feeling deep inside, and mention the unmentionable. I went through to see Jamie and Dale, sobbing my heart out, despairing of how my parents had both died alone and how I couldn't bear the same thing happening to Henry. After all he had done for our family, he had been abandoned in a terrifyingly strange place and that thought alone consumed me with grief – more than the idea of actually losing him.

Jamie's good sense was the antidote to my distress. He told

me that unlike the situation with my parents, Dale and I could make a call with Henry. We could go right away to see him and discuss with the vet whether it was time to let him go. Taking his advice, Dale and I set off around midnight for Glasgow, Wee Henry again joining us for the ride.

With all the same fears of the previous night's journey, we travelled as fast as we could, discussing the situation as calmly and rationally as any two people could in the circumstances. When we arrived, the hospital was very busy, so we walked Wee Henry round the block while we tried to clear our heads. We stopped outside the window where we knew Sir Henry was – I know it seems strange, but we just wanted Wee to get a sense that Sir was in there, before we put him back in the car.

We went in and the same staff from the previous night took us straight to Henry. My heart broke on seeing him. Unlike the last time he saw us, he was unable even to attempt to stand. We could at least tell by his face that he recognised us, and his beautiful sad eyes almost seemed tinged with relief that we were there for him. Although continuously panting heavily, a drip in situ on his front paw, he was still fully alert. The poor soul then needed attending to again as he had soiled himself and I knew that this was because he was no longer absorbing the medications. He was losing precious fluid and the entire treatment was becoming futile, with his discomfort only increasing.

Dale, I think, was just happy at that point that Henry was alert; but I could see that, clinically, Henry was losing his battle and without some form of pain relief or sedation would have a slow, laboured, alert death, feeling every agony of his rapidly failing body. Because of his pneumonia, sedation wasn't an option, as it would compromise his breathing further.

The vet and nurse stood by our sides as we tried to comfort our dog. Then I left Dale kneeling alone beside him and raised my fears with the vet. While I desperately didn't want to lose Henry, I felt positive in my heart that it was time to say goodbye. I discussed this with Dale and then asked him to talk to the vet. As he did, he strongly reinforced that under no circumstances was Henry to suffer.

On hearing the vet's opinion, Dale turned to me with tears in his eyes and said with a determined but trembling voice, 'Mum, it's the hardest decision I've ever had to make in my whole life, but I know it's time to let my dog go.'

Like the dignified, mature adult he is, Dale calmly signed the consent form to enable the vet to prepare the injection. Having been involved many times in my job in helping carers maximise that final bond and farewell to their loved ones, with the vet's help I was now able to do this for Dale. We asked him to sit on the floor and then positioned Henry's upper body and two big front paws right across Dale's lap, ensuring that Dale could see Henry's face. A nurse took a particularly yappy little dog outside, to allow us a sense of peace and quiet as I knelt down beside Dale. I held Henry's front paw, stroking and massaging it in the way he was used to. Although inside I wanted to howl with distress, I was determined to ensure that Dale was given quality time with his dog in those last few moments. I told him to make sure he kept a good hold of Henry's head and neck and talked to him in any way it felt natural.

'You're going to be all right now, Henry,' Dale told him.

'This jab will make you better.' Although struggling, he kept repeating these words over and over, kissing Henry on the head and occasionally adding that he loved him.

As soon as the vet had completed the injection, she left the room to give us some privacy.

'Dale, make sure he sees your eyes,' I reminded my son. Of the fifteen seconds it took for Henry's eyes to close and head gently flop, I stole a few moments, whispering in his ear, 'Thank you, Henry, thank you for everything. I love you.' As I choked on these last three words, I turned to Dale and told him that his dog was gone.

He hadn't realised this, and was still talking to Henry. I could only look on in desolate wonder as my once-tortured little boy, who had become such a fine young man, bade farewell to the dog who was in no small part responsible for his transformation.

We laid Henry gently down on his side, covering him with a blanket from his kennel. His battered old body was at last relaxed and he looked totally at peace – even now still a beautiful dog. I asked Dale if he wanted some time alone with his dog and he said, 'Yes, I would like that, Mum.'

I went outside the room, where the vet and nurse were waiting. I looked at them and the only words I could think of to express how I was feeling were, 'How do you let go and say goodbye to someone who has helped give you back your children?'

About ten minutes later, Dale emerged, holding Henry's blue collar with its green chip tag attached. We thanked the staff for their care and understanding, and gave instructions about receiving Henry's ashes back in a casket. Only as we left the hospital arm in arm did Dale's emotions finally break through. As he let go and cried, he looked so much younger than his seventeen years, seeming once again like my little boy lost, which in a sense he was.

When we opened the car to greet Wee Henry, we both wept copiously as we tried to hug him. He did not understand what had happened, but I think he sensed our pain. We drove back home reminiscing and openly acknowledging our disbelief that we would never see our wonderful Henry again. How on earth would we adapt to life without him?

At home, by now numb from all that had happened, I shared our experience with Jamie and couldn't help reflecting inwardly on the irony that the man who had never wanted a dog in the first place was now as devastated as Dale and me. We resolved that in the morning we would break the news together to Amy that Sir Henry had gone to join Granny Madge, Granda George and friends from Merino Court up in heaven. We knew she would be sad, but were equally sure she would bounce back in her irrepressible way.

I made some tea and took a cup up to Dale. I wanted to be sure he was all right and found him in bed stroking a sleepy Wee Henry on the duvet beside him.

We sat quietly for a few moments and then Dale asked tentatively, unsure of the maturity of the gesture, 'Mum, would it be silly if I tried to sleep with Henry's collar under my pillow?'

'Of course not,' I told him. 'Whatever you feel will help you, tonight or any night.'

And I know that last night, as every night, Dale slept with Henry's collar under his pillow.

In His Own Words

By looking back at various incidents in the past and discussing them with Dale today, I have concluded that the extent of a child's understanding should never be underestimated. When they aren't communicating, it is very easy to assume they are taking nothing in, but when Dale was ten, for example, he told me, 'If we hadn't talked through Henry, I would have chosen not to talk to you at all.' Dale's recent recollections below of events described in various chapters of this book show he understood a great deal more than we perhaps gave him credit for at the time.

Chapter 2

The obsession with water (see page 16)

I loved the feeling of water. The sensation all around me calmed me and I loved it. Nothing else mattered while I was in the water.

Tiptoe walking (see page 17)

I put a lot of effort into walking properly until I got the hang of it, mostly because I was fed up with my parents going on at me about it. After we moved to Gourock, I was sixteen and a friend of Dad's, Sammy, had noticed me tiptoe walking as I made my way home on the estate. He mentioned it to Dad, who suggested to him, 'Have a word with Dale about it – it's very obvious and could blow his cover.' Sammy's comments made me realise others noticed my strange walk, and although I'd been moaned at for years by Mum and Dad, it was Sammy's words that gave me the determination to stop.

Chariots of Fire (see page 19)

That was the house I ruined the walls in. I ran because I liked to pretend I was a train – I could see trains in the distance from the Wellpark and at Granny Dorothy's from the back garden. The running made me feel happy and calm, and I did it until I was about twelve, but my parents finally convinced me it was bizarre and made me look very autistic.

Circus spinning trick (see page 20)

I remember doing this. The eye thing was me looking at an object in the room. I liked it while I spun and loved the dizzy feeling at the end and the fact that I was in control of what was happening. It just made me feel happy.

Climbing (see page 20)

I remember doing this a lot. It was to see things from a different angle, like the cooker. I liked to see what the kitchen looked like from this different place and had no understanding at all of the danger I was putting myself in. I was just fascinated to see things from a different viewpoint.

Chapter 3

The tree (see page 28)

I remember my tree. It was big and had branches that reached almost to the ground. Granny Madge would shake them and it made me happy. She did that for me for years. My tree is still there in the Wellpark. Not long ago, while in the Wellpark with Amy and my mum, we were talking about it and Mum pointed to a tree that was similar, but it was not my tree. I will always know it from any other.

Chapter 5

Stripping off clothes (see page 50)

I was happy to wear clothes so long as I liked the look of them or they were comfortable fabrics. However, if I didn't like the look of them or they irritated my skin, I would strip them off. Sometimes just simply wearing clothes annoyed me and when this happened I would also take them all off. The Mickey logos, Mum giving me the choice of what to wear, involving me and letting me feel and touch the clothes at home helped a lot.

Chapter 6

The Waverley (see page 71)

I hate *The Waverley* now – it bores me. The circling motion of the paddles reminded me of a steam train and I liked the funnels for the same reason. I liked the way it just appeared at random times, giving me a surprise, unlike the Dunoon ferries. Also, I thought it was good when Mum joined in my excitement as I believed she liked it as much as me, which helped us to bond.

Chapter 7

The hoover (see page 82)

It wasn't the noise of the hoover I minded – I was terrified it was going to suck me up like a monster.

Chapter 8

The war (see page 93)

I think it is horrific the way my parents were treated and it really upsets me to talk about this time in my life. I can now see what they did for me, and it frightens me to think where I would be if they had not fought so hard for me. I feel so bad for any children that this might have happened to also, who maybe have not been so lucky.

Chapter 9

Non-verbal communication (see page 110)

I hated trying to work out what someone's face was telling me, especially if it was a new one or someone I didn't know very well. I found it scary as I couldn't work out if they were angry or feeling all right, and I found the whole eye-contact thing very confusing and frightening.

Thomas trains (see page 111)

I really liked Henry because he was the very first engine I saw when Dad put on my first video. I enjoyed the story of Henry's forest and how he was helpful and caring. The videos helped me play with my trains, and the way Mum and Dad taught me their names made it understandable. Helpful Henry was my favourite and I always made sure that he got to pull the big coaches. I gave Grand Gordon the Troublesome Trucks because he annoyed me, being so sure of himself all the time and boasting about how he was faster than Henry.

The tantrum at Boness Steam Railway (see page 117)

I remember that day as I was really terrified of the loud noises coming from the station – the steam and whistle, etc. I didn't realise it was coming from a real steam train. Once I saw it was a giant real steam train, I immediately became very excited at seeing it moving and working. I hadn't realised that the big trains in the Transport Museum could do that and that that is how they worked – I thought they were just giant models of trains.

Chapter 10

Discarding Henry's fleece (see page 134)

I really liked the warm and secure feeling I got when I had my cot train duvet round me. Because the pup was so young and small, I wanted something of my own to give him to make him welcome – I wanted Henry to have the same feeling I got from my train duvet.

Puppy Henry (see page 134)

I liked having the pup as company, especially the way he looked with his friendly face and the fact he was so cute and cuddly. Henry was like my living friend and always there for me.

Chapter 11

'OK' and 'proud' (see page 156)

I hated it when my mum and dad said 'OK'. Saying 'OK' and other such words really irritated me so much; it gave me a weird feeling in my head. Words like 'proud' – if I didn't understand what they meant, it really frustrated me and gave me the same irritating feeling in my head. That's why I would hit my head with my fists or bang it off the wall, to get rid of this weird irritation these words caused.

Chapter 12

Eye contact in drawings (see page 163)

I really did understand the eye-contact thing, because my mum, dad and everyone else had taught me that I should be making eye contact and looking at people's faces. That's why I did it with the train drawings. But even knowing this, I still found human faces intimidating.

Why Henry was so special

Henry was just really gentle, friendly and sociable. I liked that he had a wise look on his face and I always trusted him, which made me feel very comfortable with him. You could see all this from his eyes, as they were lovely and I could understand his feelings from looking at his eyes and face. Henry's face only had slight changes with his expressions so I understood them. It made me feel confident and secure with him. I really liked that Henry was always seeking attention, and it made me feel good when people admired him and would talk to me about him.

The kick (see page 170)

I'll never forget kicking my dog; it still upsets me even now, all these years later. I didn't think I'd really hurt him – I was just so angry at hearing the words that upset me so much and hurt my head. What Mum and Dad did that night really got to me, as I understood when the plaster was used how much I'd hurt my dog and my mum when I kicked them. I really believed Henry was going away for ever.

Chapter 14

John Turner (see page 199)

John always made me laugh and helped me relax and gave me a good hyper feeling. So I liked to copy him and join in with him. It was like having a real-life Charlie Chaplin friend. He was always so funny when he was around me.

The Thomas wreath (see page 210)

The Thomas wreath really helped me to understand what was going on. I wanted Thomas to do for Granny Madge what he did for me. I really liked Thomas and he made me feel secure. I genuinely believed that because he was a train he would be able to travel up to heaven with her. I also thought that if Gran had Thomas with her, she would always remember me.

Chapter 15

Instantly riding a bike (see page 229)

Seeing Fraser and all the other kids on the estate playing and being together on their bikes made me want to be the same. So I just got the hang of it that night, to be with them.

Chapter 17

Bullying and swearing (see page 258)

I wanted to say the swear words back in the playground, but I was scared as I had been taught not to use bad words like these. After Mum gave me the swearing lesson, I felt more comfortable because I understood the rules she taught me about how and when to use the words. The few times that I did have to swear the way I was taught actually helped me be the same as the other kids and fit in socially – especially at Gourock High as it's the way teenagers often talk.

Chapter 19

Mum and Dad tapping into friends' skills (see page 291)

I liked being with all the other people my parents arranged for me to see. It was fun and more interesting to learn from them as to me they were the experts. I didn't realise I was also learning to interact with them. It made it more real because they all knew the chosen subject so well and had the same interest in it as me. It meant it wasn't boring like it would have been if my parents had tried to teach me about things like mobile phones.

Chapter 20

The road back (see page 307)

I found the help Prospects gave me vital and I couldn't have managed everything ahead of me to do with college without it. The workshops and individual work that they did with me helped so much, making me much more relaxed and confident about my college work and especially regarding the interview for entry to the course – the thought of this alone was frightening to me.

When I think of how much everyone in my past has done for me and the support from the Scottish Society of Autism and others, I realise how they have all given me the chance of a good quality of life. Lead Scotland and the support of the James Watt College staff with my studies have helped give me the opportunity of a successful future. To everyone who has been a part of this journey that I've had to take, I will be forever grateful.

Chapter 21

On Henry's passing (see page 327)

Henry brought me through all of my childhood and because of that I was able to help him at the end, when he needed me. It was the hardest thing I have ever had to do, but due to him, I am not scared any more of the thought and responsibility of being an adult. I have decided that for the rest of my life I am never going to let my amazing dog down, so that he will be proud of me, as I will always be of him.

Dale J. Gardner
2007

Henry
17 Dec 93 to 17 April 06

A/P   Dale J gardner

Afterword

If I had to say just one thing about autism as a disability, it is this: we must never underestimate how hard a person affected has to work every day, all day to live by our society's rules and to fit in. The anxiety and effort this takes is always immense, and, like their autism, it is for the rest of their life.

We are very aware that other parents are still experiencing today what we went through fifteen years ago and what we nearly experienced with Amy. I am also aware and saddened that parents in similar situations to ourselves are still driven to the brink of suicide because of lack of support and understanding.

While my experience with my children and Henry is somewhat different, it is far from unique. Our life and struggle is typical of what all families affected by autism live with and have to cope with every day. I hope that in some way this book has helped increase awareness and understanding of the condition.

We want to thank our families and friends and all those involved who helped return our children back to us. Without their incredible professionalism and respect for us and our children's autism, Dale and Amy would not be where they are today. Because of all these people, Dale and Amy have a normal quality of life in spite of their autism. We are forever indebted.